A PORTRAIT
OF JOAN

A PORTRAIT OF JOAN

The Autobiography of

JOAN CRAWFORD

with

JANE KESNER ARDMORE

Published by Graymalkin Media, LLC

www.graymalkin.com

Book design by Timothy Shaner

Originally published by Doubleday & Company, Inc.

This edition published in 2017 by Graymalkin Media

ISBN: 978-1-63168-113-4

Printed in the United States of America

1   3   5   7   9   10   8   6   4   2

A PORTRAIT
OF JOAN

FOREWORD

As Joan Crawford's grandson, it is my honor and privilege to help champion Joan's incredible legacy as Hollywood icon and trailblazing businesswoman. May 10, 2017, marks the fortieth anniversary of her passing. Over the years I have enjoyed discussing the many films she starred in, but the role of hers that I will always cherish the most is that of devoted mother and loving grandmother.

I remember my grandmother greeting my family at her Imperial House apartment in mid-1970s Manhattan, thousands of miles and years away from her life in Hollywood. In her housecoat and slippers, she would lead me to the kitchen. Waiting was a lunch of roasted chicken, ice-cold Pepsi-Cola, and some wonderful one-on-one time with her. After lunch, it was playtime and the exchange of beloved gifts. The visits with my grandmother were always special and I will forever remember her as a warm and affectionate person.

My grandmother wrote *A Portrait of Joan* in 1962 as the definitive Joan Crawford history. Readers and fans can learn the intimate details of Joan's life from her unique perspective as a reigning queen of Hollywood. One of the things that I found so powerful in the book was learning of Joan's incredibly difficult childhood, moving from city to city as the family endured poverty and failed prospects for a better life. In my opinion, Joan's childhood account of working for her mother in a Kansas City laundry was a major turning point. From that time forward, Joan would chart her own destiny.

With *A Portrait of Joan* out of print for decades, Joan Crawford fans around the world have been asking me if I had any intention of publishing a new edition. I am proud to present the family authorized reissue of *A Portrait of Joan*. This new edition provides many familiar photographs taken from Joan's early childhood to her work at Metro-Goldwyn-Mayer and into her later years.

From childhood to her last breath, Joan's life was a complex medley of extreme highs and lows. Born into desperate poverty, she was able to achieve the pinnacle of stardom. *A Portrait of Joan* provides an insight into her life as no other could tell it, directly from the grandmother I called "JoJo."

—Casey LaLonde

ONE

LUCILLE LESUEUR YOU HAVE BEEN
PLACED UNDER CONTRACT MGM STUDIO STOP
SIX MONTH OPTION STOP SEVENTY FIVE
DOLLARS A WEEK STOP LEAVE IMMEDIATELY
FOR CALIFORNIA STOP

kept the telegram clutched in my hand as the train rattled out of Kansas City and then swam on with chugging, steady strokes across this incredibly broad land—across plains and fields and forests I'd never really known existed, toward a destination I'd never really known existed either, Hollywood. Did they dance in movies? All that mattered was dancing. I'd seen six movies in my whole life. No one danced! And I wanted to be the best dancer in the world.

Lucille LeSueur . . . a seventeen-year-old bursting with energy, with pent-up spirits. I longed to leap into the aisle and dance. Instead, I sat there sedately in my gray plaid suit, my small gray cloche hat pulled down to my eyes, my feet resting on my one suitcase. I was wearing pumps with huge bows, and inside the suitcase there were additional pumps with bows. Not many, it was a small case.

Producer Harry Rapf from MGM had seen me dancing in the chorus of *Innocent Eyes* and offered a screen test to "the girl third from the left in the back row." The girl third from the left would never even have taken the test if it hadn't been for theatrical agent Nils T. Granlund, dear old Granny Granlund, the chorus girl's friend in need. What was I thinking of, he said. Did I want to spend the rest of my life doing a time step in some Broadway chorus? Fighting for a place in the front row? So I took the test, along with eighteen others, a routine affair that consisted of walking toward the camera, stopping where a mark had been drawn on the floor, then full face to the camera, profile to the camera, after which I was to look "sad, mad, questioning, wistful and coy." It was all over in fifteen minutes, but I was called back the next day to make a second test. This time Nils Granlund practically had to drag me. This time Mr. Rapf and Bob Rubin were introduced to me. Would I like to be an actress, they asked. No, I said candidly, I'd like to be a dancer. I wasn't interested in acting.

I was far more interested in going home for Christmas. So I went home. I was helping Mother iron shirts in the laundry agency when the wire came from MGM. We read it with absolute amazement. Mother never had approved of show business, she had all the arguments most parents have to a girl away from home in a glamour business, but those seventy-five dollars a week paralyzed her negatives. Mine too. Compared with the twelve dollars a week I'd earned behind the notions counter at Kline's Department Store in Kansas City, compared with the thirty-five a week dancing in a Shubert chorus line and doubling in a nightclub—seventy-five dollars sounded a veritable fortune!

Two days later, I was on the train. New Year's Day 1925. It was a lonely ride for a homesick girl who had no home to be sick for—I'd been on my own since I was nine. And seventeen is an age of contradictory moods. You can do everything, you can do nothing, you're at once fearless, insecure, eager; you haven't the vaguest idea what's expected of you. What would Hollywood expect? I couldn't possibly foresee that awaiting me were love, laughter and disaster, power, and a lovely pinnacle. Not *awaiting* me either, experiences to be worked for, living that would demand everything I could give and that would give to me in return. I couldn't possibly foresee that Hollywood was to be my high school and college. Everything I'd ever learn was to stem from the people I worked with, the characters I played, the people I learned to love.

Seventeen is rebellious—and suppliant for reassurance. It took an endless while for the train to finally pull into the station at Los Angeles and when it did, I scanned the platform anxiously. There would be, I felt sure, a welcoming committee from the studio, people to guide me. Mr. Rapf probably. I searched the passing faces. People were rushing toward each other, hugging and kissing, there was buoyance, a sound of happiness in the air. But no one for me. Mr. Rapf had the sagacious look of a vaudeville agent, an old-time showman. I scrutinized the crowd . . . not a single sagacious look.

The crowd was thinning. Redcaps were trundling away the luggage. I quickened my pace, ran, following my suitcase. It was a long walk, and when we got to the station itself there was a bewildering crowd of people. I walked back and forth as if I were expecting someone. It grew more and more quiet. I leaned against a pillar waiting.

It must have been a strong pillar, for at this time I weighed one hundred and forty-five pounds of baby fat. I was self-conscious, unsure, and my "style" was strictly dreadful. I hated my round face, I hated my freckles, my big mouth and eyes. I tried to stretch my five feet three as tall as possible, tossed my head in the air, poked my chin out, and dared people to notice me.

When the station was virtually empty, I hid my face against the pillar sobbing. This alone I'd never been in my life. Suddenly into the loneliness came the sound of whistling. Around and around it went like the buzzing of a bee. I began to recognize the tune. I'd sung it myself at Harry Richman's nightclub in New York, "When my sweetie walks down the street, all the little birdies go tweet, tweet, tweet. . . . " I looked up to see a young man, strolling toward me, his hands in his pockets, still whistling and almost on key. He nodded politely as he approached and asked if he could be of any help. He was just a teenager too, so I blew my nose and sobbed my story.

He gave me a quick appraisal, head to toe, and whistled his surprise, the kind of whistle every girl likes to get. "Why you must be Lucille LeSueur!" he said. "Honey, I'm *looking* for you. I'm the Welcoming Committee from the studio." He was Larry Barbier, the publicity department office boy—they'd instructed him to go down to the station and meet one of Harry Rapf's "show girls" from New York.

"I was looking for a dame six feet tall with a big hat and wolfhounds," Larry said, and we both laughed. Obviously I was no show girl, I was a pony.

"Rapf usually signs show girls," Larry said. "Come along, honey, we'll find your luggage."

One nice thing—he did have a limousine waiting, with a chauffeur, and we drove out a long, long way through streets lined with palm trees. An infinity of palm trees. In nothing flat I discovered that the pretty young girls in film business were just as numerous. Business was booming. Metro had taken over the Goldwyn Studios ten months before. They were making big pictures, *The Merry Widow*, *The Unholy Three*, *The Great Divide*; they had wonderful stars like

Ramon Novarro and Lon Chaney, Mae Murray, Lillian Gish, Alice Terry, Buster Keaton and Marion Davies. But they were constantly signing new talent, searching for some face or personality that might develop into stellar box office. Besides, every studio boss had some relative or protégé who wished a job. It was routine.

We dropped my bag at the Washington Hotel in Culver City, continued on to the studio and signed the contract. It was all as unreal as a dream. What really hit me was that six-month option. I had six months to prove something. If I failed to make it, they could drop me. However, I had no time to worry about that—my screen test was scheduled for the next day. I'd never have gotten through it except for cameraman Johnny Arnold (later, for years, head of MGM's camera department) and Tommy Shagrue, the little redheaded Irish electrician. These men behind the cameras like new faces; they somehow never lose their enthusiasm. They felt then as they do now that too often, established players are cast in parts not suited to them, and they like to spot new talent. They must have been pretty disappointed in me, freckles and all. But Johnny, seeing how tense I was, insisted that I'd photograph.

"Don't be afraid of that thing," he said, pointing to the camera. "It's only got one eye, honey, and it can't talk back to you."

He and Tommy worked with all the great stars. MGM watched zealously over their stars in those days, and of first importance was the choice of cameramen, Ollie Marsh to this star, George Barnes or George Folsey to that star. . . . Johnny Arnold made the assignments with great care. But he also ran these routine tests of newcomers every week, kids who'd last six months or less. When I was told to smile, I smiled.

"Turn your profile to the camera, dear."

I turned.

"Now let's have a few lines from this play, right here." Sad lines. It was very obvious—even to me—that all I knew how to do was dance.

"Can you cry?"

I thought of that six-month option, started crying and couldn't stop.

Tommy Shagrue had once hoofed in vaudeville.

"You're a dancer, *aren't* you?" he asked. "Bet you can't do this one." He cut loose with a buck-and-wing.

"Bet I can!" And I did.

"Well, can you beat that?" Tommy said. "Say, how about this one?"

For a minute I forgot the test, forgot where I was. Tommy and I were dancing and I was laughing.

"Okay," Tommy said, "now go in there and do your scene, honey. Give it everything you've got."

I gave. What the test looked like I never knew, but Johnny told me it was okay. "A lot of girls look just alike," he said. "You don't look like anyone else. You're athletic-looking and your face is *built*" . . . whatever that meant.

Within a week, I was spending most of my time before the camera. Not the movie camera, but the still camera in publicity. I was strictly the "action queen" of cheesecake, as Greta Garbo had been. Pete Smith, head of the Publicity Department, had just bought an action Graflex for photographer Don Gilum and Don's action shots were favorites with newspaper editors. There were a number of young starlets around the studio. Don Gilum would take Dorothy Sebastian and me over to the University of Southern California track— an excuse to put us in shorts and T-shirts—and snap us while we ran the fifty-yard dash and took the hurdles. Or he'd take us out to

Santa Monica beach—an excuse for bathing suits—where we'd play volleyball, leap on the sands, kick, jump and play football, not the authentic version of course. We'd kick a football—I damn near broke my toe the first time—or toss a pass in very feminine fashion while Don's camera caught us. There was no such thing as a portable radio, but the prop man improvised a horn on a box when Dorothy and I danced, and the caption read, "to the music of a portable radio." That gave the manufacturers an idea.

Dorothy Sebastian and I became devoted friends. She was a jolly, vital girl from Alabama and we loved these excursions to the beach. We kicked, leaped, worked out with dumbbells, lifted iron weights and played with boxing gloves as if it were a game. For me it *was*. I probably had more pictures taken than any girl who'd ever been signed at the studio, because, as a dancer, I could leap the highest and jump the farthest. I threw myself into action shots with youthful abandon.

They also took pictures of me as I came out of a firecracker for the Fourth of July, climbing down a chimney in a fur-trimmed Santa Claus bathing suit with a Teddy bear in my pack, and in all sorts of chiffon scarves and beads I'd dig up in wardrobe, some of the most artistic of these for European publication. Once they took me down to Seventh and Broadway in Los Angeles, put me in a traffic cop's hat and let me stop traffic. I stopped quite a bit of traffic, and that photo broke in newspapers across country. I was in pictures, that's true, but not *moving*.

As a matter of fact, my first appearance before the moving camera was anonymous. I doubled for Norma Shearer in her dual role in *Lady of the Night*. This was the story of a reform-school graduate and a judge's daughter, both in love with the same young inventor. Full

face there's no resemblance between Norma and me, but our pro-
files did look somewhat alike. While Norma played the Tough Girl
(full front, close-up), I played the Lady (with my back to the camera);
when she did the Lady, I was the Tough Girl (with my back to the
camera). Between times, I tried to watch everything Norma did, for
she was that wonderful being, a star. Also, she dated Irving Thalberg,
who was in charge of studio production.

Thalberg would come by the set occasionally, a cool-looking, dark
young man who tossed a gold coin in the air, tossed it and tossed it,
with such concentration that you never dared speak to him. I didn't
envy Norma, but I did long for a friend at court! She had Thalberg,
Marion Davies had Mr. Hearst, Jeanette MacDonald had a good education and a hard-working mother, I . . . well, I still had never caught
sight of that vanished showman with the sagacious look.

Mr. Rapf I had seen only that once in New York. He evidently
had forgotten I was here. No one else *knew*, except, of course, Johnny
Arnold, Tommy Shagrue, the boys in publicity, Lulu, the matron in
charge of the dressing rooms, and Edith and Eleanor in hairdressing.
I was always showing up in hairdressing to experiment and watch.
I'd swipe pictures from the publicity files to study the coiffures, see
what was wrong and what was right. The grips and prop men were
my friends too. They'd try to build me up with a "Don't worry, kid,
you're okay, you can do it."

Well, I had to do it. I couldn't sit and watch those six precious
months slide by. There were dozens of girls on the lot, with contracts
and theatrical experience, *and* friends at court. I'd find out what pictures were being cast, then attempt to secure a bit part or extra work.
What I didn't grasp was that when Mr. Rapf went east looking for
talent he wasn't looking for *actresses*, he was looking for background

glamour, which is certainly what I was. In New York I'd been so far back I never did see the audience.

Now in Hollywood I was still background glamour. Carey Wilson cast me—at Mr. Rapf's suggestion!—as Miss MGM, introducing a sales film which would show clips from forthcoming MGM attractions to exhibitors at the annual convention. Mr. Wilson sent me to Sophie Watman in wardrobe for plain opera pumps—no bows—size two and a half at that time. The opening shot was of me, all legs, in high-heeled black patent leather pumps, no acting ability needed. But I liked Mr. Wilson and he became one of my self-appointed guardian angels. Later he told me why. He was used to girls in what he calls "the Hollywood pattern": brassy exteriors, a vamp technique and the ability to scheme, plan and finagle to get ahead. "You were different, you were just plain scared to death," he told me years later. "You hadn't come to a boil yet. You'd have been overwhelmed anywhere and here you were in a spot that was honestly overwhelming, the biggest studio in the business, a place teeming with the brightest stars."

I wonder what would have happened if he'd told me then. Perhaps I'd have had a whole new concept of life earlier, knowing someone understood me. Like most youngsters my age I thought no one did.

I used to wander about watching the "brightest stars" at work. Posing for still pictures didn't begin to exhaust my energy. I was at a *motion* picture studio, motion pictures were being made all around me, and, subconsciously at first, I wanted to see what was happening, get in on it, learn. . . . William Haines and Eleanor Boardman were making a picture called *Memory Lane*. Enchanting to me were the scenes they shot at night, the blue-white lights warming to life a small world out of the dark, and in this warmth actors moving toward each other, away from each other, smiling, vital, somehow more palpable than any people anywhere! I used to steal onto the back lot and stand in the shadows, watching. William Haines, Eleanor Boardman and I became close friends and we've been friends ever since. Willie shouts with laughter when I recall watching him from the shadows. According to him, my life has been strictly in the spotlight and when I stood in the dark it was probably the signal for a light to swing in my direction.

I met Marion Davies too. She was warm, generous, a delightful human being who made you feel that *you* were a delightful human being. Sweeney, the prop man, would find me behind the scenery and ask Marion if I could come on the set. Marion always agreed. She was bubbling with pert good spirits, much more animated between scenes than she was as the sweet proper heroine of her pictures. And her pictures *were* proper. Leading men were afraid to kiss Miss Davies. Mr. Hearst was far more formidable than any censor, and he was always on the set.

Marion I watched. Also Mae Murray, whom I came to admire for the measure of her tremendous discipline over her body. She was a dancer, and every facet of her dancing technique came to bear on her performance. I tried to note everything the stars did, tried to understand why, for I was beginning to realize that I wanted to become an actress, maybe a dancing actress.

My own first picture was *Pretty Ladies,* with ZaSu Pitts and Lilyan Tashman. Myrna Loy and I were chorus girls. We sat on blocks of ice—some melted faster than others—all done up in maribou, in imitation snow. We had no lines to speak. I was strictly a mummy with big eyes, watching everything. This was Metro's answer to a series of glorified Follies films Florenz Ziegfeld had been signed to do for Famous Players. It was a spectacle of the New York theatrical world, a good deal more lavish than the Shubert world I'd just left, and blended with a human-interest story. ZaSu was the human interest, Myrna and I were background. In one scene we were Japanese ladies, and in the pièce de résistance we were clinging tenaciously to a chandelier of living statues high on a Cedric Gibbons set, while down below, young director Monta Bell brooded over the effect. I kept on clinging tenaciously, not only to the chandelier but to my job at the studio.

The next picture, I remember nothing about, *The Only Thing*, starring Eleanor Boardman, who was on her way to the top (I thought she was there already). It was based on an Elinor Glyn novel about a mythical kingdom and a beautiful princess betrothed to an old king. I played the part of Young Lady Catherine, which must have been one of those bits I was begging so hard for, that Jack Conway tossed me this tiny morsel to keep me from hounding his office.

My first real part was in *Old Clothes,* produced by Jack Coogan, Sr., and starring Jackie, the child with the great black eyes, who could walk about with his hands behind his back and melt everyone's heart. For this picture, there was a tryout of one hundred and fifty girls. We were lined up, turned profile and tested. I got the part of Mary Riley, the girl who mothers the waif. Mine was a small part, but I took it big. I'd sit listening to the musicians in a coma of concentration. Director Eddie Cline'd smile around his cigar. "You'd think this scene was the most important thing in your life, girl." It was!

Once when my twins were on Spike Jones's television program, Eddie Cline was the first person I saw as we walked on stage. He was still a cigar-smoking cherub. We laughed over my early intensity, but that first part *was* a break for me. Jackie's father, Mr. Coogan, believed I'd make good and was kind enough to tell me so. Besides,

Jackie was such a big star, *Old Clothes* received a great deal of publicity and I got my picture in the papers.

But you can't eat publicity, and I was hungry—for excitement, for fun, for people, for work. I simply hadn't work enough, and my vitality was at the explosion point. In my cramped little hotel room, I'd turn on the Victrola and dance to the point of exhaustion. I borrowed money from the studio and bought a second-hand coupe— white of course—and some spangled dresses. Shirley Dorman, an extra on the lot, had become my friend, and through her, I met many other girls. Betty Jane Young (later Sally Blane), Polly Ann Young, Carole Lombard, Audrey Ferris, Doris Dawson, were all young hopefuls like myself. Except, perhaps, I wanted more than any of them to make it. I had nothing to go back *to*. Hollywood must notice me— before that six months was up.

And I loved to dance. At the Montmartre overlooking Hollywood Boulevard, the gayest people in town lunched, dined and supper-clubbed while tourists were held back by red velvet ropes. We kids wanted an important table, just as important as those occupied by the big stars, Connie and Norma Talmadge and Gloria Swanson. Wednesday nights at the Montmartre there were exhibition dances. That was for me. I was timorous about exhibition dancing—there was no chorus line to hold me up—but every time I got up on the floor and forced myself to dance, it was like winning a personal victory. I worked all day and danced all night. Tuesdays and Wednesdays at the Montmartre, Fridays at the Cocoanut Grove, the beach clubs, the Saturday tea-dance kid. The LeSueur girl got to be known as an exhibition Charleston dancer. When she did the Black Bottom, and people applauded and whistled between their teeth, I was in another world.

There was no lack of dancing partners—this town was filled with gay young men. The minute Professor Moore's orchestra would start at the Montmartre, over they'd come from the famous bachelor's table. You couldn't dance with a man without having your engagement announced in the next day's paper. Jimmy Hall . . . Danny Dowling . . . Mike Cudahy . . . Johnny Westwood . . . Don Lee's son, Tommy. . . . Tommy was the most successful beau of his day. Everyone— Carole Lombard included—competed to see who'd get a Friday night date with Tommy. I was reported engaged to everyone but Bull Montana, and that publicity seemed in step with my exuberance, my need for the dramatic. My skirts had to be a trifle shorter, my heels a little higher, my hair a tint brighter, my dancing faster. One night I lost a slipper dancing with Jack Ensley at the Grove. We didn't stop to retrieve it, and the crowd applauded and awarded us another trophy.

I danced even faster after Jerry's death. Jerry Chrysler was one of the boys in this dancing crowd. We had picnics a few times at the beach, we took motor trips along the coast on Sundays. One Wednesday night Jerry and I won a loving cup after a hectic hour of twirling. When we came out and got into Jerry's little open car, it was chilly, and I begged him to keep his coat over his shoulders. He shrugged it off. The air felt fine, he said. Two days later he had pneumonia. When I went to see him at the hospital, the minute I entered the room, I *knew*—he was so flushed, his eyes were so wild and dark— but I didn't want him to know. I don't know how well I played that scene, I really couldn't act my way out of a paper bag then. I played it more effectively eight years later in *Sadie McKee*, visiting Gene Raymond, trying to keep him from knowing he was dying. The scene was a natural then. I had only to think of gallant Jerry, whose life had ended when it had scarcely begun.

Johnny Arnold used to try to talk to me like a Dutch uncle. He'd hear people on the set inviting me here, there and everywhere.

"Don't pay any attention to those good-time Charlies," he'd say. "You can't stay up late and get up early. Besides, you have to be careful where you go and with whom."

I only half-listened. "The hotcha kid," I was called, "the hey-hey girl," those terms embarrassed me even then, but the only time I felt I belonged was when I was on the dance floor. The publicity department played this up for all it was worth. They exploited my "new beau every night" and the fact that I had "more cups than the Brown Derby." Every time I won a cup I was "engaged" to my partner. It was a day of unbuttoned journalism and the stories about me got increasingly out of hand. There were stories that said I'd had my eyes slit to make them bigger . . . that I'd ruined my health by drastic dieting . . . and other unsavory items harder to disprove . . . that I'd danced at smokers . . . that I'd made a stag reel of film . . . that I floated easily from one romance to another. As one writer said, "She wears her escort of the evening like a corsage and passes from one love to another with equal ease." This reputation for easy romance haunted me for years. It couldn't have been less true.

You never found me dating a boy who couldn't dance. I went out with boys because I wanted only to dance. There was no such thing as a Hollywood romance until I met and fell in love with dashing Mike Cudahy. He was startlingly handsome, tall, dark, gallant, a graceful dancer; my happiness and unhappiness hinged totally on Michael for the next two years.

He was kind and gentle and weak. He lacked the strength for self-discipline, for facing life, but he could dance. One evening at the Montmartre we won the Charleston contest. Michael insisted we stay on and dance until dawn. For me this was impossible, I had to work the next morning. For him, work meant nothing, he'd never had to work; he'd been very casual about school. "You and your work!" he fumed.

Eventually I grew angry and went home alone; but I never slept, I worried about our quarrel. We argued about my working, we argued about his drinking, but Michael was beguiling and we made up so happily I gave up all other dates to be with him.

He showed up each evening wearing an immaculate dinner jacket, and he either sent flowers or brought them—a gesture I've always adored. To me he seemed a dream prince. I overlooked the weak chin, the slight puffiness about his young face that presaged trouble ahead.

His family hoped I'd marry Mike, although newspaper columnists kept insisting that Mrs. Cudahy would have none of me. In fact, she and his sisters and I were good friends. Michael used to take me to his home for tea. His father was dead, I had been told that his mother hadn't been out of the house for twenty years, literally since Michael was born. But I still wasn't quite prepared. . . .

Their house sat on a hill above Hollywood and Sunset, a great old mansion with at least thirty-five rooms. We came in out of the sunshine and bracing air, and every window in this house was locked tight, every drape drawn. It was as eerie as a tomb. And sitting in a raised straight-backed chair in the wan electric light sat a woman who might have been an empress—Michael's mother. She was tall, massive—he was six three and she couldn't have been much less— dressed in an elegant emerald-green chiffon hostess gown. I never saw her in anything except hostess gowns, and I never saw her in any light save artificial. Her skin was white and languid as linen.

Obviously she *hadn't* been out of the house in twenty years. But people came to her, people of wealth and society attended her salons.

And I came to tea—and drank tea. I'm sure she didn't. This belle dame sans merci lived in the past, dressed unlike other mortals, and the whole atmosphere was strictly Sunset Boulevard. I often wondered if we raised the blinds, flung back the drapes, opened the windows, would the ornate cushions gleam satin as they seemed, or would they be revealed in shreds and tatters.

Mrs. Cudahy eschewed publicity and preferred not to see her son's name in the papers, but she liked me, since I was the one person who could keep Michael off the bottle. Sometimes, even I couldn't. There were many nights when this young Errol Flynn with his flare for gaiety would drink himself into insensibility. I'd drive him home in his car, park him in his driveway, ring the doorbell so the butler would know he was there, then go home in a cab.

I never blamed him, only tried to help him, worried over him and let the future blur out of focus in the back of my mind. This was a tumultuous romance which could have ruined my life. I tried to win Michael to my way. I won . . . over a hundred cups for the Charleston. My new little apartment on Ogden Drive was stuffed with trophies and silver cups, with woolly animals and dolls, the treasures of a child. Perhaps Michael was a child's hero.

He was the reckless scion of the F. Scott Fitzgerald era just as I was the flapper of the John Held, Jr., cartoons. At nineteen, he had a roaring blue Packard roadster, an unlimited allowance, the most beautiful manners I'd ever seen, and an insatiable taste for night life. We had some glorious times making the rounds of cafés and hotels. Adela Rogers St. Johns saw us one evening when she visited the Montmartre with Tom and Virginia Mix and the town's pet bride and groom, Harold and Mildred Lloyd. She found herself staring, she said, "at an unknown girl dancing with that tall dark youth, Mike Cudahy, heir to the Chicago packing fortune. From her too-high heels to her too-frizzy hair, she was all wrong, yet she stood out as though the light was too bright for anyone but her. Terribly young, showing off rather crudely, laughing too loudly, she had a fierce and wonderful vitality and grace. Lucille LeSueur has done a few bits at MGM, I hear she may be on her way." Adela was a keen observer, and my insecurities *were* showing.

She wasn't the only one who noticed us whirling around the local dance floors. One night, director Edmund Goulding saw us at the Grove. He said that when I Charlestoned, it was as if I were intoxicated with joy. It *was* joy—I never touched liquor. I barely touched earth!

"That girl's under contract to us, isn't she?" Mr. Goulding said. "Well, she's a natural. She's Irene."

He was speaking of the forthcoming production, *Sally, Irene and Mary*, for which a lavish set was already being built for a full-stage Charleston number. Constance Bennett had drawn the role of Sally, Sally O'Neil would play Mary. We were three hardworking ambitious youngsters in the script, earning a living in a chorus and coming home at night to corned beef and cabbage. It was a good picture of back-stage chorus-girl life with bits of comedy and pathos, and the characters made sense. This had been my old life. As it turned out, *Sally, Irene and Mary* was the beginning of my new life, and my new name.

Pete Smith in Publicity had never liked "Lucille LeSueur." It may have been the name I was born with but it sounded contrived, he said, too theatrical. The top brass evidently agreed with him. So the studio sponsored a contest in *Movie Weekly*, a roto Macfadden publication, with one thousand dollars in prizes, five hundred dollars for the person who came up with a name "simple to pronounce," "euphonious," and a match for my personality, which the editors described as "energetic, ambitious and typically American." The judges were to be Florence Lawrence, drama editor of the Los Angeles *Examiner*, Edwin Schallert, drama editor of the Los Angeles *Times*, Harry Rapf of MGM and Adele Whitley Fletcher, editor of *Movie Weekly*. The contest closed May 2, 1925. The winning name—Joan Arden. Within a week after I'd reported for work on *Sally, Irene and Mary* we discovered an extra on the lot whose name *was* Joan Arden. Studio and magazine agreed to use the second prize name suggested by Mrs. Marie M. Tisdale, a little crippled lady of Albany, New York. She used the money for hospital bills and gave me the name I love now but hated then.

"Crawford, Crawford, it sounds like crawfish," I mourned.

"You're lucky it isn't cranberry," Willie Haines said. "You could be dished up every Thanksgiving with the turkey." And he promptly dubbed me "Cranberry," which he calls me to this day.

But Joan Crawford I *was*. My name was changed on two unreleased pictures, and there it appeared every day on the call sheet. I plucked my eyebrows wide apart, fashioned my mouth into a coy cupid's bow. Director Goulding insisted my hair be parted in the middle, and I wept while Edith Hubner did it—I thought it made my baby face look even rounder. I observed Connie Bennett's svelte figure and started dancing harder than ever and dieting like mad to lose weight. I ate crackers and mustard, drank gallons of black coffee. Totally absorbed in the picture, I didn't even know when I was hungry.

The only one of us with any assurance before the camera was Constance Bennett, who'd had stage experience. Willie Haines, who played Sally O'Neil's sweetheart, took his lead with easy philosophy. He thought we were getting paid to have a good time. But to me each moment was deadly serious. I remember working myself up for one big emotional scene, and how, at the last minute, Johnny Arnold left his camera and took me aside. He said, "Pretend that the news you hear in this scene concerns someone close to you and you've just heard it for the first time. No matter how many times you've rehearsed it, hear it now for the first time."

In all my early pictures I overacted horribly, moved too much, cried too much and photographed like a caricature. It was all part of my education. Mine was an inadequate taste and poor makeup. We had no makeup men then—the stars had makeup men—but we had a makeup department where we were given supplies. Then we were on our own, trial and error. My errors were countless. I tried to make my eyes and mouth look smaller. But one mistake I didn't make—I never tried to imitate anyone else. Johnny Arnold shot one closeup of a scene so my face filled the entire screen, and when I saw it, I went into a frenzy of experimentation. But it was the day of the question-mark eyebrow, the tiny mouth. I didn't have the courage to let nature take its course, and no one ever said, "Take off your makeup, let's see how you *look*." We didn't have time for costume tests or makeup tests, we made six or eight pictures a year, and I studied my script in a concentrated panic, for *Sally, Irene and Mary* or no, that six-month clause was still staring me in the face. There wasn't a peaceful moment until the studio renewed my option on the first day of July and raised my salary to one hundred—a week!

I learned from everyone. From director Bill Wellman on *The Boob,* in which I had only a bit, from Goulding who also directed *Paris.* I played a French gamin in *Paris,* and in one scene Mr. Goulding suddenly said:

"Take off your shoes, Joan."

I obeyed.

"Now . . . spread your feet and take a good grip of the earth with your feet and toes."

I obeyed.

"Draw the strength of the earth right into you! Strength is there, use it."

I've played many big scenes shoeless and found a wonderful sense of strength and stillness. Just when everything was under control, another director shouted for *high* heels. I felt like Samson after the haircut.

"I'll be taller than my leading man," I protested.

"I'll stand him on a box. Put on your heels! You'll stand straighter. With heels on, a ramrod goes right up your . . . !"

And you know, he was right!

What saved me in *Paris* was working with Charles Ray. As the gallant millionaire he was so shy and soft-spoken he put me at ease. He never seemed to speak above a whisper, never threw his weight around. He realized what an amateur I was. I broke my ankle during the apache dance, which we rehearsed seventy times in a narrow camera range, but I wanted the part so badly, I said it was *nothing*, nothing at all. My ankle was bound up and I went on dancing. I was desperate for work—almost a year at the studio and only *Sally, Irene and Mary* to show for it.

The studio's publicity build-up only increased my apprehension. I understand that the paeans of praise a studio trumpets forth as publicity makes some players feel assured. More than that, they believe it. But publicity intimidated this newcomer. I kept thinking, Suppose I'm not that good? The Baby Wampas stars had just been named for

1926—the girls most likely for stardom in the opinion of one hundred publicity men. One by one, we each stepped timidly out of Cinderella's coach and bowed to the audience of the Western Association of Motion Picture Advertisers. We'd been marcelled within an inch of our scalps, manicured, splendidly gowned. But suppose the publicity men were wrong. Suppose we never made it?

Looking back, I must give those publicists credit. Their choice, alphabetically:

Mary Astor
Mary Brian
Joyce Compton
Dolores Costello
Joan Crawford
Marcelline Day
Dolores del Rio
Janet Gaynor
Sally Long
Edna Marion
Sally O'Neil
Vera Reynolds
Fay Wray

My nomination gave Pete Smith and his new assistant, Howard Strickling, a chance to flood the country with publicity art, pictures of me dancing the Charleston in beaded dresses, pictures of me dressed as Hamlet contemplating my silver cups. I spent so much time posing in bathing suits on the windy back lot, I developed tonsillitis that only ended when my tonsils were removed. This was my first meeting with Dr. Bill Branch, who has kept his eye on me ever since. I told him my dreams about being an actress. He told me about the clinic he wanted to build to care for patients who needed help. I made up my mind that if I managed to stay in this business, I'd contribute to his clinic each time I received a raise. And there came a day in the thirties when Dr. Branch invited me to lunch. He had called rather urgently. I thought perhaps he had a problem and dropped everything to go. But he mentioned no problem. He marched me in the door of Hollywood Presbyterian Hospital, down one corridor and another, turned me around to face a wall, and there was a plaque inscribed: *This wing dedicated to Joan Crawford who has dedicated every bed in this wing.*

But at the time of the tonsillectomy the question was, would I survive in this business? Would I ever last to the next six-month option?

At this point, I returned home one day to find my brother, Hal, newly arrived from Kansas City. He'd seen my pictures in the paper. "If you can make it, kid, with that funny face of yours and all those freckles, I sure can," he said, and studying him across the little table in my kitchen that night as we ate our dinner, I quite agreed. He was certainly as handsome as any boy in Hollywood with his blond, curly hair and charming presence. Girls had always flocked after him. They were captive to his boyish appeal. Mother was captive also—Hal could do no wrong. As a child I had idolized this older brother, but I knew his weaknesses now, and between Hal and a career lay the question of hard work, the ability to stand on his own feet and fight for it. The only job he'd held to date was jerking sodas.

I greeted Hal with mixed emotions. It was wonderful to feel part of a family. On the other hand, my apartment was tiny. I slept on the pull-down bed and made up his bed on the couch. I had to see that he had dinner and transportation and laundry and a job. I who wasn't yet responsible for myself was now responsible for him. The next day I took him around to the casting department, where they gave him a job as an extra. That didn't daunt Hal. He was cocky, optimistic, within a few days he'd found some pretty girl friends and felt quite at home. Before the end of the year Mother joined us, as soon as I was able to rent a small house on Genessee.

Now we could be a family, like other people, I thought. Mother was a magnificent cook. She could keep house in a home of her own, no laundry agency attached, and for the first time we could all be happy together. I'd had a salary raise. I rented a little bungalow and started furnishing on the installment plan. It was a nightmare of fringe, lace, tassels, pink taffeta drapes and long-legged dolls. It was also a very solid establishment with stove, icebox, washing machine and upholstered furniture, all slowly to be paid for.

Pressure is something I welcome, but sending money home to Kansas City had been one thing, while this was another. Having them with me, knowing that if I didn't make good, not only I but they were sunk, was far from contributing to my peace of mind.

And there were problems. One morning I got up to go to work and discovered, at a quarter to six, no car. Hal had wrecked it the night before.

Getting to the studio on time is a must. You keep dozens of people waiting and run production costs up thousands of dollars a minute. I'd never been late, but I was that morning. Hollywood is a long way from Culver City, across town. I took a bus and streetcars, arriving shamefaced. That night I gave Hal the word. This was my car and since I was the family breadwinner, that car had to be at *my* disposal.

"But, Lucille, he couldn't help it," Mother said.

And of course after a while I relented, and he took the car again, and it happened over and over. I'd wake in the morning not knowing whether I had a car or not.

One day I received notification of a lawsuit from the Broadway Department Store, and almost immediately similar notifications came from Bullocks' and from the May Company. Mother adored the department stores. She enjoyed shopping and, bless her heart, she was spending money as if it were going out of style. Hats, shoes, bags, clothes . . . she never showed me the bills. She hid them and hid them until now we were threatened with these lawsuits. Five hundred dollars at one place, four hundred at another.

"Mother, why haven't you told me?" I asked, but she looked so like a little girl, I sat down and wrote letters explaining that the bill would be paid, I'd pay it off so much a week. That's when Shirley Dorman came to live with us. She and I shared my room. With the money Shirley contributed, I helped pay off the bills.

We still had problems. Nights when I needed to rest for an early call at the studio, there would be friends of mother's visiting. And there were additional incidents with the car. Finally, one day I'd had it. My nature is to accept a situation, gloss over it, endure it, take it for just so long. Then suddenly, *Finis!* I was through—I couldn't live that way.

Hal was doing a lot of work. He was on call for all crowd scenes in pictures at the studio, he now had a stock contract. If he wanted a car, he could buy one. I had to have some rest and I could no longer go to bed worrying about whether or not my car'd be there in the morning. With the help of a friend of Mother's, Scotty Welch, a real estate man, I found a little house on Roxbury Drive and went to see Mr. Mayer.

Louis B. Mayer was head of the studio and, I'd heard, an astute businessman. I told Mr. Mayer about the house, it was lovely, with a garden all concealed from the street, but it cost a tremendous amount of money, eighteen *thousand* dollars! Could I get the money for a down payment from a bank? From the studio? And before I borrowed a nickel, was I—did Mr. Mayer feel I was doing well enough at the studio to risk this kind of an investment?

It was the first advice I'd ever asked of him, and Mr. Mayer gave me immediate sanction. He knew of my car situation. There'd been items in the paper about Joan Crawford's car and Joan Crawford's brother and the accidents. Mr. Mayer knew better than I the old story of bit players who dream of starring parts and worry more than they admit and drink more than they should. He told me to go ahead and buy the house, and the studio would lend me the down payment and, yes, I was doing very well.

This I tried to remember when MGM loaned me to First National. Not too optimistic a sign—studios didn't lend valuable properties at that time. The picture was *Tramp, Tramp, Tramp* with stage star Harry Langdon. It was my first comedy. There was, however, more to this plot than laughter—there was a cyclone.

In one scene Harry and I had to run through the town. He found a manhole, pushed me in and slammed the lid. I didn't know the word claustrophobia then, but I had known the sensation since I was five and Hal locked me in a closet—it was several hours before Mother found me. *Years* passed while I cowered in that manhole during the cyclone. When the wind machines finally stopped, and Harry pulled me out limp, director Frank Capra said, *"Just once more, please."*

I wasn't so sure I wanted to be in the movies. The one that almost sent me back to Kansas City was *Winners of the Wilderness* with Tim McCoy. Not that I didn't like Tim, I did. He'd been a government liaison man with no acting ambition, now he was a cowboy star in such tight britches he couldn't mount a horse without the help of a three-foot ladder—out of camera range, of course. But this was a period western and the minute I met my first horse I knew I was not destined to be a female Buck Jones. I was sure of it after the runaway scene when, at the director's instruction, two wranglers seized me, threw me over the horse and away I went without benefit of stirrups, and a few gallops later, without benefit of *horse*. Whatever had happened to dancing?

Now I was assigned to *The Unknown*, to a star known as the horror man of films, a man who literally made the lights tremble on the marquee—Mr. Lon Chaney. Here was the most tense, exciting individual I'd ever met, a man mesmerized into this part. Between pictures when you met him on the lot you saw a grave, mild-mannered man with laughing black eyes who seldom laughed, but when he did, his laughter was irresistible. When he worked, it was as if God were working, he had such profound concentration. It was then I became aware for the first time of the difference between standing in front of a camera, and acting. Lon Chaney's concentration, the complete absorption he gave to his character, filled all of us with such awe we never even considered addressing him with the usual pleasantries until he became aware of and addressed us. He was armless in this picture—his arms strapped to his sides—and he learned to eat, even to hold a cigarette using his feet and toes. He was in a world of his own, a world in which he'd had those arms amputated for love of a gypsy girl who abhors men's arms. And when he returns to the circus, he finds her—me—in the arms of the strong man! Mr. Chaney could have unstrapped his arms between scenes. He did not. He kept them strapped one day for five hours, enduring such numbness, such torture, that when we got to this scene, he was able to convey not just realism but such emotional agony that it was shocking . . . and fascinating.

With new determination, I jumped into *Twelve Miles Out*, a rum-running yarn in which I became the tug-of-war between John Gilbert and Ernest Torrence. Jack was a top star, a renowned screen lover. It was fortuitous to be cast with him—I was star-conscious now and looked forward to an epic picture—but I was in for quick disappointment. John Gilbert wasn't interested in this film. He was madly in love with Garbo, the love affair wasn't going well, and he was obsessed—a caged lion. After an evening with this exquisite woman, he'd stride onto the set in his stomping, military manner, rush to the phone to call her, only to find that her phone had been yanked out of the wall or her phone number changed—since last night! He fretted like thunder. He was impatient with the picture, the director, and as for me, the moment I'd read my lines, I'd rush to my dressing room. The moment he finished a scene, he'd rush to her set, to her dressing room, or he'd attempt again to call her. Thwarted, he was fury incarnate.

He resented every minute on the set away from her. Ernest Torrence kept up my morale. He was the lamb of the world, the meekest, sweetest, fiercest-looking villain. Thanks to him and to director Jack Conway, I survived, and *Variety* gave me a valued plug, "A classic for form, appearance, looks and ability . . . two more pictures like this and JC's set." They didn't say for what.

Incidentally, when I worked with Jack later in *Four Walls*, he was a completely different man, vivid, vital and dynamic. The curly black head tilted back, when he laughed, his hearty chortle could have been heard from Culver City to Santa Monica. His eyes were like radar. From Lon Chaney I had learned concentration. From John Gilbert I learned to keep my vitality undiluted on the screen, never to let down for a moment.

William Haines exemplified the same principle. I was his leading lady in *Spring Fever* and *West Point*. He had great naturalness
and charm and an overwhelming sense of humor. He would take you
in his arms in a love scene, joking so that you had to brace yourself
not to laugh, but his mood for a sad scene of *yours* was immediately
responsive. I was strictly secondary in both these pictures. Complete
with bows on my satin shoes, an ankle bracelet and one-eighth yard
of printed chiffon dress, well above the knees, when I arrived at West
Point that first day at sundown and came out to catch dress parade,
Willie Haines says the whole military line went serpentine. But I was
furious because the wardrobe department insisted I wear a bra, and I
was terrified of breaking my tissues, I was also furious because I was
background scenery. You couldn't ask for snappier direction than we
had from Ed Sedgwick, or more dulcet love scenes—despite Willie's
wisecracks. But essentially what made a Haines picture was always
Willie himself, like Puck, the symbol of eternal, cocky, lovable youth.

His was the first movie star's house I ever visited, and there you
encountered another facet of the man—his talent as a decorator. He
gave beautiful, elaborate parties with different décor each time, huge
candelabra of Georgian silver, bacchanalian bowls of fruit. Once he
gave a Southern party with butlers in knee breeches and magnolia
blossoms throughout the "manse," fried chicken, corn pone, mustard greens. Whatever the décor, the food was served to match. One
party was strictly collegiate. Cliff Edwards played the uke, Clara Bow
was there, everyone was whooping it up. One of Willie's friends made
a remark to me Willie didn't like and he threw him out, then pro-
ceeded to fight him in the street. Willie knocked out some of the fellow's teeth that night, insisted on paying to have them replaced, and
then tried to collect half from me!

It was the flaming youth period, the jazz era—we know that now. We had no name for ourselves then. Today they are called teenagers, and everyone tries to help them understand their responsibilities and rationalize their problems. We weren't supposed to have problems. We didn't rationalize that as an aftermath to war, old standards had broken down, that ours was a freedom our parents had never had, that young women were free for the first time to choose a way of life after centuries of having life arranged *for* them, first by their fathers, then by their husbands. We only knew we were free and we wanted to try everything, do everything, have everything.

On my birthday I hosted a party at the Montmartre, crammed my girl friends in a taxi, took them to lunch and didn't have sufficient money for the taxi home. I was spending twice as much as I earned, but that was all part of the tempo. Everything had to be fast. I made most of my own clothes, and they looked it—loving hands at home. This was hardly difficult dressmaking, a bit of chiffon or crepe de Chine or satin, some drapery and a bow or two, and because they were extreme they were imitated. I went stockingless while others were experimenting with half-socks. I wore bright red nail polish on fingers and toes, and the minute others did, I switched to pale pink. Pink and white blondes were the prototype of Hollywood pictures. I went to the beach, oiled, and acquired a deep dark tan.

I wanted to be noticed, I was. I received so much publicity that it made me the target for disappointed wives, and the next thing I knew my name and face were on the front pages in two divorce actions. One of the suits concerned a man I'd met once. The other was brought by the wife of a quiet, unprepossessing set musician. He had received a sweater from me for Christmas, she said, and with the gift an affectionate note. Everyone on the set received a gift from me that Christmas, *with* an affectionate note. When I autographed pictures they were always to the "dearest boy" or "the sweetest boy" or "the sweetest girl." I used only superlatives. All the stories stressed my dancing, my Charleston cups, my squabbles with Mike Cudahy, my "engagements," the fact that I played hard.

Maybe I did play harder than anyone else—I worked harder, too. Perhaps because I had such an inferiority complex, because I was trying to compensate for all I lacked in education, poise and background. I wanted something out of life and this was the only way I knew to acquire it. The studio thought me a crazy kid who got into jams because I was interested in nothing but pleasure.

One day I was summoned to Paul Bern's office. Paul was Irving Thalberg's assistant in production. He had seen me standing around observing the stars at work. He sensed a need, and asked what my problems were.

Since he was the first person who had ever asked, I poured it all out. I was getting nowhere. The films I'd made since *Sally, Irene and Mary* were cheaply and quickly made. Direction was given the male stars. Sally O'Neil and I had started with identical contracts. Now she had been given star status.

His lips twitched. "Improve yourself, my dear, study, work, have patience and faith in yourself." He was a quiet man. He studied me with his dark brooding eyes.

I didn't know he meant books or art or the theater. Then one night he took me to the El Capitan Theater on Hollywood Boulevard to see the great Pauline Frederick. I watched her artistry, her confidence, her beauty. I wished I could make people love me as she made the audience love her. She was taking off her makeup when we came into her dressing room. I could only stand, staring.

Paul said, "Polly, speak to this foolish little girl. She wants to conquer the world in an hour. Tell her what hard work it is, how long it takes."

The glorious Miss Frederick turned to look at me. She rose, crossed the room, took my face in her two hands. "Go on, dream your dreams, little one. Conquer the world in an hour. If you feel that you can accomplish things, never allow anyone or anything to destroy your thought."

I held her words close. I fought for pictures. I fought for Michael. But he couldn't share my dreams. Work meant nothing to this boy. He couldn't see why I was so engrossed. He'd come with me, sneak in the side door of the West Lake Theater and watch previews, but at nineteen he was interested in pictures just for fun. He couldn't understand this necessity of mine to work. He couldn't understand my need for love. Mike would never have noticed me if it hadn't been for the Grove or the Montmartre, the dancing, the flamboyant personality. That was what mattered to him—the jazz, café-society life mattered—and so it was important to me. But not for long. It wore thin; it wasn't the answer. Being in love had to be more than this round of fun, it had to be something fine.

I kept thinking I could make him stop drinking. That it was a losing battle was indicated by my increasing unhappiness. I never believed in Michael, really. I didn't trust him. When he'd alibi an absence, I'd try to laugh it off, but he knew I didn't believe it. You can't build happiness out of uncertainty. There were quarrels and bitterness. We'd patch it up and go on. We were very like the rootless young people of *Our Dancing Daughters, Our Modern Maidens* and *Our Blushing Brides,* in constant motion, not knowing where they were going.

It wasn't all Michael's fault. I was looking for a dream prince, and I was sensitive and impulsive, two qualities that bring a wide variety of joy and pain. Michael fell in love with a brash hoyden. He never understood that behind the façade was an uncertain child whose need was love.

TWO

The child was Billie Cassin and I remember her acutely. She lingers in me as childhood lingers in each of us. When I'm tired, Billie's child voice, Southern accent and all, rises in my throat. I remember working on an early Mankiewicz picture. We'd been shooting all day, now it was nearing six, and Mr. Mankiewicz stopped me in the middle of a scene.

What I'd said was, "I'm the new woman repohtah."

"Reporter, Miss Crawford."

"Yeayus, that's what I said—*repohtah.*"

We tried it a couple of times. Finally I said, "I cain't say *repohtah,* but I cain say newspapah womannn."

Don't ask me where I got my Southern accent. I left good old Texas at the age of six weeks, but my mother had a soft accent, some of my uncles and aunts must have had too, because Billie grew up speakin' Southern. I catch back her voice in weariness. When I need tears for an emotional scene in a picture, I catch back her memories. There was, for example, my daddy. His name was Henry Cassin and he was the center of my child's world—a short stocky man, black-haired, with small brown eyes and a pervasive quietness. A mature man, he was not the type to romp with children, but I could always crawl on his lap—he made room right inside his newspaper. And I knew he loved me. His two memorable gifts were this love and the privilege of playing in the barn where he stored scenery and costumes for his vaudeville house.

I must have been stagestruck from the first. It was entrancing to watch the dancers backstage at the theater. Once a ballerina in flaming-red tarlatan let me kneel before the lighted mirror on her dressing table while she put purple eye shadow and pink rouge on my face. I inhaled the smell of greasepaint, the musty scent of scenery, the dancers flying about, light dazzling in their spangled skirts. And I literally danced through the days, a butterfly, a bird. I never walked. I ran, danced, jumped, leaped, skipped rope, shinnied up a tree, "flew" down. Mother classed these as tomboy antics and did not approve. My legs were switched—my legs were switched whenever anything went wrong.

It seemed to me I was always blamed, not my brother, not Hal. One day the boy next door, Leslie Powell, threw a ball into the yard. Hal ran to catch it and trampled the nasturtiums. When mother saw the flower bed she immediately assumed that I'd been running again or trying to walk the "tightrope" on the fence. That day my legs were switched again and I was put in the corner.

"I did not do it," I muttered through clenched teeth. "I did *not* do it. Why doesn't Hal tell the truth? I did *not* do it." The continuous muttering earned me another switching, and, as always, unwarranted punishment only made me rebellious.

Mother had lost one child, which is probably why she worried about me—a daughter who died two and a half years before I was born. Her name was Daisy and she must have been a dear little thing, black eyes, black hair—pure French that one, not a trace of our Irish ancestry showing. But I was Irish as *well* as French and stubborn for my way. I trooped along with Hal and his boyfriends and helped put on shows with the scenery in the barn. My brother was five years older and my hero—a curly-haired boy with a handsome face—but he thought dragging little sister around was purely for the birds. I was always running after him, begging him to like me, begging him to play with me. In my eyes he was a veritable Jesse James and I was Pavlova. That was the world I lived in.

Actually, we lived in Lawton, Oklahoma, in a house like every other on the block, frame, with a couch swing on the front porch and eight steps from porch to pavement. Up and down those steps a hundred times a day skipped lightsome Billie. One day, aged six, she skipped out barefoot into the cool wet grass and twirled onto a broken bottle. It was the end of dancing for a long time. A big boy from across the street saw me lying there bleeding. He raced over, picked me up and carried me into the house, where a tourniquet was applied. Then he ran for a doctor.

The boy responsible for my rescue was Don Blanding, a senior at Lawton High. He grew up to be a poet, and years later we met when he returned from the South Seas and the Orient and was doing celebrity interviews in Hollywood. When he arrived on the set of *The Gorgeous Hussy* I said, "Hello, Don Blanding, do you know you once saved my life?"

He looked blank.

"I was Billie Cassin from . . ."

"The little girl across the street!" and he wrote a poem that was published soon after:

She was just the little girl who lived across the street,
All legs and curls and great big eyes and restless, dancing feet,
As vivid as a hummingbird, as bright and swift and gay,
A child who played at make believe . . .

But that broken bottle cost the hummingbird a year and a half of
inactivity. Every time I'd try to step, the wound would burst open.
Skin should have been grafted. Heaven knows, had it been done
properly, I'd have leaped up and executed an entrechat for the doctor. Instead, he sewed the gaping wound, and since the arch of the
foot needs pliability, stitches failed to hold. The doctor said I'd not
only never dance again, he doubted that I'd ever walk. I heard this
through the ether. But did you have to walk in order to dance?

There is something intuitive about childhood, a blending of
heredity, environment and dreams. You never know where the child
is going, but the child half knows, guesses, yearns toward the color of
a promise, wriggles fishlike toward some subterranean pool of memory. My mother had nothing of the volatile in her, neither did my
father. I dreamed only of dancing. To pass the time, I'd dream, lying
on the sleeping porch, smelling our morning glory and honeysuckle.
Dew translated them to the fragrance of jasmine.

Mother took tender care of me that year and a half. Like many
mothers she adored her son and favored him, but during that time
she felt genuine compassion for her daughter. A tiny woman, very
dainty, she never weighed over a hundred and ten pounds; I was a
heavy child for her to carry. But she carried me back and forth about
the house during the day—Daddy Cassin carried me at night—until I
was well enough to hop. Mother spent time with me. She brushed my

hair until it was glossy, it was long enough to sit on and she braided it in two pigtails and tied them with ribbons.

I remember her as happy at this time. One day when she handed Daddy Cassin his hat at the door, I saw him give her a good-bye kiss, then reach around and give her a little pat on the derrière. It was the most astonishing moment of my childhood. I had considered one's rear something strictly to sit on. My reaction might have been out-rage. It was, rather, curiosity, since mother obviously approved the gesture. I could hear her whistling in the kitchen while she cooked.

Mother's was a contagious, bell-like laugh, a sweet soprano. As time passed, she laughed less and less. My "buried treasure" put an end to laughter. When I was almost well, I was playing in the cel-lar one day. Our cellar was lined with shelves of Mother's preserved peaches, apricots and pickles, but we had used most of the pickles, and behind these shelves were mysterious apertures that tunneled beneath the house. Crawling in, I discovered some dirty old canvas bags, hauled one out, found it too heavy to hold, and when I dropped it, an avalanche of bright shiny coins spilled across the cellar floor. I didn't know it was gold, but I knew it was pretty, and scooping up two handfuls, went screaming excitedly to Mother. She turned white, swayed as if she might faint, then pulled herself together and ran with me to the cellar. When she saw the gold, she was frantic. Instead of pouring riches on our heads, my "treasure" brought calamity.

Daddy, it seemed, in addition to his theater, was involved in an insurance business with a partner. This partner had stolen the gold and Daddy had hidden it in fear of being held as accessory to the crime. Faced with Mother's hysterics he promised to turn the money over to the police. I overheard this, lying sleepless on the sleeping porch. The honeysuckle lost its fragrance as I listened to my parents' awful conversation and tried to find a solution. Before I could be of any help, Hal and I were hustled off on a train to visit our Grandmother Johnson, on a farm near Phoenix.

I couldn't understand what was happening. Trouble or no trouble, I wanted to be with Daddy Cassin. Any threat to him caused the bottom to drop out of my world. Twice before, this had happened. I remembered the one outing we'd all ever had together. We'd had a flat tire and while Daddy was out on the road fixing it, a car whizzed by, grazing him. The propulsive force threw him off balance and sent him turning over and over and over. I'd thought he was killed!

Another time, he'd climbed a big tree to saw off a branch. First he'd tested the limb on which to stand, but the sawing evidently had weakened it, for it broke with a mighty crack, dropping him at least twenty feet. In both accidents my response was identical: "Are you hurt, Daddy? Are you hurt, are you hurt!"

But this was worse, much worse. For the first time in my seven and a half years I was aware of a hurt beyond physical pain. Daddy Cassin hadn't fallen from a tree, I hadn't cut my foot, but we were both terribly wounded. Some weird mental anguish had warped him and me. We were in this together. I felt he needed me to help him.

As the train pulled out for Phoenix, I waved to Daddy until there was nothing to wave to but houses scudding by in a blur of tears. After a while Hal said it was time for lunch and got me settled with a paper napkin on my lap. As we ate, he must have teased me about something for I yelled:

"You wait till we get home, Hal Cassin. I'm gonna tell my daddy on you."

"Aw, he isn't even your daddy," Hal said.

I stared at him.

"You heard me. He isn't your daddy at all," Hal said.

I didn't understand. I had been fooled or left out of something. I was lost. The train bounced on the tracks. The smell of oranges and fried chicken was nauseating. Hal got under the seat, dragged out his suitcase and produced a picture of three people: himself as a small boy, Mother, and some man with great haunted eyes. That, he said, was our real daddy. I took one look at the eyes, the prominent cheekbones and bold eyebrows, and hid them deep down inside me where I hoped no one would ever see them again. Daddy Cassin *was* my daddy.

He was cleared of any complicity in the matter of the buried treasure, but that was the end of our life in Lawton. It was the end of order, of happiness, of family. Mother so feared any attendant publicity that although Daddy had been totally absolved she persuaded him to move. He sold out, took a loss on everything and we moved to Kansas City, to a shabby hotel he and Mother were to manage. It couldn't have been very profitable. Often I heard quarreling in the night.

Then one day Daddy vanished. No need to get his slippers ready, no need to run for his paper, no safe place to nestle up on his lap with the newspaper as a screen blocking out the world. I don't give up people easily. I didn't then, either. I loved and missed him so, and one summer afternoon I went out to find him. I walked the long way from where we lived to downtown Kansas City, keeping my eyes on the pavement, watching the feet. The streets were so crowded I was afraid I'd miss his face, but I could never miss those shoes. Daddy Cassin had very small feet and he was special about his shoes.

And suddenly in the midst of those thousands of feet, I walked right into them! Daddy and I grabbed and kissed each other and talked . . . we had ice-cream sodas . . . he gave me money to ride home. I didn't. I walked along, slowly, savoring the joy of our meeting, victorious because I'd found him myself. I could do it. I could *always* do it. He'd said, "I'll see you!" and as I walked along, my little mind was plotting and planning the moment when I'd bring him home, back to his chair and his newspaper, back to happiness. We would all be content together.

I never saw him again.

Years later, I met my own father, Thomas LeSueur of San Antonio, Texas. By then I knew that San Antonio was my birthplace, that my name originally had been Lucille Fay LeSueur, that my parents had separated before I was born. Many stories had appeared in print in which I mentioned never having seen my own father, many men wrote letters stating that they were my father and sending along pictures to substantiate the claim. Among them was a letter and a picture exactly like the picture Hal had shown me long ago on the train. When Mother verified his identity, I started corresponding with my father. I also started supporting him. We wrote at length trying to become acquainted. Finally, I asked him to come to Hollywood.

We met on the set of *Chained.* I looked over during a take and there stood a tall man with enormous eyes and hollows in his cheeks big enough for Katharine Hepburn and me together. Walking toward him, I wondered what to do. Embrace? Shake hands? My father decided it for me. He picked up my hand, kissed it and said, "Baby, you're everything I thought and hoped you'd be." We stood together, exchanging pleasantries as you would with a stranger . . . details of his trip . . . the California weather. Then I was called back to finish the scene. When I looked in his direction, he was gone. Writing had been more facile than talking.

Mother loved me, I know that now, but she had problems of her own when Hal and I were small. Life isn't easy with two broken marriages and two children. She went to work, and we moved into a laundry agency across from the cheap little hotel where we first stayed in Kansas City. Mother and I waited on customers in the front and did hand laundry and ironing in the back, in the big room which was also our sitting room, kitchen and bedroom. Later we built a balcony, a ladder extended to the floor above and we improvised a bedroom up there for Mother and me. From upstairs we could see into the laundry agency entrance and Mother could hear the tinkling of the bell that hung on the door. I slept on a pallet—we had so little room—bathed in the laundry tub and helped with the laundry.

At first, customers couldn't see me above the counter. I couldn't reach the shelves without standing on a chair, and customers would have to help me. As time went by, I learned to iron; I could wash and iron a shirt very nicely. Mother was expert. She could even execute accordion pleats on ladies' blouses and she was very strict about my ironing. Six shirts, seventy-nine cents. I wonder about the identity of those men whose shirts I ironed. I wonder if our paths have ever crossed again.

Because Daddy Cassin was Catholic, I had been sent to a school I liked very much, St. Agnes Academy. But after he left, we were very poor; I heard Mother telling the Sisters she could no longer pay my tuition. That's when I began my apprenticeship as a private school helper. The Sisters suggested I wait on tables, wash dishes and make beds for my tuition. I've never minded housework. Strangely enough, I still enjoy it. What I did not enjoy at St. Agnes' was being relegated to the position of an outcast. For a youngster the paramount issue each and every school semester is: Will *they* like me? It is so necessary to be liked, accepted, wanted, made to feel a part of it. Children can be cruel. They are certainly aware of class distinctions. The minute I started serving them at table it was a step down into the menial class. I'd lost Daddy Cassin and now I didn't even belong here.

I was destined to remain in that class awhile. For when Mother found another school, Rockingham, which supposedly had a better curriculum, I found myself "going to school" by keeping a fourteen-room house, cooking, making beds and washing dishes for thirty other boys and girls. This was far worse than St. Agnes'! My status as helper was strictly a misnomer. I was the only working student. Head master was a timid bookworm, but his wife, a huge, lumbering creature with gray eyes and gray hair, was either a sadist or a bully, or both. She treated me like a slavey in a sob story and wielded a broom handle in a manner not to be believed. When she overheard me asking another girl to hand me a dustpan, she grabbed me by the hair, threw me down a flight of stairs to the basement and beat me with that broom handle until I was dazed.

"I'll teach you to work if I have to kill you," she shrilled. How's that for dialogue?

I ran away. I ran several times, ran around in circles trying to escape. I didn't go home because I didn't want to worry Mother, and I always returned voluntarily, half starved, to additional floggings with the broom handle.

When I did visit home, we weren't alone, Mother, Hal and I. Our new stepfather, I realized then, was the reason I'd gone to Rocking-ham. Instead of adding to our family, this man made me feel more alone than ever. Mr. Hough was moody, he seldom spoke to me. I wondered if Mother really liked him. I didn't know. She was still Mother, but she was living behind some glass partition I couldn't penetrate. From the time Daddy Cassin left, Mother, Hal and I never were able to communicate. All the time I was at Rockingham, four years, when I'd come home we seemed to be speaking to each other from a distance, through the glass partitions. I didn't know what they were thinking about anything.

Hal couldn't be bothered with me. Five years is a lot of difference when a boy is sixteen and his sister a girl of eleven. Occasionally he would take me to Electric Park where Sally Rand was working. Intimidated by the noise and action I'd wander around while Hal watched Sally Rand, show after show. I wanted and needed my big brother and at this point I felt more orphaned than Annie.

My one regret about childhood is that living away from home so much I didn't really get to know my mother until much later and only realized then how much she wanted to give, how great her capacity was. The happiest I ever saw her was on the set of a picture, feeding the whole crew her homemade pies—lemon meringue, boysenberry, banana, chocolate. But in my childhood we lacked communication. The only way human beings can know each other is by talking and listening, but there was no use telling Mother about my hardships at school, there was nothing she could do about them, and I sensed that she had difficulties enough of her own. There was no use telling her about my dancing dreams. We lived in different worlds. She felt sure life would pick up for us when she married Mr. Hough. I never did tell her that I ran away finally because the one thing Mr. Hough tried to pick up was *me*.

Life has a way of compensating, and lacking a father, I've not been fatherless. When I left Rockingham, my path crossed that of a man who was to have a profound influence on my whole life—James Madison Wood, president for many years of Stephens College, the college

I attended for a few brief months until it became obvious that I was simply not equipped.

As helper at Rockingham I was supposed to work like a little horse and learn in between times. The hitch: there was so much work to do, no time remained for studying or learning. I don't remember getting to classes more than two or three times a year. The chores I've never regretted. Scrubbing, cooking and ironing taught me a self-sufficiency I've tried to pass along to my own children, but I didn't learn very much reading, writing or arithmetic—nothing to pass along to my children here—and since the headmaster's wife couldn't admit I'd not had my classes, she gave me forged high-school credits.

My proud mother! I was so young she thought she'd brought a mental giant into the world. Stephens College was my next step, she decided, and I didn't dare tell her how unprepared I was. We packed my suitcase and I was off for Columbia, Missouri, where it had been arranged that I could wait on tables in the dining room to pay my tuition.

It was the same old story. Some of the girls *were* cordial—one friend even suggested my name to her sorority, but her sorority sisters, like most girls, wouldn't accept a "waitress." I'd had a brief feeling of elation; when I wasn't accepted, I grew defiant. Who needed them? Well . . . I did. Even more than joining the sorority, I longed to stay at this school, but the classes were Greek to me. College was only comprehensible when I was dancing . . . into the kitchen with a tray of dishes, into the classrooms, across the campus.

There were glorious dances at the University of Missouri and at the College Inn where Orville Knapp's orchestra played. Often we got home way past curfew. Mr. Lake, the watchman, was a dear, pint-sized man who guarded the whole campus. While he was making his rounds he'd leave a window open and we girls would help each other through it. When I was broke—which was frequently—he'd lend me a dollar. Repaying him was my first obligation when I started working.

But no one could help me in class, where I was in dire need. With midterm exams coming up, I fled. There was no point in taking them. I packed my suitcase, left the dorm and ran all the way to the railroad station. There—waiting for the train—was where I encountered the president. He was a man of consummate dignity. He was also a man round and ruddy of face with genial blue eyes and a true Santa Claus jollity—a man with whom you felt free to level.

"Where are you going, Billie?" he said.

"Home! I can't stand it any longer. I don't belong here."

"That isn't true," he said. "You're one of the nicest girls we've had on this campus, Billie. You have courage and dignity and a lot to give. Someday you'll understand what I'm talking about. You're not a quitter. Don't behave like one. Do this properly."

"But my mother works very hard. I mustn't hurt her by flunking."

"You come with me," he said. He took me back to the college, phoned my mother and told her I was coming home, that I wasn't equipped to handle college, my education was too sketchy. Then he gave me three rules for living:

Never stop a job until you finish it.

The world is not interested in your problems. When your problems are the deepest, let your laughter be the merriest.

If you find you can do a job, let it alone, because you are bigger than the job already, and that means you will shrink up to the size of that job. If the job is impossible, you may never get it accomplished but you'll grow in trying to accomplish it.

The job at Stephens was too hard at the time, with my lack of background, but I'm grateful for the experience because Daddy Wood became my staunch friend. He wrote me until the week of his death, "Dear Billie . . ." and because of him I've tried never to run away from anything since.

Through the years he explained to me the essentials of education. He had been influenced by John Dewey to what, I eventually discovered, was the pragmatic approach—curricula are valueless unless they prepare women for the life they are destined to live. During his tenure at Stephens (1911–1947) his leadership built the college from a student body of fifty girls and five teachers to a group of twenty-two hundred students and faculty of five hundred. Later, as President of the Women's Foundation, he devised even more advanced curricula, about which he constantly kept me advised.

My college has had to be people, and second only to Daddy Wood as an early influence was Ray Sterling, my first beau, the confidant of my dreams. Ray was the one I called when anything went wrong, and I loved him with my whole fourteen-year-old heart. Ray wanted me to go out and get my dreams. Once I was in the process of realizing them, I lost him.

It is interesting how first love can set a pattern. Ray knew so much more than I. He was five years older. He was not only a student but a good one. He made learning sound like an adventure—what's more, an adventure I'd be able to take some day. Ray understood how I felt. He was cognizant of the beatings, the snubbings, the laundry, the stepfather, the fiasco at Stephens College, *and* the dancing. I'd won a cup at a fraternity dance at the Jack O'Lantern Café when I was still at Rockingham. It was Ray who had taken me to my first big hop at the old Kansas City College; and much as I loved dancing, I sat out a couple just to hear him talk. He had a beat-up jalopy in which we rode all over town. We'd drive along the muddy Missouri, and he'd point out how beautiful it looked in the changing light.

Somehow Ray knew me better than I knew myself. I did everything headlong, pretended that I didn't care what people thought. Ray explained that I had brash ways not because I didn't care what people thought but because I cared too much. He gave me faith in myself. He made me long to be the beautiful entity he thought I could be.

Then one noon there was a chorus tryout at the Baltimore Hotel. Sixteen girls were needed for a little revue with Katherine Emerine as prima donna. Luck was with me. I was one of the sixteen chosen and for a week was on the road, in show business. Then we folded in Springfield, and I went back home, back to Kline's Department Store, ladies' dress department this time.

Restless, energetic, I was only waiting until I'd saved enough money to make a try for the big time—Chicago. I went sooner than I'd planned. Mother and I quarreled because I came home late from a dance. I packed my bag and walked out for the last time.

Ray took me to the train. "Go ahead, Billie, and good luck. You're like a little filly you're so high-strung. I want to marry you, but you have to want me too. I'll wait."

He did.

But I was on my way. My plan was to look up Katherine Emerine, who'd felt so badly when our revue folded. She'd said, "Any of you kids come to Chicago, look me up. I know a producer, Ernie Young, he'll get you a job."

I stared out the train window to avoid seeing any of my fellow passengers. Suppose someone talked to me. Asked my name. Should

I say, "Lucille LeSueur?" It sounded more show-business. When we pulled into the station, someone did speak. An elderly gentleman—as I recall, he was probably forty—asked if I were all right. Did I know Chicago? Where was I going? When he heard Katherine's address, he said he was going that way, he'd be happy to drop me off. Ray had said *never talk to strangers,* but I had less than four dollars. Once in the cab, I sat watching the meter, mesmerized. I wanted to pay half the taxi fare but it kept clicking higher and higher. As we pulled up to Katherine's the meter jumped to five dollars. Embarrassed, not wanting to give more than half my money. I jumped out of the cab. Without a word. I hope the kind "elderly" gentleman knew I meant to say, "Thank you."

It was fortunate I hadn't paid my share of that fare. Katherine wasn't home. She was away on tour. I remembered the name Young, found him in the telephone directory, and in his office, played my first big scene unrehearsed.

The outer office was filled with pretty girls, all slim, chic, the most beautiful and attractively dressed girls I'd ever seen. And here I was in a cheap blue suit too tight at the seams, service-weight hose, a hole in my glove. Unless I got into that office before those girls did, I was sunk. The next time the inner door opened, I raced through it like a guided missile and burst into the room, tears streaming down my face. The two people who stood facing me—a small man and a sweet plump woman—were both totally astounded.

"I know I'm not as tall or pretty as those other girls but I have less than two dollars and no experience and I can't go back to Kansas City!" I cried, without introducing myself. "Please won't you give me a tryout?"

Mrs. Young, Ernie's wife, came from behind the desk and put her arms around me. "Come on, honey, cry it out," she said. "When did you eat last?"

I played that scene again in *Dancing Lady*—pushed my way into Clark Gable's office—and one critic ridiculed it as overdone. Believe me, I didn't begin to show the desperation of the original scene, and if I didn't move that critic, I did move the Youngs. They gave me dinner and found me a week's job at the Friar's Inn, where I sang and danced for what looked like an extravagant pay check—twenty-five dollars a week. Then there was a two-week job in Oklahoma City. From there, Ernie Young sent me to the Oriole Terrace, Detroit—thirty-two girls, eight routines a night.

One week we had a gypsy number with multicolored skirts, slave bracelets, beads around our necks, and poppies in our hair. As we revolved among the tables the first night, my twirling skirt knocked a glass off a table and onto J. J. Shubert. There have been suggestions that this incident was more than accidental. Not only did I not have that much sense, I didn't even know who J. J. Shubert *was*. All that occurred to me was that I had drenched a cash customer and might get fired. But Mr. Shubert came backstage afterward looking for "the little fat girl with the blue eyes." He wanted to offer her a chorus job in his show, *Innocent Eyes*. He invited me to see the matinee next day. I was captivated! The company was leaving the following afternoon and they'd open in New York in ten days. Just in case the boss of the Oriole Terrace wouldn't let me go, I committed a theatrical crime, I *jumped the show.*

Exactly twelve weeks to the day I'd left Kansas City—Broadway! I wrote to Ray in superlatives. New York was electric, the tempo was fast, the people seemed different, warmer, more knowledgeable. The girls in the show liked me, in fact, I was their "baby." Five of us shared one room in an old brownstone on Fiftieth Street just off Fifth Avenue. Our beds stood in a row like the dwarfs' in *Snow White*. You could tell which corner was mine—the window was plastered with my hankies, panties and stockings (I had two pairs). When it was cold enough, they froze.

Mistinguette was the star of the show. She had been very beautiful when she was young and even now, when she was (to us) very old, she had a magic of her own and the most beautiful legs in the world. That's all I ever saw, dancing behind her, or peering from the wings, the lady of the fabled legs. She was Pat Stanley, Ethel Merman and Kay Thompson all rolled into one—any wonder that Maurice Chevalier adored her?

Someday I wanted to be out in front kicking, and I thought I was on my way when the stage manager, instead of roaring, "Come on, get the lead out of your feet!" roared, "Get out there in the front row, honey, Janice is home sick today." The chorus was a life unto itself and not always the way you've seen it pictured in movies. Stage-door Johnnies and butter-and-egg men did exist, but they didn't interest me, and the other girls would shoo them away with "Leave her alone, let her grow up, she has plenty of time for you." The girls looked after me, were very strict, and I adored it because I felt cared for.

My heart was still with Ray Sterling. I wrote him constantly and he wrote me. He'd never been to New York, but he wrote, "New York is like a melting pot of all classes, a cesspool of licentiousness, Billie. There are bound to be flies gathering around a sugar bowl like show business; but there must be many good people in the city too. May God keep you and give you the aid I cannot."

Of the good people was my one escort and companion at this time, Jack Oakie, who was also in the chorus of *Innocent Eyes*. Together we'd ride the bus up Riverside Drive or stroll down Fifth Avenue window-shopping. We both had great hopes for our careers. Ours was no romance. As a matter of fact, knowing Jack taught me that girls and fellows can be friends, that there is a wealth of sharing for two people who have a relationship uncluttered with coquetry. This is something every girl should learn, that every woman, especially an unmarried woman, depends on. A man's point of view is stimulating. A man and woman can have an existing community of interests. Girls who feel every relationship with the opposite sex has to be flirtation are missing a great deal.

As a matter of fact I was working too hard to be emotionally involved. To earn the extra money, which would take me home for Christmas, I had asked advice of agent Nils T. Granlund. "Granny" introduced me to Harry Richman, loaned me fourteen dollars to buy a dress and steered me to Tin Pan Alley to find some songs. We played *Innocent Eyes* six nights and three afternoons a week and after the show every night now I danced at Harry Richman's and sang my little song, "When my sweetie walks down the street. . . ." It was quite a schedule.

Then, two days before my Christmas holiday, Harry Rapf and Bob Rubin of MGM came in to catch *Innocent Eyes*. The first I knew of it was when the note arrived backstage offering me a screen test. Years later I asked Mr. Rapf what in the world he had seen in me. His answer: "Structure and vitality." Believe me, that's *all* I had. Ray had said I was like a young colt? Well, he was right—an eager, expectant, overemotional colt running across the field with no idea that there could be barbed wires.

THREE

No wonder Daddy Wood worried about me. Hollywood is like life, you face it with the sum total of your equipment. And mine was meager. He told me later, "Given the right breaks, Billie, I knew you'd come through with flying colors, but you were tragically sensitive. I felt that if the breaks were bitter, you were in definite danger."

Some of the breaks seemed bitter. Every morning of my life I stopped by St. Augustine's Church across from MGM to pray. I prayed for my career, I prayed for love. Sometimes on my lunch hour I was again in church. Father John O'Donnell often spoke with me. He knew I wasn't a Catholic, but he also knew I needed all the spiritual guidance I could get.

At night Michael Cudahy and I would drive along the moonlit Pacific, and I counseled him as Ray Sterling had counseled me beside the muddy Missouri. I wanted Michael to be perfect, I wanted to convey to him the faith in life Ray'd given me. But he laughed away all my sermons, closed my lips with kisses and gunned his car up the coast or down the coast to the nearest night spot. At Christmas that first year we had a big emotional blowup, patched it up and went on, blew up and patched it again. Each time, I thought my life was ended. I was trying to prove something every moment and every moment was *the last*.

Carey Wilson kept an eye on me, Paul Bern kept an eye on me, but they were busy people, I didn't want to intrude on them. Daddy Wood kept the letters coming, letters about life's significance, about friendship—the kind of letters a father should write. In the early fall of 1927, he came out to the coast on business and we met for dinner at the Biltmore Hotel, I in my most colorful dress. As we talked, he studied me across the table.

"Am I still your Billie, Daddy Wood?"

"Yes and no. There is an even more apparent surface happiness. You are certainly more beautiful. But there's an expression that troubles me, a sort of cynicism. Why, Billie?"

Hollywood was a sham, I told him, life was a dream without substance. I wanted real friends my own age. I was showered with affection and compliments, but people seemed to come and go. Who were my friends? The fear of criticism . . . the fear of failure . . . my secret engagement. When I was with Michael, he exerted compelling charm. When I hadn't seen him for an hour, he ceased to exist. "He doesn't love me," I told Daddy Wood. "Not the way I want to be loved."

"And you love him, Billie?"

I didn't know. I hated to face it.

Daddy Wood offered no advice. "You're thinking, which means you'll work it out. Hollywood's no more sham than life anywhere, Billie. You're reflecting your own insecurity."

Paul Bern continued guiding me. Immersed as he was in production, he was a kindly soul who somehow managed to carry another full-time load—the problems of those who were miserable. He was the one, I'd heard, who stood by Barbara LaMarr during her brief stormy career. He understood talent, he also understood the undisciplined, uneducated girls who were unable to handle that talent. He certainly understood me. As I came to the parting of the ways with Michael, he observed my increasing unhappiness. I danced all night, worked in pictures all day, flaunted a sort of defiant zest.

It was at this time that F. Scott Fitzgerald wrote, "Joan Crawford is doubtless the best example of the flapper, the girl you see at smart night clubs, gowned to the apex of sophistication, toying iced glasses with a remote, faintly bitter expression, dancing deliciously, laughing a great deal, with wide, hurt eyes. Young things with a talent for living."

I fooled him. Talent for living, indeed! But I didn't fool Paul. Exhibitionism was mere camouflage for heartbreak. Paul sensed that I was daily becoming more and more sentient. He made it his business to divert me, to introduce new values. Bringing me a beautiful black fan that had belonged to Barbara LaMarr, he said, "I want you to have this, Joan. *Barbara* would want you to have it." I treasured that fan.

One night when he picked me up at the house, I entered the living room to see him staring at my prize possession, a wall tapestry of black velvet with a dancing girl emblazoned in rhinestones. Paul couldn't help himself, his lips twitched.

"What's wrong?" I demanded. "What's wrong in wanting beautiful things?"

"Nothing, Joan. And because you want them so much, you will someday have them," he said.

The wall hanging came down that night.

Another time, we went to the Cocoanut Grove with Corinne Griffith. While she was dancing, I looked at her white ermine coat thrown back over the chair. I touched it, the most luxurious garment I'd ever seen.

"You love that, don't you, Joan?" Paul said.

Love it? I couldn't take my hands off it. What a contrast to the inexpensive polo coat I'd just checked.

Excusing himself, Paul left the table and by the time he returned, the entertainment had begun. But as we left the Grove that night and paused at the check stand, I was handed a coat . . . of ermine. I sent that coat back to Paul—don't think it didn't take will power—but I kept his friendship, and he took Ray Sterling's place as keeper of the dreams. His impeccable taste guided me as it guided so many others. His tragic death robbed everyone in the industry of a genuine friend. It especially robbed the newcomers, for Paul was a script searcher, talent finder, troubleshooter, and their veritable anchor.

Rumors attending his death were ridiculous. Paul was no mystery man. He had shared an apartment for years with Jack Gilbert and Carey Wilson; they were steadfast comrades and a mutual inspiration society. When they first bunked together, they were earning a combined $800 a week. Within five years they were earning $18,000 a week. Very different men, this trio, but typical of the Hollywood of that day—talented, valiant, hardworking, hard-playing and creatively unique. They were pioneers in the promised land. They spent money as if they'd invented it. They adored women. They were chivalry personified. Even Paul's last gesture was a gallant one to save the woman he loved, Jean Harlow, from scandal threatened by a woman with whom he'd been involved before he knew Jean.

Paul imbued me with his own keen perspective on this business. I wanted to be a star? Sometimes it was hard to differentiate between rising star and rocket, he said. Self-improvement wasn't limited to

experimentation with makeup or hair styles. It meant learning. The
motion-picture industry represented a mosaic of talents—you could
learn from each of them if you wished. Well, I wished. Later there
was a raft of publicity about the new Joan, the changed Joan. I don't
think for a moment that I deliberately planned my *self*. I simply had
a passion for living, and when one activity didn't prove fulfilling, I
tried another. I wanted to acquire understanding, feel, grow, discover
who I was and who I could be.

Not long ago I came across an old clipping of an interview given
in 1927. "I want the Joan Crawford I am this year to be only a building block for the Joan Crawford of next year," went the interview. "I
want to be prepared for those years that come when youth is gone.
If you're prepared for them, they never catch up with you. I never
want to be second best. I haven't even begun to be what I want to be.
I haven't done anything, not a single thing, with which I'm content."
The world of dancing cups and jazz music had lost allure. As a matter
of fact, it had begun to seem rather cheap.

Two weeks after I'd broken with Michael, Paul escorted me to the
Vine Street Playhouse to see Douglas Fairbanks, Jr., in *Young Woodley*.
Douglas and I had met casually at the studio commissary and he had
seemed rather stuffy, but what a deeply touching, tender performance
he gave that night! Paul took me backstage. I refused to go to supper,
went home and dreamed of *Young Woodley*. In the middle of the night
I picked up the phone and sent Douglas a congratulatory telegram.

He answered in person, dropping by at teatime the next day. Monday, we had dinner at the Biltmore. How can I describe Douglas? He
was very tall, very thin and boyish, but also the epitome of suaveness.
His had been a comprehensive education in France and England. He
could write, paint, had a gay delicious wit, exquisite manners, and so

much knowledge that it was hard for me to reconcile his conversation with his youth. Puck and the Poet!

After dinner that Monday night he took me backstage to see his play from the wings. From then on I sat in a box every night. We dined together, bronzed on the beach, played golf and tennis, danced Saturday nights at the Biltmore or the Palomar Tennis Club. When Douglas was working at First National, we'd rush across town to meet for lunch. Later, when he was working at MGM, we were on each other's sets during every break. Now I knew what I wanted out of life—everything—a full career, love, marriage, lots of children, and Douglas looked like the answer.

He has since proved he can be that answer. He *has* a good marriage and a happy life. But I wasn't the right wife. Or perhaps we were too young. There were obstacles against us from the beginning. We were both in our late teens, not exactly a time when a boy's parents want him to marry, *and* we were both very involved in show business. Douglas, at thirteen, had starred in a picture called *Stephen Steps Out,* but that merely represented an attempt on the part of Paramount to capitalize on a well-known name. Douglas didn't want to trade on his father's name, he wanted to prove himself, and certainly anyone who saw *Young Woodley* recognized an actor with a future unlimited. It was a performance convincing to his dad, who up until then had opposed his career.

Being the son of a famous father has its own problems. For all his talent, Douglas was living under his father's shadow and his mother's thumb. Douglas Senior was one of the all-time greats of the business. *The Thief of Bagdad* had just won the International Film Exposition in Warsaw; *The Black Pirate* had introduced Technicolor, had been voted one of the ten best films of 1926 and was still a top moneymaker in '27; *The Gaucho* had just been released to tremendous publicity. The son of such a star not only had to face constant comparison, he was regarded as a second edition by everyone, including Doug Senior.

Living abroad with his mother, Douglas hadn't known his father well during his childhood. It was only now that they were becoming close, and they grew constantly closer during the next few years, something heartening to see and share. It isn't easy for adults to pick up the parent-child relationship, as I found in the case of my own father. Douglas Senior disliked being called "Dad," he found it uncomfortable, and my Douglas equally disliked "Junior." So one day they rechristened each other—"Pete" for Doug and "Jayar" for Junior. That seemed to set them free; they'd become exhilarating companions, and my Douglas was very much the heir apparent at Pickfair.

But a serious romance for a boy this age was hardly what his father had in mind, whether he felt paternal or not. And as for Douglas' mother! Beth and I are sympathetic to each other now. She is, incidentally, one of the most beautiful women I have ever seen, white-haired with skin of alabaster, and she had since had a richly fulfilled life with her husband Jack Whiting. But she was a lonely woman then, Douglas was her baby and she was bitterly opposed to any thought of his marriage.

Nothing, however, not production schedules, parents or publicity could deter us. Shortly after we met, I traveled to Yosemite on location for *Rose Marie* and Douglas came up to surprise me. Picture me standing on a huge rock bellowing "The Indian Love Call" across the mountains at the top of my voice—it was a silent picture, but that didn't stop me—while Douglas stood below just out of camera range, waiting to take me to lunch.

From this I jumped into the billowing skirts and modest bonnets of *Across to Singapore*. What I resented about this picture was that it took us out to sea, away from Douglas. He drove me down to the pier at Long Beach, saw me safely on board that majestic square-rigger, "the good ship *Nathan Ross*" bound for "China," wrote me, radio-grammed me, and on Christmas morning, Ramon Novarro delivered the lovely jade earrings Douglas had entrusted to him, for me.

This picture was based on Ben Ames Williams' *All the Brothers Were Valiant*—but they weren't, they were three sheets to the wind, except for Ramon, who was whimsical, noble and kept throwing me at his drunken brother, Ernest Torrence, until that old salt was rubbed out by mutineers. I'll never forget that when I first met Alfred Lunt and Lynn Fontanne—it must have been about 1933—Lynn said, "I love you in pictures, Joan," and I, so gratified, asked her what she'd last seen. By then I'd done pictures like *Paid* and *Grand Hotel*. Imagine my dismay when she said *Across to Singapore!*

The one important moment on the picture was when we docked at Long Beach—the great hulk finally stopped rocking on a choppy sea—and Douglas took me in his arms. It was almost midnight, December 31, 1927. As the whistles sounded, he asked me to be his wife. Two days later we went shopping for my platinum wedding band. An engagement ring, Douglas said, he'd give me when we were married. Wedding ring and diamond anklet were engraved *To my darling wife,* and I wore them from that minute. We couldn't understand the storm of publicity about this ring. . . . We said nothing. Our engagement was a "secret." How naïve we were!

I was *Billie* and he was *Dodo*. We invented a language of our own that went something like OPI LOPOVE YOPOU—how nauseating can you get?—which we talked incessantly to everyone's confusion, no matter where we were . . . on the set . . . across the dinner table . . . backstage at *Saturday's Children,* Douglas' new play.

There's a certain spontaneous combustion that happens once in a lifetime, when two very young people fall very passionately in love and nothing else matters. Even another western with Tim McCoy didn't matter. I galloped through it, dreaming of Douglas. Next came *Four Walls,* in which I played my first heavy, and when Douglas was signed for A *Woman of Affairs,* with Garbo and Gilbert, we were together at MGM, our sets next door to each other, and he could come rushing in and kiss me, frantic because we'd been apart seven minutes.

Douglas and I were interviewed daily. Reporters hounded the studio. Our preoccupation, our clasped hands, our kisses occasioned an avalanche of publicity and conjecture. We'd been rumored engaged from our first date, then there was the mysterious ring I wore, and the rumors that Douglas Senior and Mary Pickford, the royal family of Hollywood, did not approve the romance of the "crown prince" and the "Charleston queen." According to the fan mail, this just made the public love us more. We were Cinderella and the Prince, the lovers all the world adores. MGM publicity bragged that my picture appeared more often in print that year than that of any girl in the world.

But Douglas and I were absorbed in each other, in a sphere of our own. He read poetry aloud. I had written verse, but I'd never read anything like Sara Teasdale and Edna St. Vincent Millay! He mentioned books he'd read, and I tried to devour Shaw, Ibsen, Proust and Nietzsche all at once. I read my way to mental indigestion. We were young, ambitious, we seemed to be each other's good luck charm. Douglas was signed to a new contract at First National, I was given the best part I'd ever had, in a picture called *Our Dancing Daughters.* I'd read the story, which was running serially in the Hearst papers.

I'd stolen the script, gone to producer Hunt Stromberg, begged for it and was given it.

This much fun making a picture, I've never had. We were a group of young moderns and it was a way of life I knew. As Diana, I was the *flapper*, wild on the surface, a girl who shakes her windblown bob (mine started a craze) and dances herself into a frenzy while the saxes shriek and the trombones wail, a girl drunk on her own youth and vitality. Under it all, she's far more sound than the *baby vamp*, Anita Page, who would never dance like Diana does, but was perfectly willing to jump into any male's bed. Johnny Mack Brown played the *handsome hero*, who deserts *flapper* for *baby vamp* and lives to regret it. Dorothy Sebastian was the *modern girl* who tells the *villain* all—and lives to regret it. Nils Asther was the *villain*.

If the characters sound stereotyped, remember, they were inno-vating those types and director Harry Beaumont kept each charac-terization fresh and sharp. I was just beginning to understand how important a director is! Mr. Beaumont was meticulous, but he was also something of a pixie and he wanted to capture the very young spontaneous quality we all had. His strategy consisted in giving us the freedom *to* capture it. Ask Gwen Verdon's dad, he remembers, he was the chief gaffer* on *Our Dancing Daughters*.

Everything about this picture was inspired. I'd never seen such clothes, I'd never seen such sets as those Cedric Gibbons created. Our location at Carmel was idyllic—to make it more so, Douglas was able to drive up for a visit. Sound was just coming in and our sound score included the noise of ping-pong balls, door knocks, sobbing saxophones and wild waves.

---

* head electrician

Our Dancing Daughters opened at the Capitol in October, to a $40,000 weekend, then to a big Monday matinee, and Monday night by nine thirty, standees were five deep behind the last row with a solid crowd filling the lobby to the doors. It was all the ushers could do, said *Variety*, to keep an aisle for the fire laws.

This was my turning point. None of us were starred in the picture, but theater owners, sensing the audience response, "starred" me. My name went up on their marquees and I'd drive around with a small box camera taking pictures of "Joan Crawford" in lights. I didn't even tell Douglas about those pictures, but I phoned him, wildly excited, from the studio when Mr. Mayer called me in, doubled my salary, "Beginning Saturday, Joan, you will have five hundred a week." He kindly advised me to save my money and told me someday I'd be a star.

Reviews and fan letters were pouring in. The studio gave me bundles of them every day and I read every word. I had found that incredible thing, a public. People wrote to me as if they *knew* me. I answered every letter personally, addressed and stamped the envelopes and took them to the post office myself. In my little house on Roxbury, the fight burned late. No bedtime for me until every letter was answered. From this moment on I had a sense of audience, warm living people who would care for me in direct proportion to the energy and talent I could give, a public to whom I owed a loyalty and from whom I've always received loyalty.

From this moment on, life was never again carefree. On screen for some time I had specialized in carefree, blithe young girls and like them I had been sure of myself in a brash, juvenile way, but now I began to doubt, study and observe myself. I had sense enough to know that I must work, and work hard. From that moment to this I've kept setting the goal higher.

I wanted Douglas to be proud of me. I craved valid pictures, significant parts. Not *Dream of Love*, another load of romantic slush in which I was strictly subordinated to giving Nils Asther a build-up. Not *The Duke Steps Out*, in which I was again background, for Willie Haines.

This picture was one of the big grossers of its day because Willie epitomized the *wise guy* and he did it to perfection, but it wasn't a very good picture. One of the reviewers wrote, "Following *Our Dancing Daughters,* this girl seemed well on her way, and the impetus of that one makes the dual names Crawford and Haines strong. But the sidewalk Don Juans and kitchen Cleopatras are going to be disappointed in their Joan. It's a reverse situation for her, she has nothing to do, she'll have to make it up on the next one if she's going anywhere in a fast moving field that's moving faster."

The next one, luckily, was *Our Modern Maidens,* further adventures of the dancing daughters. Douglas and I had announced our engagement October 8. On November 21 Mr. Mayer advised me that *Our Modern Maidens* was next, I would be given star billing, and Douglas was to appear in the picture with me, the climax to our year-and-a-half courtship. What a lark! This, we knew, would be our sole picture together. We planned to be married immediately afterward, and we didn't want to commercialize our love, but for this one time, we were together.

Our characters were ultralighthearted, ultrasophisticated and buoyant, but I'd corner Sam Zimbalist, then a film editor, to ask him how yesterday's scene had played. How did it *look?* Where was I *wrong?* I must say that the more I studied the rushes the more aware I became of my imperfections. No one ever walks and they seldom sit in this picture. We all bounced, skipped, danced and hippety-hopper, which I guess was our way of showing animation, but we also exhibited a rather touching sincerity. I had one spectacular scene, a solo dance in a costume by Adrian—my first—and Douglas had a scene where he accurately impersonated John Barrymore, John Gilbert and Douglas Senior. These impersonations stand up today.

As soon as the picture was finished, we put our footprints in the courtyard at Grauman's Chinese Theater and slipped away to New York. It was a quiet serene wedding, in the rectory of St. Malachy's Roman Catholic Church, the actors' church. The only ones with us were Douglas' mother, Beth, who had finally recognized our love, and Jack Whiting, whom she married two months later. Father Edward F. Leonard, Douglas' friend and counsellor, was deeply sympathetic to us. Before the service, we went to him and he gave me a little prayer book and his blessing. A few minutes later we were married. June 3, 1929. We were both very young and the world was ours! We spent our honeymoon at the Algonquin Hotel owned by our dear friends, Bertha and Frank Case, and the day after the wedding they helped us receive our friends. My gift to Douglas was a wafer-thin platinum watch with diamond-studded hands. His gift to me, a gold cigarette box and lighter. We sent wires back to the studio.

Douglas' read: JOAN AND I WERE MARRIED YESTERDAY, NOW THAT I HAVE A WIFE TO SUPPORT NEED RAISE IN SALARY.

Mine: IF I HAVE WORKED HARD IN THE PAST WATCH ME NOW.

The answer to this was my first appearance in a talking picture—as a singer. Mr. Rapf was producing *The Hollywood Revue,* a gigantic effort to outdo anything yet seen, on a screen which had suddenly gone all-talking, all-singing and all-dancing. Every studio was launching extravaganzas. MGM had already scored with *Broadway Melody; this* was to make *that* look pale. Plans included a chorus of two hundred, the participation of twenty-five stars—everyone from Marie Dressler rising from the sea in a burlesque ballet, to Nacio Herb Brown playing his own "Singin' in the Rain" and Shearer and Gilbert giving their all in a scene from *Romeo and Juliet.* Producer Rapf and director Charles Reisner were brave men. Neither of them were brave enough to tell me what was expected of *me.*

It was musician David Snell, later conductor at the studio, who summoned me and broke the news. I was going to do the first tap dance ever audible on the screen and *sing* a song—"Gotta Feeling for You." The Biltmore Trio would back me up. Mr. Snell thereupon handed me a sheet of music and suggested rehearsal. I couldn't sing! With my face to the wall I made some assorted sounds, to my ears woefully inadequate, but David insisted my low guttural voice had what he called recording quality, and after weeks of patient effort he finally had me singing. However, I wouldn't go on stage without him—everything was direct recording in those days—so David was in the picture too. I was also among those present in the "Singin' in the Rain" number and Buster Keaton, Marion Davies, myself and George K. Arthur, in rain hats and coats, did our melodic best.

Evidently my voice failed to violate the sound barrier because my next picture, *Untamed,* opened with me singing "Languid and plaintive, hear the chant of the jungle!" and later in that picture I sang

"That Wonderful Something." Between songs I coped with the part of the little jungle flower.

Hollywood, at this moment, was in a state of jitters over talking pictures. It was the age of the pear-shaped tone and everyone talked as if they were playing the tuba. Before talkies began, the studio imported vaudevillian Oliver Hinsdale from Battle Creek, Michigan, and all contract players were to study with him an hour a day. I was working steadily, there *was* no hour a day. We also acquired a Spanish teacher because Hollywood wasn't about to give up the South American market and the studio saw no reason why players couldn't dub their own dialogue in Spanish. We couldn't speak English let alone Spanish! Willie Haines took the first test in dubbing. As a consequence, the teacher was quietly fired and Spanish was dubbed by Spaniards.

A frantic search was on for young girls with the sex appeal of Garbo and the voice of Katharine Cornell, young actors with the appeal of Valentino and the enunciation of Walter Hampden. Luckily for me, *Our Dancing Daughters, Four Walls* and *Our Modern Maidens* scored so well at the box office that a deluge of jazz-age pictures were under way, and I was the one person in 1929 made a star without a talking picture. Top executives were so busy worrying about what would happen to Garbo, Shearer and Gilbert, they had no time to worry about me. Dr. Marafiotta, Caruso's voice coach, was transplanted to the studio now and we all were told to take lessons from him.

"There's no such thing as diction, it's enunciation," was Dr. Marafiotta's slogan.

Before *Untamed,* I went to his office and asked for an appointment. I waited a long time, he was so busy. Finally I was ushered in.

"What do you want to learn, child?" he said.

"To speak for talking pictures, Dr. Marafiotta."

"Here is my book," he said. "Read it, child, study it."

"Learn to talk from a book?"

"Study the book, *then* we begin."

"But Dr. Marafiotta, I start a talking picture tomorrow!"

I never saw the man again.

Douglas, of course, had an excellent speaking voice and stage experience to assure his continued career. He was of the fortunate few. Some top stars panicked, among them Lon Chaney and John Gilbert. I didn't panic because I didn't have enough sense. I'd been talking all my life; it seemed perfectly natural.

Johnny Arnold had been pulled off a camera and put in charge of the whole process of synchronizing photography with the new demands of sound. He'd had experience with Edison as far back as 1908, he told me; he'd made talking pictures with Ethel Barrymore and others, but sound then had been on Victrola records with a metronome swinging back and forth to cue the projectionist. This hadn't worked well. Now that an electrical device had been perfected so the sound track could run on the film, talkies were in. But cameras made so much noise that Johnny had to lock them up—and himself—in big booths that resembled insulated ice houses.

Before talkies, the cameraman had taken a long shot, then moved up for a close shot; now cameras had to be stationary and four cameras were used on each scene to get a long shot, a medium shot, a close-up and an angle shot. Where one cameraman and one assistant had been sufficient, now we used four cameramen, four assistants, four sound men and four boom men. Because cameras were stationary, the actors couldn't move around and their positions were chalk-marked on the floor. Since I had no stage experience to unlearn I had no trouble staying within the marks. After about six months Johnny found a way to encase the camera in a little blimp, a device patented and used ever since. That did away with four cameras and the static area imposed on the actors. The camera could go wherever it wished and so could we. By the time we were filming *Montana Moon* our camera was able to follow the action as cowboys galloped all over the range and Ricardo Cortez and I tangoed—all over the range.

Douglas was on location with me in the San Jacinto mountains. He'd rise at five to light the fire in our little cabin. Shooting started at sunup. By four in the afternoon, sunlight was gone, then the whole gang would play football or handball, or what have you. At night there were roaring fires, and we'd sit around laughing, talking and singing, while I hooked rugs. When the last scene was shot, Douglas and I left for New York for a quick round of theaters and nightclubs. We were like pilgrims come to Mecca.

But we were never away from Hollywood long. Studios had busy production schedules and no time out. *Dawn Patrol* was waiting for Douglas, *Our Blushing Brides* for me. *Photoplay* named mine "the best performance of the month," as they had similarly honored most of my *dancing daughter* roles. But personally, I had wearied of the part—to me it was totally passé.

If I'd proved I could play the dancing girl I'd once been, fine. Now let's have a new objective. I went to Mr. Mayer and asked for a serious acting part. Mr. Mayer listened, understood, but Irving Thalberg had requested me for the ingénue in an expensive musical, *Great Day*, using Vincent Youman's fine music. The part wasn't well defined, I had never played an ingénue and I went into the picture with grave misgivings. After ten days, I viewed the rushes with mounting concern—they were God-awful. Mr. Thalberg hadn't seen them. Again, I went to Mr. Mayer.

"Have you seen the rushes?" I asked.

"No, Joan, I haven't. I always think no news is good news."

"Well, I'm dreadful, Mr. Mayer. Southern drawl I can do, but I just can't talk baby talk!"

Mr. Mayer viewed the rushes that evening, got an earful of my attempted baby talk and without more ado, shelved the picture. It represented a loss of $280,000 to the studio—a tremendous amount of money—but Mr. Mayer knew how to build and protect his "properties" and he had consideration for them as people. He also had a canny sense of star material.

He often kidded me that at this time, if I heard of a director or producer or writer who had a part that might be right for me, I'd camp on his front doorstep until I got it. The fact is, I watched the front door *and* the back. The time had come to move forward, meet a new challenge; that stasis in destructive, I knew instinctively. I wanted to be a serious dramatic actress. I was Mrs. Douglas Fairbanks,

FOUR

What glorious fun we *had* during that first year of our marriage. We called our house "El Jodo" after ourselves—the ten-room house I'd rushed out and bought after *Our Dancing Daughters*—the living room carpeted in green, with rich brocaded silk drapes of rose, ivory and green hanging from ceiling to floor at the French windows, gold brocaded settees, tiny Italian occasional tables, and a grand piano covered with a rich Burmese drape on which stood always a vase of fresh flowers and a large picture of—ourselves. To us then it all seemed the apotheosis of taste, but when I think back, what a hodgepodge—everything from Early American to baroque.

On a pretentious table near a very uncomfortable chair were books such as Wells's *Outline of History* and Ludwig's *Napoleon*. Every book Douglas mentioned, I promptly bought and read. Between Wells and Ludwig, we exercised, skipped rope, sunbathed, studied, worked, loved and played together, played wild games of Russian bank, and snap and double solitaire.

The sun porch was the room we enjoyed most, so bright and comfy with sun pouring in from three windows, illuminating the hooked rugs and the shelves crammed with toys: a life-sized hen that cackled and laid an egg, a life-sized baby pig that grunted and walked, teddy bears of every size and shape, clowns that sang, a monster electric railroad with complete equipment—my Christmas gift to Douglas—and dolls of every shape and size, two thousand dolls and I was still collecting like mad. For the children I dreamed of? What a headshrinker could do with this phase of my life!

Ours was strictly a dollhouse marriage. While Douglas read poetry aloud, I sewed constantly, everything from the daintiest embroidered napkins to shower curtains for the bathroom, depending on what he read. I hooked rugs for every room in the house, remodeled dresses, hemmed and initialed his handkerchiefs, knitted his sweaters.

There are those who within marriage keep part of themselves intact, but for me there was only totality. The motivation since childhood had been toward belonging. Now there was someone to belong to. I was strictly the wife I felt Douglas wanted me to be. I wouldn't even have a housekeeper that first year. I kept the house myself with not a trace of dust or disorder. Bessie cooked and did the heavy work, but I planned each meal and supervised each detail, ran all the household errands in my little white Ford, and managed finances for both of us. My young husband knew very little about finance; he'd been in debt $14,000 two months before we were married. What was that to a boy who'd found himself broke in the most interesting cities in the world? Money was something about which I was not too astute either, but for Douglas, I learned.

To have a more luxurious home I cut down on clothes, made most of my own, and they were clothes unlike those I'd once worn. I was cultivating simplicity. My hair was its natural brown, almost shoulder-length, and it shone from brushing. We were mahogany brown from the sun; I used no powder, let the freckles show, used only lipstick. My radical self-improvement campaign included daily dancing lessons, music lessons, Spanish and French when I wasn't working, and I was never three inches removed from a dictionary.

I couldn't wait to get home from the studio. Many nights we'd go to the Hollywood Bowl up in the topmost tiers, bring blankets and stretch out full-length, head to head, holding hands over our shoulders, watching the stars. He bellowed grand opera in the shower . . . loved music and couldn't carry a tune . . . wore beautiful clothes and an ancient seven-year-old hat he wouldn't permit to be cleaned . . . was an emcee at parties . . . loved to initiate follow-the-leader and led everyone through stunts no one could follow, climbing the roof of a house, leaping into an awning, sliding down into a pool. He did card tricks and imitations, wrote poetry, sculptured, sketched, left his clothes wherever he stepped out of them, and promoted all sorts of friendly arguments, taking either side for fun. I'd never *known* how to laugh until Douglas taught me, and I needed that laughter.

Pickfair was a formal and sumptuous house to which came some of the world's most renowned people. Going there was an ordeal for me but it became an essential part of our life. My Douglas and his father were now realizing the intimacy they'd both missed for so long. They enjoyed golfing together, exercising together, and when finally the ice was broken—it was more than a year before we were admitted into good graces—we went to Pickfair every Sunday. *All* day. It was a ritual.

We'd arrive there at ten in the morning, Douglas would join his father, usually out of doors, while I took my place in the living room alone to knit. We would all assemble for an imposing gourmet luncheon and, believe me, I never selected a fork until I'd checked to see which one Miss Pickford used. After lunch, the two Douglases would go over to United Artists Studio for steam baths while I'd sit in the living room, alone again, working at needlepoint or knitting. Miss Pickford would have retired to her room. Knitting helped me survive those Sundays. Gwen Pickford, Mary's niece, helped me survive when she happened to be there. Gwen and I became fast friends. She was younger than I, yet she sensed and appreciated my acute self-consciousness.

About six, the Douglases would return, Mary would descend, beautifully gowned for the evening, guests would begin to arrive, and there I sat in that same damned chair, in the same damned dress I'd put on that morning, feeling anything but chic, anything but poised, in fact, gruesome. Of course I should have gone home during the day and changed. I didn't because I was terrified that while Uncle Douglas and my Douglas were over at the gym, Miss Pickford might *possibly* come downstairs and think me rude. There had been a breach, I wouldn't for the world open it again, so there I sat. Finally I gathered sufficient courage to bring along a cocktail dress and change in the downstairs powder room.

Then we'd have dinner, another formal and elaborate meal, complete with menus, later a movie would be shown and I could subside into the dark beside my Douglas, hold his hand and be at ease. But the lights would go on again and anything could happen.

What kept the atmosphere perking at Pickfair was Uncle Douglas' sense of humor. Even with the titled guests, the gold plates, orchids and waiters in knee breeches, he played practical jokes like a small boy. You never knew, when he held a chair for you, whether or not it was a breakaway. He had chairs wired to give distinguished visitors the hot seat. He had breakaway knives and forks at the table. A guest might pick up a salad fork, stab at a green, and the rubber prongs would double up. Guests were astonished, Uncle Douglas, gleeful, and Miss Pickford would say, "Oh, Douglas, you've done it again."

On one occasion our host approached a guest, seated her, then signaled the majordomo to turn on the electricity. The visitor gave no evidence of shock! Uncle Douglas signaled again. Still the lady sat her ground. "Would you stand for just a moment?" he asked. The lady stood. Our host took the chair and promptly jumped.

"Didn't you feel *any*thing?" he asked.

"Well, yes," admitted the guest, "but I thought that's just how you felt meeting a movie star."

He enjoyed kidding me. In front of people like Lord and Lady Mountbatten he'd say, "Billie, you tell them which of my pictures you like best," knowing I'd seen none of them, that I was just beginning to see pictures, knowing too that I didn't dare open my mouth in front of his distinguished guests. Until now I'd customarily uttered whatever came into my head, but the brilliant international conversation at Pickfair not only gave me pause, it committed me to muteness. Uncle Douglas was amused at my discomfiture. If he saw me watching Miss Pickford and counting my forks, left to right, he'd attract my attention, "Oh, by the way, Billie . . ." getting me so confused I once used a dessert spoon for the fish course, at which he burst into gales of laughter.

His sense of humor was that of a Walt Disney character, his poise absolute. The night of the first great ball to which we'd been invited, my debut as it were, I was descending the long staircase on Uncle Douglas' arm when the lady in back stepped on the train of my dress. I heard the rip, I felt it straight up my back. My grand manner faltered and began to rip too. Uncle Douglas never missed a step. He leaned back, swung my torn train over his arm and kept right on, suavely guiding me down and through the long line of guests. This man became my close friend and I loved him.

Mary and I became friendly after my divorce from Douglas, but during the time of that marriage we never had a word of conversation save in a group of people. Newspaper columnists harped on the fact that Mary couldn't tolerate the idea I might make her a grandmother, but I've no idea whether or not that was true. She was still very young, very girlish, with her hair piled high and soft curls dangling at the back of her head. Exuberant Uncle Douglas would come whirling into a room, pick her up and hold her high in the air while she laughed her girlish laugh and cried, "Now, Douglas, put me down." She was enchanting with him, and he was obviously enchanted with her. She had the manner and bearing of a little queen.

Several times during the years, Gwen or Miss Pickford's cousin, Verna Chaliff, would bring me up to her room before dinner and I would sit on the chaise longue while Miss Pickford decided what clothes to wear—soft, feminine fluffy clothes—and chatted with Verna or Gwen. These girls seemed quite at home and not the least overawed. Gwen called her "Aunt Mary," Verna called her "Mary," but I called her "Ma'am" . . . "Yes, ma'am" . . . "No, ma'am." I wasn't risking the chance of saying the wrong thing, estranging my Douglas from his Douglas.

Long after Douglas ceased to be mine, I continued meeting Mary at Hollywood social functions, and as time went by there was a growing cordiality. We correspond. As a matter of fact, when we met several years ago at the Eastman Awards presentation, Mary came to me at once, across the room, kissed me, and said, "Billie, my darling, I am so proud of what you've done with your life. You not only set yourself a great goal, you've surpassed that goal!" I wouldn't have believed it *then*, but I know now that Mary has a great capacity for friendship.

There is a warmth that goes with greatness. Uncle Douglas had it, so did Corinne Griffith and Gloria Swanson, Marion Davies and Ruth Chatterton. They lived in fabulous castles, these stars, they had a flair for living. In retrospect I adored being their guest; in actuality, I stood in reverence like my children when we first drove through the redwoods. The children couldn't wait to tell their schoolmates about the redwoods and the salmon run in Oregon, but they were restless and fidgety while they were seeing it—as I was at San Simeon.

Marion tried to put me at ease. We'd become friends during *Our Dancing Daughters* and she always greeted me with, "How's my daughter?" I did not drink, she did, but without Mr. Hearst's approval, so when he'd enter the room, sometimes she'd thrust her glass into my hand. One night Mr. Hearst said:

"I've never seen you take a drink before, Joan."

"I thought I'd try it," I said, blushing.

"Well, try it!" And he stood there to watch me choke it down.

Douglas loved society. On his birthday I gave him a surprise party at the Biltmore: Connie Bennett and Hank de la Falaise, Ruth and Leslie Howard, Norma Shearer and Irving Thalberg, Florence and Fredric March. But I preferred the evenings we spent at home with our closer friends: Ann Harding and Harry Bannister, Kay Hammond and her husband, Hope Loring and her husband Bud Leighton, Dorothy Sebastian and Bill Boyd. Willie Haines was with us a great deal and Katherine Albert. They and Dorothy Sebastian were the three friends I'd kept from my first years in Hollywood. Everyone else I lost track of when I married Douglas.

Gradually our entertaining increased. "Cielito Lindo" we called the house now, "Little Heaven," and to it Douglas invited a rush of celebrities, young sophisticates and literary fights. We acquired a domestic staff. I learned to organize dinner parties quite successfully. Saturday nights were usually formal, virtually the same group would return for a swim on Sunday, we'd have an early buffet, show a movie and to bed for Monday and work. Larry and Jill Olivier and Larry's son, Tarquin, were close to us, Barbara Stanwyck and Frank Faye, Cesar Romero, Julie and George Murphy, Sally and Norman Foster, Dick Cromwell, Claudette Colbert, Bob Young, Alexander Kirkland and Helen Hayes. But I constantly made other friends too, script clerks and publicity people such as able Jerry Asher.

Betty Barker, now my secretary, was one of our first fans. Bettina was a little twelve-year-old freckle-faced child. We'd find her sitting out on the curb after Sunday School. Bennett the chauffeur would slow down and Betty would chat with us; sometimes she'd come into the kitchen and have a glass of milk and a cookie. She was a gay, friendly girl and she obviously loved us. You couldn't resist that. I think that when Douglas and I split up, Bettina was bereft. We had looked as happy-ever-after to her as we did to ourselves.

It took me a long time to realize that what had started out a thrilling and rhapsodic romance had turned into a marriage that was neither. What happened? Basically, I think, there was no middle ground for us. Never were two people more intense *every minute*. Every minute was never or forever. We were the most discussed bride and groom in the world and we were too high-keyed, too absorbed, too dramatic. Love can't continue at that pitch. Ours was flaming youth in earnest, we couldn't keep our hands or our eyes off each other, but in the matter of day-to-day living, we were young and inexperienced. My becoming totally Mrs. Douglas Fairbanks, Jr., was no pose. It was true. I didn't want to be separated from Douglas for a moment, I was completely dedicated to being his wife, but neither of us knew how to live once the year of honeymoon was over.

He really didn't want his wife to work. Isn't it strange—a man marries a woman for certain qualities and then wants to change them. And much as I loved him, working was essential to me. As a matter of fact, marriage gave me tremendous incentive. I worked so hard, tried so hard—for him—my career had to accelerate. As one columnist wrote, "Douglas Fairbanks, Jr.'s name had been better known than Joan's, but she became a box office star while he remained a leading man. It's the rock ninety per cent of the industry's ruined marriages split on."

Douglas *wasn't* as ambitious as I. He didn't have the same necessity to compensate. He was a dreamy, poetic boy. For his career he could at times evince a burn-up enthusiasm, but for a role he didn't like, total indifference. He gave rare feeling to his roles in *The Barker* and *Dawn Patrol,* but *I Like Your Nerve* was a slipshod performance and he didn't care. He could give one of the six best performances one month, one of the six worst the next. I couldn't. No matter what the role or what the picture, I was driven to do my utmost, as if by a whip. No matter how lousy the dialogue, I believed every word of it.

Douglas had a dozen talents to my one. He could paint and sculpture and write, he'd written subtitles for *The Gaucho.* He agreed once to write a series of articles for *Vanity Fair,* but he'd come home, curl up in a chair and read.

"Get out your typewriter, darling," I'd say.

He'd stretch, laugh, say he was lazy.

He hadn't developed the muscles for fighting because he hadn't had to fight.

I craved children and for years people have asked why we had none. I was plagued with miscarriages is why—a brutal disappointment, to me, at least. Columnists rumored that the Fairbanks Seniors didn't sanction our having children. They were both still active in pictures and glamorous symbols. Nonsense. Each couple must work out their own destiny. I was the one who wanted children; I was the one who lacked the physical strength to have them. It left, I felt, a sad void in our lives.

Douglas and I might have hurdled even this gap, but gradually we were taking diverse paths. I loved people, but at the end of a working day I longed to be alone with my husband. He increasingly craved the company of jovial, witty people. Douglas was trying to prove something, that he was as good a man as his father, that *he* was a wit, a practical joker in his own right. He didn't have to prove this to me. I was his best audience; but that wasn't enough, he needed a larger audience, and entertaining constantly, he'd dispel his energy. When the guests would leave, alas, we were without communication. There was nothing left to say.

Silence is a precious thing. It can be the most personal communication if two people are implicitly giving to that silence. But the rigor of studio demands, the social pace, militated against this. Once upon a time I'd worked all day and danced all night, but not since my career had gotten under way. Now I wanted to devote myself to the job and to my home, but Douglas wanted work all day and people all night. We were growing further and further apart.

Several times I suggested we spend a quiet weekend at home alone. Each time, Douglas agreed enthusiastically, then forgot and invited people. The tempo continued at the usual pace, games, laughter.... I suggested we spend a weekend alone at Carmel where we had been so happy. By the time the weekend arrived, Douglas had invited half a dozen other people. He couldn't see why I was perturbed. I jumped in the car and drove the three hundred and fifty miles to Carmel myself, trying to find an answer.

Constantly in the public eye, I became quieter and quieter, so subdued.... What did the hotcha girl think, some writers asked, that she was cultured? And let me say that the press, for the most part, has always been level with me, always professional. But there are a few hatchet boys too. They said I had a chip on my shoulder. In my Charleston days I'd been called the hey-hey girl. Now that I read serious literature I was called high-hat. When I fraternized with electricians on the set, they said I was posing, when I cultivated celebrities, a snob.

My dear friend, writer Katherine Albert, expressed it very well. "Today they say Joan is high-hat, ritzy. But nothing can stop her remarkable journey to success. What she came here with was a hardboiled veneer and an easy manner not her own. Today's Joan Crawford is no more that girl than Will Rogers is Mahatma Gandhi." She had taught me, in the beginning, not to believe my publicity, now she urged me not to be hurt by criticism. But there were those who said I had married Douglas because I was trying to make it from chorus girl to lady.

In my scheme of things, being a lady has never seemed as important as being a woman. As a woman I could never love a man to whom I couldn't look up. What *I* mean by lady has nothing to do with which rung she stands on the social ladder. Lady indicates a woman of innate breeding. She's read and absorbed what she's read, she's cognizant of other people, she's kind to people regardless of situations or circumstances, she understands them and understands herself. That's the kind of woman I wanted to be. The sorriest tragedy that could befall me would be the lack of ability to feel.

Criticism tortured me and drove me away from people. And where was Douglas and my love? That tortured me even more. I'm not feline or female enough to pout, use my femininity and walk away. I wanted to talk it out, give it every chance. We discussed it for six months—in our rare moments together—then took the "honeymoon trip" we'd always wanted and for which we'd never had time. We went to Paris and London trying to recapture what was lost.

In New York, Mayor Jimmy Walker provided a police escort of eight motorcycles to escort us to the pier, a wild, careening ride, the sirens shrieking. Crowds at the pier tore at our clothes, women fainted scrambling over each other to see what I was wearing and to plant kisses on Douglas' new moustache. When we finally achieved our cabin with police help, a man tried to climb through the porthole. "I'm gonna see you, Joan, I don't care if they arrest me!" he shouted as they carted him off. Jill Esmond and Laurence Olivier were on the *Bremen* with us and Heather Thatcher and Noel Coward met us all at Southampton. I was introduced to the London Douglas knew, and Heather and Noel, the Duke of Kent and Ivor Novello were with us every night; it couldn't have been more exciting.

Everywhere we went, crowds followed us, flashbulbs exploded, the press kept pace. I had presumed no one would know me outside the U.S.A. It wasn't true! English people peered in the restaurant windows to watch me dance with the Duke and with Noel. There is no other movie audience in the world to compare with the English. They are more alert to personalities than people in New York or Hollywood. At Noel Coward's *Cavalcade* they tore my evening coat off my back and I basked in their fond attention. Noel, Douglas and a corps of bobbies carried me into the theater on their shoulders. This is the public without which an actress cannot exist, and I had a ball.

We had planned to visit Venice, but the closest we came was the picture we'd had painted of us in a gondola. Douglas was summoned to Hollywood for *Revolt* and we came home, rested, exhilarated, but with the same basic problems. In a different country our pattern had been no different: people, people, people. When one person craves an audience and one craves intimacy, there is an inevitable loss of rapport. I simply was growing up faster than Douglas. I needed less outside stimulation.

Our divorce was a constant rumor. A famed columnist announced it as a scoop on the air and had to retract. Gossip persisted as it had from the day I sent Douglas that first telegram and Hollywood tagged it "puppy love." The world loves lovers; it welcomes, as well, their disillusionment. Douglas did not want a divorce, but I did. I couldn't go on.

I turned in this crisis to Uncle Douglas, the one person closest to my Douglas. I phoned him, we met at the Derby for lunch, and I told him the truth, that all the lovely laughter had disappeared from the doll's house. It had, as a matter of fact, been gone for some time.

Jovial Uncle Douglas could laugh off anything. This was the first time I ever saw him devoutly serious. He studied my face. "Billie," he said, "when two people are this unhappy, they shouldn't stay together."

His words freed me. I filed quietly for divorce and left for Malibu. The Frank Cases gave me the keys to their beach house. It was late February, cool, the Malibu colony was all but deserted. I walked the beach the whole first day, scarcely knowing where I was. Night dropped down, isolating me. I sat in the dark house, terribly alone, not a light visible the length of the beach! Just then a car's headlights swirled through the room. I rushed to the door. And there was, not a foe but a friend, Bill (Alexander) Kirkland, then in *Strange Interlude*. He brought in armloads of flowers and strewed them at my feet. That brought me back to normal. I put on the fights and cooked dinner.

I stayed at Malibu for some time. Day after day, friends came out to keep me company—Bill, Bob Young with whom I'd recently made *Today We Live* and Jerry Asher, three of the most sympathetic people on earth. Jerry, who had once felt like a lost soul himself, understood one. We'd sit on the beach at dusk eating hot dogs and beans, drinking lemonade. They listened and tried to help me.

Douglas and I feared divorce publicity. It seemed best to let Katherine Albert write the story for her magazine—that would be our official announcement and its good taste would be insured. But fan magazines have a deadline three months ahead of issue. We separated officially in March, a trial separation, we said, and Douglas vowed he was going to woo me all over again and win me back. He was very sweet. He took me dancing, we spent my birthday together, along with Mother and Hal. But there is no going back. I knew that and I'm sure Douglas did.

Then, just before Katherine's story was published, Douglas was the target of a $50,000 alienation of affections suit, a nuisance suit. Douglas was the victim of publicity as I once had been. I'd never have chosen this moment to announce our divorce, but nothing could be done. Katherine's story was already on the presses.

What hurt most in the next weeks were those questions that harped on the failure of our marriage. How could you call it a failure?

Through marriage to Douglas I learned tolerance, understanding, self-respect. I learned to view life from numerous angles. No question, we brought out and polished each other's latent qualities. When I'd first known Douglas and told him of the foolish mistakes I'd made, he said, "Nothing is important from yesterday save what we learn for tomorrow." When I left Judge Minor Moore's courtroom that day with Jerry Giesler, May 13, 1933, I was a different person from the girl who'd gone backstage at the Vine Street Playhouse, immeasurably sadder, immeasurably richer in character and nothing *was* important save what I'd learned. An actress, I felt, should never marry, but what Douglas and I had known was no failure.

Proof that it wasn't—we're still friends. We've always kept in touch, always been proud of each other. While this book was being written, he was in New York, en route to the Island of Palmas. Jane Ardmore and I were lunching at Twenty One when Douglas walked in. I asked him if he would consent to being interviewed, and he was most gracious.

He alluded to himself as "Old Woodley," but that isn't true. He's very young Woodley still, a trifle gray at the temples, but you don't believe it, they've just powdered him up for a last act. We spoke of many things . . . of people whom life defeats, and thank heaven, he's not one. He's kept his handsome presence, his personality and charm in focus. He's developed business acumen and far more polish, but he's young in heart and boyish.

Janie asked Douglas how I had changed in the years and he said:

"I'll have to go all around Robin Hood's barn to tell you. I once said to Lady Mendl, 'I must be a case of arrested development because all my basic attitudes, all my basic feelings are the same as when I was twenty.' Lady Mendl answered, 'Douglas, I have passed my ninety-third birthday. I won't tell you by how much, but I have passed my ninety-third birthday. I still have my teeth, my eyesight and my hair . . . I limp a little . . . but when I see a handsome young man pass by, going into a ballroom, I think how delightful he'd be to spend the weekend with. And *then,* I remember I'm ninety-three. No, Douglas, you're no case of arrested development.'

"So . . . my tastes and my reactions are the same now as when I was twenty and the people for whom I cared deeply, seem as I knew them then. Billie," and he turned to face me across the luncheon table, "still looks to me as she did at nineteen. You're so lovely, Billie. You were always grown-up. You always had guts. More than that, you had the ability to transfuse those guts to others. To *me.* That I didn't flounder and fall under my father's shadow, I owe to you, Billie. Remember how you used to pound your fist on the table and cry, 'Stand on your own feet!' You gave me faith in myself. Yes, *you.*"

I'm very grateful for those words, grateful that I gave something to someone who gave me so much.

FIVE

Where does the woman end and the actress begin? I can't answer that. A little of every part rubs off on you. Bogart could never have been Bogart without the parts he played, I could never have become Joan Crawford. But the reverse is equally true. When I first married Douglas, I was fighting for emotional, dramatic parts because I am dramatic and emotional. I wanted self-expression.

My first chance came in a picture that for years was my favorite—*Paid*. The remake from the famous old play *Within the Law* had been planned for Norma Shearer, but Norma became pregnant and I begged to take her place. Here was a melodrama that had made Jane Cowl a star on Broadway, Alice Joyce, then Norma Talmadge had translated it to the screen, now the play had been rewritten with Charlie MacArthur doing the dialogue.

How did I get hold of that script? I was always a script stealer. Totally engrossed, I read this story of the department-store clerk railroaded to prison, who emerges with one thought, revenge. I pleaded with Hunt Stromberg, the producer, pleaded with Mr. Mayer, and against their better judgment, the part was mine. This moment was crucial careerwise. I knew if I scored a triumph I'd surprise my fans and attract a new audience. I knew too that if I failed I'd lose the audience I had built up and gain nothing. My dancing-daughter days were over, so far as I was concerned.

The distinguished Charles Bickford, whom I'd never met, was visiting on the set. He came up and kissed my hand after the courtroom scene. I wonder if he knows what confidence he gave me, that dynamic actor with his shock of red hair!

"You're going to be a great star," he said.

I'd begun to feel the prickles of stardom already. "But am I going to be a good actress?" I cried.

Some critics said yes. *Variety* said, "Histrionically she impresses us as about ready to stand up under any sort of dramatic assignment."

I treasured that. I pasted it into the scrapbook stuffed with clippings, and right next to it, the telegram from Marlene Dietrich, whom I had never met. *She* liked *Paid* too.

But parts like that of Mary Turner didn't come along every day to me. They came, but to Miss Garbo and Miss Shearer. To compensate, I gave everything I had to each character, trying to make *her* real and living. My next was the rich girl turned newspaper reporter in *Dance, Fools, Dance*. It was based on two high spots in Chicago's then current crime history, still being used over and over today in pictures and on television: the shooting of Jake Lingle and the St. Valentine's Day massacre.

The picture was memorable for the presence of an electrifying man, one who couldn't miss stardom—Clark Gable. Clark had a comparatively small part in *Dance, Fools, Dance*. He played Jake Luva, the gangster heavy, but in the one scene where he grabbed me and threatened the life of my brother, his nearness had such impact, my knees buckled. If he hadn't held me by both shoulders I'd have dropped. I wasn't the only one who noticed Clark. Every girl on the lot noticed him. So did Mr. Mayer with his unerring eye for talent; and the consequence was fairly unique in the industry.

My next picture was *Complete Surrender,* with Johnny Mack Brown as the Salvation Army man who restores this cabaret girl's self-confidence. After the preview, Mr. Mayer called us back for a total remake. Johnny's performance was excellent, but Mr. Mayer had seen the chemistry between Clark and me and thought he scented box-office dynamite. This time the picture was called *Laughing Sinners* and Clark Gable was the Salvation Army man. We didn't have too many scenes together, but they were powerful ones and went well.

As in all MGM pictures at this time, our supporting cast was made up of superb actors. Look over the casts of all those early pictures. They included such contract players as: Edward Arnold, Lionel Barrymore, Billie Burke, Cliff Edwards, Wallace Ford, Ralph Forbes, Louise Closser Hale, Ted Healy, Jean Hersholt, Hedda Hopper, Guy Kibbee, Otto Kruger, Una Merkel, John Miljan, Frank Morgan, Edna May Oliver, Una O'Connor, Reginald Owen, May Robson, Lewis Stone and Arthur Treacher. Studios today have stables, but not stables of thoroughbreds like this. If you couldn't learn to run in this race you'd better be put back to pasture, and some young players *were.*

Marjorie Rambeau played my mother in *Laughing Sinners*— I became blonde to further the resemblance—and she was cast as my mother again in *This Modern Age.* But Marjorie became ill and was replaced by my adored Pauline Frederick. Pauline was chosen because many people had noted our resemblance, and the publicity department flooded rotogravure sections with pictures of Pauline and me, profile next to profile. However, the entire picture could not be remade because of cost, just the Marjorie Rambeau scenes, so I had to play dark-haired Pauline's daughter with blonde hair.

Acting with Pauline Frederick was a stirring experience for me. The celebrated actress I'd met backstage with Paul Bern when I was a novice in Hollywood, the first legitimate theater I'd ever seen—now we were working together every day and I had the opportunity of knowing her, savoring her quality. Her voice had the tone and range of a rare instrument, but that was just one adjunct of her charm, as were her physical beauty and dramatic ability. At the core of this woman was an exquisite maturity. She had utilized her intelligence, expanded it, she was living proof of what a woman and an actress could become. Imagine my reaction when she told everyone, "If they'll give this child a chance she'll do big things. Joan is an actress."

Neither she nor I had any illusions about *This Modern Age*. It was hopelessly artificial, especially for a depression year. Critics called it "a shop girl's delight" and said, "Pretty thin ice for a release to be skating on *this* season." It would be my first starrer that failed to hit big grosses and it wasn't my fault, they said. I deserved something less ridiculous in the way of a story, they said. They were right about the story, wrong about the grosses. There must have been a lot of shop girls, bless 'em. It had taken my career a long time to start rolling, but it was on its way like some lovely snowball. Everything we did made money. Occasionally we even made a good picture.

Possessed, for example. The story was hardly original or significant, but director Clarence Brown was. A small man, professorial in appearance, he kept us geared to his slightest expression of approval or disapproval. Reserved, dignified, I've never known a director with more respect for each minute detail in each and every scene. He was an engineer before he came to pictures and like an engineer he evaluated his tools and used them. He sensed the volcanic attraction between his stars and used that for all it was worth.

In this picture Clark and I hit our stride. In *spite* of the fact that I was emotionally distraught. The shadow of divorce colored my mood, I felt saturated with defeat—all very good for the picture, in which I was supposed to register pathos. My forced gaiety in between scenes, however, failed to convince Clark. He studied me one day when I arrived hollow-eyed on the set, tilted my face up and said:

"You didn't sleep again last night."

"How did you know?"

"Joan," he said, "whatever's bothering you isn't worth it."

He let me talk it out. He'd experienced heartbreak himself and we'd been friends from the first—if you could call it friendship. This magnetic man had more sheer male magic than anyone in the world and every woman knew it, every woman looked at him with desire. He knew it too. It was as much a part of him as his own breathing.

With Douglas I had played the part of a girl in love and lived it. With Clark I lacked the courage to live it. My misgiving was that he might be one of those men who desire a woman they can't have; once they attain her they lose interest. Perhaps Carole Lombard voiced the answer years later: "The men who *work* with us see us at our best, exciting, glamorous, meticulous. The men we *marry* see us at our worst, dead-tired, at the day's end, with makeup off and the curlers on." I had no qualms about giving Clark the wife he wanted. He was happiest in the mountains, in the woods, fishing, hunting, and I've participated in these outdoor sports since. I did occasionally then. I was just afraid it wouldn't last, that I couldn't make it last, that every girl who ever worked with Clark would feel the same way I did.

Here I was, lonely, dejected over the failure of my marriage, and every day Clark Gable walked onto the set—earlier than necessary. We took to arriving earlier just to have a little more time with each other. In the picture, we were madly in love. When the scenes ended, the emotion didn't—we were each playing characters very close to our own. It was a love bounded by the flats on the set. Perhaps twice a week we lunched together—he couldn't absent himself oftener from the publicity table where he and Spencer Tracy always ate, without being conspicuous. Occasionally we'd break away early, go for a quiet ride along the sea. And all day long we'd seek each other's eyes. It was glorious and hopeless. There seemed nothing we could do about it. There was no chance for us.

Clark insisted that I was wrong, that there was hope, that we could marry. We talked of marriage, of coarse. But I dared not ruin the dreams. I'd rather live with them unfulfilled than have them broken.

Outside the studio we never even held hands, never held more than a momentary glance. Clark was married. I was often in groups with him and Rhea socially. She was a charming lady, so happy in Clark's success, so anxious not to intrude on his glamour, and you felt like a heel cherishing this emotion for her husband. I wouldn't have hurt her for the world. Neither would Clark. And yet the rumors were rampant. "What star is interested in her leading man?" "There's a top actress and a grand gal who's running a couple of risks. She's wide-eyed in another hubby's direction."

I'll never forget lunching at a popular restaurant with Rhea Gable. A writer rushed up to the table and gushed, "I just saw you in *Pos-*

sessed. Joan, you were wonderful, inspired, the way you look at Clark, anyone can tell you're *crazy* about him."

I blanched, turned quickly to the writer and said, "May I present my good friend, Mrs. Clark Gable?"

It was like living over a lighted powder keg, but it was worth it. I've said that Clark could melt you with a look. Well, he could talk, too, and we had a great deal to talk about. His job, like mine, was the most serious thing in the world to him. When we went into a scene, everything else ceased to exist. When still-photographer George Hurrell took pictures of us, he'd simply have the lights set up . . . sometimes we were oblivious of the fact that he'd finished shooting. We could talk or not talk. There was nothing in the world Clark couldn't understand about me save my uncertainty about us.

He was extremely sensitive, but like most physically big guys, afraid to show it. There is probably only one other man of our time whose personality incorporated the same blend of toughness and tenderness, the same ability to be a woman's man and a man's man— Ernest Hemingway.

The only time I could be with Clark was on the set, and I was disconsolate that I was cast in *Letty Lynton*—without him. Clarence Brown, who also directed *Letty,* knew. He came up to me one day just before a big scene and said, sotto voce, "I understand, Joan, I know who you're missing." I threw my arms about his dear professorial neck and went right into my crying scene, my own unhappy tears for unhappy Letty.

But the next assignment had to be a thrill, even without Clark. I hadn't had a proven play since *Paid.* Now I stepped into a great play, a picture into which the studio had funneled its top talent. I'm speaking, of course, of *Grand Hotel.* Imagine working with Lionel Barrymore . . . John Barrymore . . . Wallace Beery . . . Lewis Stone . . . Jean Hersholt . . . Greta Garbo.

Garbo was my favorite actress in the world, a fascinating woman. To this day I deplore the fact that she is unable to share herself with the world. Such a waste! If anywhere along the line she'd been able to find a person who would have pulled her out of her fears, she'd have continued giving such great artistry, such joy to the world. There are those who need a leader. She did. I never believed she was a recluse, she didn't want to be alone, that was a publicity gag—only look how she adored Stiller, Gilbert, Stokowski. These were strong men and she was a strong woman; if only she hadn't been so afraid, she wouldn't today be a lonely stranger on Fifth Avenue, fleeing before recognition, and to those who ask about her making movies, replying, "I've said no for so long and now it's too late."

She was a fascinating actress whom I adored from a distance. For three years I'd come out of my dressing room every day, run past hers, and call, "Good morning!" I could hear her deep voice talking to Lulu, the maid, but she never did speak to me. I'd see her occasionally on the lot. Never a word. Then one morning there was a rush call, someone was ill and couldn't show up for still art in the gallery, would I come and pose in their place? I went sprinting past Garbo's dressing room in such a hurry I forgot to yell *good morning*. An instant later I heard her door open, then a resonant "'Alloooo!"

In *Grand Hotel* I was just sad that Garbo as the renowned ballerina, Grusinskaya, and I, Flaemmchen, the little whore-stenographer, had no scene together. We frequented Grand Hotel, but in different worlds. We frequented different worlds at the studio as well. Miss Garbo worked days and left at five; I came to work at six and shot all night. One evening I was just starting to the set when she came up the stairs to her dressing room. I was with Jerry Asher and I literally shoved him into a corner and followed him into it so we would both be out of her way. She'd just finished working, she'd be tired and wouldn't want to be greeted. Just then, the vibrant voice said, "'Allooooo!" I murmured hello and bolted for the stairs from which she'd just emerged, but she caught me in passing. There suddenly above me was that beautiful face with those compelling eyes, and the woman I'd thought so aloof was saying:

"I'm so sorry we are not working together. What a pity, eh? Our first picture together and not one scene."

What I'd have done if we'd *had* the scene, I don't know. As it was, I was exhausting every resource I had and drawing on ones I didn't know existed. Can you imagine the dancing daughter in a scene with Beery and two Barrymores? The upstaging was historic. John was like Peck's Bad Boy. He was usually "hung-over" and would appear on the set with a shy appealing quality. He would use four-letter words, then giggle like a little boy. But play ended the instant the camera started rolling. Then he became beauteous and fiery. Wally Beery was wrapped up in his part of General Director Preysing and never emerged from it.

What made *Grand Hotel* memorable for me was Lionel Barrymore. He was a dream to work with. Later, *in The Gorgeous Hussy*, he was more difficult because he had grown older and very arthritic, but old or young, difficult or dreamy, this was an actor to venerate. He was utterly simple, nothing of the poseur. He'd sit hunched in a corner peering over those funny little glasses, he was forever losing his false moustache. We were constantly poking about in corners, peering under the feet of extras, under tables and chairs, hunting the thing. When we'd find it, he'd slap it on his lip without even looking in the mirror, crying, impatiently, "All right, all right, all right, let's go!" As if *we'd* kept *him* waiting. His performance as the shabby, abject Kringelein, with only a short while to live, ran the gamut from comedy to profound pathos. One of my most poignant experiences was the scene where he asks me to come away with him—Flaemmchen who has been used so badly by Beery's Preysing, who has been smitten with John Barrymore's Baron and lost him, first to Garbo's ballerina, then to death! Asking me to come away with him, Kringelein was so appealing, so gentle and joyous, he all but broke my heart. Any wonder these scenes were believable?

Edmund Goulding who had directed *Sally, Irene and Mary* and *Paris,* directed *Grand Hotel,* and what a joy to work with him again. Six years before he'd had to tell me so much, now he told me so little. "You're thinking with your heart, Joan, it shows in your eyes." He told me how much I'd changed. "You've grown quiet, you've gained strength, Joan." I listened, I sat quietly, watching every actor, every nuance, every scene.

The picture with all those stars was, of course, a tremendous hit. While it was still playing road shows, *Letty Lynton* was released also to big business and rave notices. And where did I go from there? Down into the fiasco of *Rain,* familiar, alas, to everyone who watches the late, late show on television.

I was haunted by my inferiority to famous Sadie Thompsons of the past, Jeanne Eagels, who created the part on the stage, and Gloria Swanson, who appeared in the early silent-film version. I hadn't seen them, but they were constantly held up to me by my co-workers. Mr. Joe Schenck thought I was worried unnecessarily, he told me to listen to my director, but Lewis Milestone frightened me. I wasn't wise enough about acting to understand how brilliant a man this was or how talented a director. He had worked out blueprints for every scene, precisely what I was to do and how to do it; but to me, no actress worthy of the name could be a puppet in anyone's hands. I was no Method actress, I was an emotional one—in *Rain,* far too emotional. All you have to do is check the excellent pictures Mr. Milestone has made to see who was right. I was wrong.

There were critics who praised my Sadie, called her "florid and fraught with all the passions that made Sadie what she was," but most reviews were written in acid and I grieved over them. I grieved over the letters that poured in from fans hating my mouth makeup. It was broad, it was bold and blatant, that's the kind of woman I thought Sadie was, but I hadn't the vaguest idea what she was like inside. I didn't even know then that you could work from the interior to the exterior. I was still working from the exterior. My fans wouldn't accept her. They would accept me as Letty Lynton who was just as vulgar, but she had style. Cheapness *and* vulgarity they would not accept. Oh, who am I kidding, I just gave a lousy performance!

The cameras of Hollywood kept turning. By the time of the premiere of *Rain* we were already deep in production on *Today We Live,* a story of young Britons caught up in the vortex of war: Bob Young, my fiancé, Gary Cooper, the American who wins me; my brother was played by a young man from the distinguished Group Theatre in New York. I'd seen his test, he had such an eloquent speaking voice! Franchot Tone, of course. I tried not to let him down, for this was the first movie role of a dedicated and talented actor. I needn't have worried about Franchot, he stole the picture.

He was the only one who got a line of commendation. Critics found *Today We Live* overlong and they chastised Howard Hawks for resorting to his Howard Hughes file of flying shots from *Hell's Angels.*

As an English girl, I didn't register. I was miscast, they said. I certainly was. With *Rain* and *Today We Live* on the debit side, drastic measures were needed to reinstate me, at least that's what I felt. Mr. Mayer supplied the antidote. *Possessed* had established Clark Gable and me as a good box-office combination, now he paired us again in *Dancing Lady*, and poured into the picture all the talent, the acumen and resources that made working at MGM so exhilarating at that time.

Ours was like a faculty of experts. There was Jack Dawn in makeup, Howard Strickling in publicity, Clarence Bull in still photography, a little later I found hair stylist Sydney Guilaroff at Saks and Mr. Mayer brought him to the studio. Ramon Novarro discovered photographer George Hurrell at Laguna and he was brought to the studio, introducing to the motion picture business, photography with an all-dark background, one light on the face. I'd scrub until my skin shone. Great fashion designer Adrian for fourteen years designed everything I wore in pictures and most of what I wore personally. The clothes he created had great impact on the styles of the whole country. He toned me down in color and line and gave me the tailored look women have treasured ever since. Trying to cope with my broad shoulders he decided to emphasize them: result, the broad-shouldered suit look that became an overnight sensation and dominated women's styles throughout the thirties. I frankly don't remember any "fashion" before Adrian.

Mr. Mayer wanted only the best. I esteemed all the gifted people with whom we worked and him most of all. In the many years he guided my career I valued his judgment, his patience and the fact that he never played games. I always stood in his presence, I stand now in his memory. I'm sick and tired of his current detractors and their snide detractions. The dolt he's been described since his death, by writers nursing old grudges, could never have built the star system and administered the studio that during the thirties and forties was without peer. How powerful Mr. Mayer was I didn't realize until I'd been a star for some time. Then I began to comprehend the power pictures have, the power an actress can have, the power of a studio and the obligation to your public. *Dancing Lady* was one of the happy experiences he made possible for all of us.

I loved working with Clark. We were cheerful and effervescent on a set and it must have reflected on the screen because up until his recent and shocking death, there never has been a week without letters urging me to make another picture "with Mr. Gable." *Dancing Lady* started shooting on July 15. A week later Clark was rushed from the set for an emergency appendectomy and came back to work too soon. The first day, the doctor only allowed him to work an hour—he was so weak, the cold perspiration would break out on his face. I was never so sorry for anyone.

And then, I broke my ankle. In the script I was supposed to *sprain* it. I guess I overacted *that* scene. The second day I took off the cast to dance with Fred Astaire, and was so thrilled to be dancing with him that I could have danced on my head. When the dance was filmed, the cast went back on. This was Fred's first movie, a sort of trial balloon. It was one of those incredible breaks for me, both to dance with him and have him there. For Fred and his wife, Phyllis, had the most perfect marriage I'd ever known.

Fred is a shy man; Phyllis was shy too. They reinforced each other. Each morning Phyllis would drive him to the studio, wait quietly in the car, reading, until he finished in makeup, then while he worked she'd sit in a far corner of the set doing needlepoint. He always treated her like the great lady she was.

On Saturday nights she'd pick him up, with a picnic lunch and a hot thermos of soup or coffee. They'd have their dinner by the sea, then drive to their ranch, Fred curled up on the seat with his head on her lap. Some men can't allow a woman to drive, but Fred didn't compete with his wife, he enjoyed her prowess. She was a fragile, tiny person, but she could drive a golf ball two hundred yards. And at tennis . . . she, Fred, Cary Grant and Randy Scott were a foursome, and on the golf course or the tennis court this dainty woman whaled these men. They fought to have her as a partner.

Fred, you see, is such a virile man, he's never had to prove it. In all his years in show business, I've never known him to be rude and never have seen him make a pass at a girl. Pleasant he is, to everyone, and invites pleasantness, but no one moves in on Fred Astaire. He's kept himself intact, and he could because he's been a fulfilled man in his personal life. I'd never seen two people work with such minimum effort at happiness. It was good for me to know that a marriage like theirs could happen in show business. I made a mental note: it could happen because they spent their time quietly together, as they continued to do, so long as Phyllis lived. Actors have enough temptations in their business, they must have security and contentment with the person of their choice, and deep convictions.

Much as I cared for Clark, the deep conviction that it could last was lacking within me and I knew it. I settled for friendship. We always worked well together, and harmoniously . . . our only argument when I refused to do *Parnell* . . . we met often socially . . . Carole Lombard and I were good friends.

After Carole's death, it was a long while before Clark came back to work and when he did come to the studio, he was solitary, he wouldn't even go to lunch in the commissary, his set was closed, and with policemen standing guard to insure his privacy, he'd occasionally sit out in the sun. I'd check with his secretary to ask how he was. Finally one day I wrote a note—he was leaving the lot every day about four thirty or five—and asked if he'd like to stop by the house for a cocktail. He wrote back saying he'd be there.

That night he talked for hours, talked and talked and talked. He'd listened to me once, now I listened to him, knitted, listened, and filled the ice bucket. The next day I received twelve-dozen red roses with the longest stems I'd ever seen. From then on for the next four or five months, Clark stopped by the house every single day. He wasn't the gay romantic Clark I'd first known, he wasn't the easy-going Clark, he was a moody man who needed friendship.

"You're living in the past," I told him. "You have a guilt complex because you didn't go with Carole on that trip. You couldn't go, you were working! You've had your grief, Clark, now pull yourself out of it."

Gradually he did.

And no one was more pleased than I when he married Kay. I love Kay, she's wonderful and she made him happier than he'd ever been in his life. They made each other happy. There had been many men in love with Kay, many girls adored Clark, but when the two got together, it was just right . . . the kind of close harmony that makes for deep contentment. I'm glad "the King" had that.

SIX

never worked harder than on *Dancing Lady*. I was knocking
myself out to dance as well as the chorus girls, who were in prac-
tice. I was surrounded by hardworking, inciting talent and I had
to pull my career back up after its first slide down. I was the one who
a year or so before had said that if I ever reached the top I'd stop right
then and there, I'd never want to take a step down! A star can be terribly afraid of failure, but you keep your shoulders back, your chin
high. There was one person who saw beyond that chin.

Franchot Tone had a quiet way of looking at me across a set, a
capacity for giving more than a scene required. One day he said to me:

"Gee, you're a nice dame."

I was insulted.

"Hurt your feelings?" he asked, surprised.

"Yes. The word *dame* sounds rough."

"Well, it isn't rough. It's the nicest compliment a guy can pay a lady."

He asked me to have dinner with him and Tommy (Ernest)
Thompson with whom he shared an apartment. Franchot, Tommy
and I had dinner several times. That's how it started.

I didn't fall in love with Franchot—not then—but I respected and admired him. My existence was pretty circumscribed at the time, evenings filled with reading, sewing, days away from the studio spent in the sun. Whenever possible, I'd go skimming up the coast to Carmel to walk for hours on the beach, to read and think, absorb the sunlight. My skin was so tanned that when we came to the pool scene in *Dancing Lady* we had to shoot around Franchot for two days so he could get tanned to match.

During my marriage to Douglas I had adapted totally to his world and his circle of acquaintances. When our marriage ended, the young sophisticates and visiting celebrities promptly ceased calling and I discovered to my surprise that they had never been my friends at all. Letters came from *my* friends, letters I've treasured from friends I had not forgotten, but had neglected. They didn't want to intrude on my unhappiness but they wanted me to know they were thinking of me. Could they help? They began dropping by, they were worried about my being constantly alone. Not that they said so, but I sensed their concern and was grateful to . . . Jerry Asher, Ricardo Cortez, Bill Kirkland, Gene Raymond, Bob Young, Lynn Riggs—the accomplished author of *Green Grow the Lilacs*—and now Franchot.

He was tonic to me, this remarkable young man with his individuality of thought and imagination, who understood and was very patient with me, whose two hands were always filled with beauty. Franchot was of a different fiber from anyone in Hollywood. He'd been to the manor born . . . the son of society . . . of wealth . . . he'd been graduated from Cornell with a Phi Beta Kappa key . . . and he had and has a truly golden talent. This became apparent in student plays at Cornell, and after graduation he'd chosen Broadway rather than the Carborundum Company, which his family owned. By the time he came to Hollywood he had served his apprenticeship in the New Playwrights' Theater, he'd played uptown with Katharine Cornell in *The Age of Innocence* and had starred in the Theatre Guild's production of *Green Grow the Lilacs*. From there he could have chosen his parts anywhere, but Franchot left the Theatre Guild for the newly formed Group Theatre, an earnest organization of stage students with whom he did *The House of Connelly*—(his favorite play)—and *Success Story*. For these people the theater was art and they were dedicated beyond the comprehension of the ordinary run of actors. Franchot *believed* in the Group Theatre, that's why he accepted a one-year contract in Hollywood, just to earn money for the Group!

I don't believe he had ever seen me on the screen until we met. His "introduction" came via Tallulah Bankhead, who amused her clan with what I understand was a devastating satire of me being utterly Doug-domestic, knitting, reading, as she had once seen me. Franchot witnessed her imitation and howled with laughter.

"That woman must be impossible," he said.

At which Willie Haines turned on him in fury.

"Listen, you, do you know Miss Crawford?" growled Willie.

"No," said Franchot, "nor do I wish to."

"Well, I *do* know her. We're not speaking at the moment, but she's my dearest friend, no one can criticize her but me. Now you never say another word about Miss C. until you meet her. And when you do, you know what? You'll not only like her, you'll fall in love with her."

Franchot had to tell me the story because what Willie'd said is exactly what happened. He fell in love, he says, the day we started shooting *Today We Live*. I would sometimes see him watching me, his great thinking eyes so penetrating, a little crooked smile on his aesthetic face. But he was biding his time. He was self-contained, he carried with him an aura of peace, as if he knew some safe harbor; and his well-trained, scintillating mind stimulated mine. I'd never heard of Stanislavsky! I knew little or nothing about Shakespeare, even though I'd read many of his plays with Douglas. Before the grate fire in the library, Franchot would read aloud from Shakespeare, Ibsen and Shaw, while I hooked a rug. Then we'd discuss what we'd read. He taught me to respect my own mind, not just to absorb things emotionally, but to *think*. He showed me new areas in books and music. There are such hidden meanings in Shakespeare, you learn more each time you reread a play. It's like walking through a forest and becoming aware of each individual tree. Within his works is a complete education. In short order the rugs went unhooked and we were reading the plays together.

I had purchased the lot in back of my house and now planned a theater where a small group of us could actually produce the classics or rehearse our current filmscripts. Franchot introduced me to thinkers and artists. We both started studying opera. His basso profundo was as beautiful as his speaking voice, which is one of the most liquid and sonorous in this world. Franchot doesn't have just a voice, he has a hundred-piece orchestra inside that rib cage, and like a fine conductor he has every nuance of the music, every instrument under complete control.

He was imaginative and charming, this man, and his love for me made me quite—as he would say—a *dame*. The first night we went dancing I wore a collar of gardenias around my throat and he a gardenia in his lapel. The fragrant blooms were my favorites, they meant luck and love, and he always had the house and my studio dressing rooms filled with them. Photographers flashed a few pictures of us that first night dancing, but this man had a dignity that forbade intrusion.

When *Dancing Lady* was finished, Franchot made an appealing suggestion. He urged me to come to New York for the opening of the Group Theatre's *Men in White*. Movie money of his had helped finance summer rehearsals of this play by Sidney Kingsley. In Franchot's eyes this would be an exciting production, making the most complete use to date of the resources of the living theater and combining the acting talents of Luther Adler, J. Edward Bromberg, my friend Bill Kirkland in one of the leads, Morris Camovsky, Phoebe Brand, and in bit parts, Clifford Odets and Elia Kazan. The play would open September 26 at the Broadhurst.

His enthusiasm was contagious. I was only apprehensive of the press. If we went to New York together, wouldn't that invite a raft of romantic publicity? Franchot had an answer for that. New York wasn't Hollywood, we'd be inconspicuous, he felt. As for the train, he'd ride at one end and I at the other. He was very persuasive.

When the New York Central pulled into Grand Central Station, however, I found myself facing a veritable battery of photographers. MGM publicity men tried to fight their way through to me. Impossible. My fan group was waving and shouting in the background—Marian Dommer, who ran my fan club, and all her cohorts. I tried to call back to them. Flashbulbs popped, so did the questions. Was I going to marry Franchot Tone? Were we engaged? Where was Franchot? When would I marry Franchot? I was frankly flustered, I had thought we'd been so circumspect . . . and Franchot was *on this train!* Suppose at any minute he emerged and they found him?

A voice like the voice of destiny, suddenly hymned:

"Time will tell. Joan . . . tell them 'Time will tell.'"

Everyone started to laugh.

The voice belonged to a Western Union messenger boy who came shouldering his way through the crowd to hand me a telegram.

"Thanks!" I said and they laughed even harder. MGM men were able to reach me now and we plowed our way through the mob. I didn't have time to ask the boy's name. I phoned Western Union later and inquired who he was. They explained patiently the difficulties involved in tracing one of thousands of messengers who might have gone to Grand Central Station. But he'd rescued me from a tight spot and for three days I pestered the telegraph company until they found out who he was—Dore Freeman, now a publicity man at MGM and always my friend.

The next night, Franchot and I saw the opening of *Men in White*. We stood, as did the entire audience, cheering and stamping and Franchot whispered, "Here's where we'll be some day, you and I, Joan, in the theater where you belong." The idea was alarming as well as inviting, but carried away by the tumult I believed it. "Yes, of course!" I heard myself saying. This dream of the theater Franchot never lost.

When we arrived in Hollywood, because of all the publicity— we'd been far from anonymous in New York—he was cast at once as the lord of the manor opposite me as a housemaid in *Sadie McKee*. This was the Cinderella-type story that critics had come to call "the Crawford formula." Franchot was excellent, so was comedienne Jean Dixon, Edward Arnold was superb. Since the plot was so familiar, I determined at least to look a little different. I slicked my hair back, Adrian and I discussed my clothes and made them even simpler, I let my eyebrows grow in normally without benefit of tweezers.

Franchot and I were more and more constantly together, on the set and off. He'd moved up from Santa Monica to take a house in Brentwood not far from mine. I helped him decorate his house and make it comfortable, then I began tearing mine apart and remodeling it. You can't live with the past. My personality had changed, and a house must reflect and complement. This time my friend Willie Haines, now one of the top decorators in Hollywood, helped me. The drawing room was gardenia white with Wedgewood-blue corner cabinets, long lovely modern couches and English antiques. The old dining room was converted to a music room, servants' quarters were moved upstairs and we built a whole new wing with spacious dining room, kitchen, etc. This time there was a continuity of thought, of furnishings and décor throughout. My vast collection of dolls I gave to children's hospitals. It was a different Joan with sedate Franchot at the Beverly Wilshire or the Grove. Franchot was no dancer, but he learned. His dignity, his culture and charm were entrancing. Why fight it?

Then one day on *Sadie* I was rehearsing a scene where I have to walk to a table, pick up a movie magazine and glance casually through its pages. Just as the director said, "Action," I started to read, DOUG AND I ARE MARRIED THE MODERN WAY, SAYS JOAN CRAWFORD—in bold, black print. It happened to be two years old, that story. I'd let myself go in the interview as I had many times because, growing up publicly, I believed I owed my private thoughts, my life and emotions to the public who'd been so kind to me. I asked Clarence Brown if I might have a minute to adjust my makeup before the take. What I adjusted was my emotions. I clenched my jaw, determined I'd never be quoted again on anything pertaining to my personal life that I might live to regret.

There were reporters on the set that day. The representative from *Photoplay* asked if I were going to marry Franchot and my reply was that I did not believe in marriage for two people involved in Hollywood. "It isn't fair for a woman who wants a career as much as I do to marry," I said. "It wouldn't be fair to Franchot. I don't believe I'll ever marry again. Love demands so much . . . you want to give even more . . . but I'm afraid marriage makes lovers just people. They do all the romantic things until they attain each other. Then the little thoughts and attentions that mean so much are forgotten. Life loses glamour, possession becomes an empty word."

Franchot stood by letting me speak my piece. And he spoke his. He told whoever asked that he wanted to marry me and he'd keep on asking me until I said yes. He said many other things too. He wasn't interested in glamour, he said, nor in me as a symbol of glamour. He was interested in a human being. There was no reason why daily life couldn't be beautiful. I was afraid of marriage, he said, because I lacked confidence in myself.

This was certainly true. When someone made a witty remark, I'd think it a crack. If I asked people to dinner and they couldn't come, I'd wonder if they still liked me. I was much too easily hurt, and since all my little idiosyncrasies invited criticism, I was constantly cut and bleeding—I thought. Franchot gently explained that these small neuroses had come slowly and would cure slowly.

He humored me when I was morose. At other times he'd try a reverse technique. He'd flare out purposely to make me angry. Angry? Furious. Then, just as I'd reach a peak of fury, he'd start to laugh—and so would I, my tension dissipated through anger, as he'd known it would be. Why Franchot still goes to a psychiatrist I'll never guess. He's as knowledgeable as any psychiatrist and I'm sure the reason I never needed one was because of him. He understands the human mind and its reactions. This was the Group Theatre's approach to acting as it is the Actors' Studio approach today. We discussed acting ad infinitum.

He always wanted me to do a play with him in New York. His theory was that the artist needs encouragement, needs challenge, a highly creative background of work. He felt that Hollywood did nothing to encourage my inner creativity, that I was put into Adrian gowns, beautifully lighted and photographed *but* inner creativity was something I had to do all by myself. The Group Theatre was devised to stimulate the acting artist, he said. "No actor is better than his director and the quality of his material." I have never studied acting, but Franchot insisted that I have an instinct, what the French call "intelligence of the heart." He kept pointing out scenes in which, he said, I'd instinctively done the right thing.

Those words were sweet. So was the success of *Dancing lady,* which put me back where I'd been before *Rain.* Then came *Chained*— with Clark Gable and Otto Kruger—and *Forsaking All Others*— Gable and Bob Montgomery. They were tremendous box-office successes but unfortunately neither picture was much more than a fashion layout.

No More Ladies did bring a challenge—George Cukor, who took over when director E. H. Griffith collapsed with pneumonia. Mr. Cukor was a dialogue director, a perfectionist, a gentleman from the theater; at that time he merely tolerated motion-picture stars, and he began the picture quite certain I was artistically incompetent. He was also unimpressed by my brand-new artificial eyelashes.

The script was a routine husband-and-wife affair in a society setting, with one very long speech I'll never forget. Before making the speech to Bob Montgomery, I rehearsed with Mr. Cukor, giving it, I thought, an authentic emotional blast.

"Did I get it?" I asked, breathless.

"Very fine, Miss Crawford. Now could we please repeat?" Cukor said. "You've remembered the words, let's put some meaning into them."

He took me over the coals until I gave every word *meaning*, but we ended up good friends and Mr. Cukor was to have a major part in eventually springing my career into a new direction. *No More Ladies* wasn't my picture. It went strictly to Edna May Oliver as a highball-drinking grandmother, a grandam who wore trains and said "Scram." Another excellent performance was turned in by Gail Patrick, whom I had asked to have cast as the beautiful, intelligent girl who takes Bob away from me.

Franchot was in this picture and it was illuminating to watch him work with Cukor, both of them from the theater, speaking the same language. It was another mediocre part for him, but we were together, and this had come to mean everything to me. Interestingly, the romance with Douglas which started as a Fourth of July explosion, slowly quieted down into friendship. The friendship with Franchot which had gone on for two years, slowly kindled into what I felt was the love of my life. How I respected this man! What poise and sanity he had. Yet I hesitated. *Could* two careers make for a happy marriage?

One night in New York, Franchot and I went to supper at Alfred Lunt and Lynn Fontanne's. The evening had the quality of a talisman, for they are inspiring people, and in real life as on stage, present each other in the most gracious light. Seeing how happy they were, I was ready to believe two careers could blend. Franchot and I became engaged.

I went into another formula picture, *I Live My Life*, with Brian Aherne. Franchot sailed off to Catalina to *Mutiny on the Bounty*. It was his last good part for ages. It was a part that should have made him a star—certainly he was a star to me.

We slipped off to New York, arriving September 30, 1935. This time not only did Franchot ride in a different part of the train, he left it at Harmon, New York, to avoid reporters. We had come east ostensibly for radio appearances, I on Radio Theatre as Mary Turner in *Paid*, Franchot to appear in *East Meets West* for the Cavalcade of America.

To anyone who had known me, the fact that I was finally going to appear on radio was a dead giveaway that I was completely under Franchot's spell. Every other star in Hollywood was appearing on radio shows but I'd turned down each offer without question. Mike fright was only part of it. My alarm had to do with the studio audience and no major broadcast was without one. This was something I could not face. To this day I've never accepted a stage part, much as I'm tempted, because I haven't the guts. When I was a chorus girl, there was a whole line of us to bolster each other, but when I walk across an empty stage today, on my way to visit for a moment, after performances, with Ethel Merman, Helen Hayes or Mary Martin, my heart pounds just imagining them, walking out there on their own! Sometimes I stand studying the empty dark theater and speak a line or two. Then I conjure up the image of those seats filled with people and I *run* backstage to Ethel's or Helen's or Mary's dressing room.

Franchot classed this with all my other fears. "The only way to overcome fear is to pull its teeth," he said. We'd had a trial run in Hollywood on the Bing Crosby show with an audience of only fifty. Believe me, I'd never have made it without him. This was as big for me as a premiere. I'd planned my clothes, rehearsed my few lines for a month. All I had to do was speak a few words about music, but I was Joan Crawford, no character to hide behind. I was so nervous they nailed a chair to the floor, later we used a chrome bar like a towel rack for me to hang onto, and every line was printed on cardboard—paper might have rattled in my shaking hands. At the last minute I implored them to close the curtains so the audience couldn't see me, or I them, but that wasn't possible. We went on the air, Franchot watching over me like an angel. I'd have given a great deal for hauteur like his. He didn't care what people said or thought. I did, and I couldn't bear to fail in front of them. Carroll Carroll, Bing's writer, actually held me up, Franchot stood in the wings, my good friend Dr. Branch did too, and, somehow we made it.

Now Franchot convinced me that it would be easier to do a dramatic performance on radio, that I'd lose myself in the character. We rehearsed our shows—and watched for an opportunity to get married. Nick Schenck was making all arrangements, but every time we tried to obtain a license or leave town we were trailed by members of the press. For weeks we played hares and hounds with reporters. Franchot wasn't about to have our marriage made into a Roman holiday, a three-ring circus or a county fair. He reasoned that however we started out would set a pattern for the future. I was certainly *with* him—I'd been half of the most publicized marriage in the world.

We made a break for it on October 11, and for once, caught the press off guard. Mayor Herbert W. Jenkins of Fort Lee, New Jersey, married us in his mayoral residence . . . Nick Schenck and Leo Friedman of MGM were witnesses . . . I wore a blue wool suit and hat and carried a bride's bouquet. That afternoon, back at Columbia Broadcasting Studio, I was rehearsing Mary Turner with my gloves on to hide my wedding ring. We spent our honeymoon at the Waldorf, and

Franchot's family came down from Niagara Falls to visit us, as they continued to do whenever we were in town.

There was only one discordant note. On our wedding night I received an anonymous phone call. I'd received such calls before and had been afraid to tell anyone. Two men said they had in their possession a stag reel in which I danced. They wanted to sell it to me. I had made no such movie; I suggested they contact Mr. Mayer in Hollywood or MGM's legal wizard, J. Robert Rubin in New York. Mr. Rubin viewed the film and assured the men that "If that's Joan Crawford, I'm Greta Garbo." The threats of blackmail which had followed me for so long, ended the minute Mr. Rubin saw that film.

Franchot and I returned to Hollywood to establish our life. He was longing to buy a schooner and sail with me around the world— *Mutiny on the Bounty* had had its effect. Somewhere, in some part of the Pacific or Indian Ocean, he dreamed of a Pitcairn Island where we could live totally immersed in each other, without publicity, without taxes, without money or politics. He'd dreamed of a place like that from the time he was old enough to read Sir Thomas More. Now I read Sir Thomas More. Like Franchot, he was politically an idealist, he believed in the possibility of a perfect state and the achievement of universal plenty.

I heard a great many discussions of politics. Our friends now included the whole impassioned Group Theatre. They'd visit us and spend weekends lying beside our pool denouncing capitalism, while I'd trot about, serving them from trays of caviar and paté. I began thinking about politics too. I liked the Group Theatre people but I failed to see what was wrong with capitalism. When Vittorio Mussolini, son of the Italian Premier, visited the studio, I refused to continue work until he left the set.

Franchot also dreamed of a cabin in the Canadian woods north of Toronto where we could vacation, and he meant *vacation,* as he had at Muskoka Lake and at the Lake of Bays when he was a boy. From the time he was three, his father and uncle would take him every summer into the Canadian woods to rough it: fish, hunt, camp and water-ski, as he takes his own sons now. We also thought of a home in New England protected by tall trees and staunch tradition. We'd come to Hollywood to make films, go to New York to do stage plays, even sing in opera together.

We had worked very hard on our voices, taking daily singing lessons with Signor and Madame Morando, respectively. Now we were studying with Rosa Ponselle's coach, Romano Romano, and our house resounded with arias. When Rosa Ponselle visited from the east, she and I sang a duet from *Tales of Hoffmann.* I recorded several songs at the studio, Douglas MacPhail and I singing duets from *La Traviata* and *Don Giovanni.* Singing was just one facet of our busy days. Trainer Bob Howard came over to run, swim, play badminton with us, and we worked out on a rowing machine. What a lovely Christmas we had that year. Franchot gave me a star-sapphire pendant and bracelet, I surprised him with a sixteen-cylinder car which he didn't see until three thirty Christmas Eve morning, after the guests had gone home. We had our own Christmas alone.

At the studio my direction was influenced by our discussions at home, by my contact with Franchot and the Group Theatre. I wanted something different from the tired formula in which the rich girl married the poor—usually newspaperman—or the poor girl marries the rich man. I read the criticisms. Some critics always raved, "You'll love Joan. This is the kind of picture you expect from her."

But others, more discerning, remarked, "Crawford needs a new deal. Out of all her films only three are good ones. The game will be won when two consecutive pictures are not exclusively machine-made exploitations of her physical appearance and emotional vitality. Is she irrevocably doomed to explore the emotional misfortunes of the supersexed modern young woman?"

To break away from the pattern, I sought the part of Peggy O'Neal in *The Gorgeous Hussy,* the tavern-keeper's daughter who influenced the political destiny of America and captivated Old Hickory himself. Lionel Barrymore had already been cast as Old Hickory, Melvyn Douglas as distinguished John Randolph—with whom Peggy falls in love—and Bob Taylor as Timberlake—the dashing lieutenant who catches Peggy on the rebound, marries her and is killed on their wedding night.

David Selznick laughed at me.

"You can't do a costume picture," he said. "You're too modern."

But Joe Mankiewicz was willing to give me a chance, and so was director Clarence Brown. So I was Peggy. Jimmy Stewart played the lovelorn "Rowdy" Dow. I adored working with Jimmy. I wish I could again. He's such an endearing character, a perfectionist at his job, but with a droll sense of humor and a shy way of watching to see if you react to that humor. And no one who saw the film will ever forget Beulah Bondi, as Andrew Jackson's pipe-smoking wife.

Then to complete the great cast, Franchot was signed as War Secretary John Eaton, whom Peggy finally marries. This was a twenty-six line part—for one of the most brilliant actors in the business! It wasn't fair. I was horrified. And I went to Mr. Mayer and told him so. Mr. Mayer was adamant.

"We can't have a great cast like this, Joan," he explained, "and then have you walk away into the sunset with some unknown actor. We *have* to have an important actor."

That's why he'd signed Franchot. He also had known that I'd object. That's why I hadn't been told. No other major actor would have taken so small a part.

Franchot did it for my sake. It was a major mistake. It was the breaking point in his career and the breaking point in our marriage, although we didn't realize it at the time. I only knew that Franchot hated this part, loathed it. He didn't complain, he just closed up like a clam, and both at home and at the studio we were living in a state of tension. One night he didn't come home. I walked the floor, grieving, wishing that I could do something. But Franchot wouldn't let me help. This was *his* problem. He didn't show up on the set next morning until eleven o'clock. With this I could not be sympathetic—it seemed to me unprofessional and intolerable—but looking back I can see how thwarted this fine actor must have felt, playing a twenty-six line part in his wife's starring picture.

Whatever the personal problems on *The Gorgeous Hussy,* performances were strong, and the picture gave me another big boost in dramatic prestige. As after *Grand Hotel,* I had started a "new" career. It was also the beginning of a long and gratifying association with producer Joe Mankiewicz. Gable, Franchot and I were with him in *Love on the Run,* we all had a ball and Franchot walked off with the picture. Franchot and I were with Joe again in *The Bride Wore Red,* another Crawford formula film, this time with a Viennese background.

This wasn't the kind of picture I wanted. I coveted a *Dark Victory* or an *Ethan Frome,* but it was a lark, working with Franchot, living with him in the cold out-of-doors, on location in the High Sierra. We were in perfect harmony. . . .

From the beginning we had tried to build a life together, independent of our careers. Perhaps subconsciously I realized how important this was for him. Franchot stayed in Hollywood only because of me and here his personal happiness was marred by one flaw, his professional unhappiness. He had good parts, but not the kind for which he was best suited. In the first test, which had brought him west with such fanfare, he played a truck driver. He never had a chance at that kind of part. Because of our marriage, he was often one of the leading men assigned to a "Crawford picture," whether the part was satisfactory to him or not. Franchot's and my love cost him his rightful career in pictures. He could play anything with that sensitive face and heart, but he was constantly cast as a sophisticated drawing room character. He grew discouraged, his face more sophisticated, his heart more sensitive.

I wanted so to have his children. Again I had two miscarriages. A dancer's muscles, I thought, should be good for childbearing. As any competent gynecologist will tell you, they are excellent for the birth of children, but during pregnancy, unfortunately, any extremely active person is more likely to sustain a loss. You come to the point where rest and care might be the wise course, but I was engaged in a career where the hours were long and the demands strenuous. I never went to a doctor in the early stages of pregnancy. I was never advised, so I never knew you should. I grieved over my losses, and Franchot grieved over his career.

For a while we found solace in our home. We entertained on Saturday nights, small dinner parties of ten or twelve—the Fred Astaires, the Gables, the Irving Berlins, Dorothy Parker, Willie Haines, Jimmy

Shields, Jerry Asher, Helen Hayes when she was in town, Lynn Riggs, sometimes Gene Markey and Joan Bennett, the Gary Coopers and Frances and Sam Goldwyn. Occasionally we entertained more elaborately. We had a cook, butler and upstairs maid and could accommodate forty for a buffet dinner, or even more for a garden buffet. When we had the reception for Leopold Stokowski, we gave it at the Ambassador. But we were never too social. I had to share Franchot so much at the studio and in our work that I didn't want the social life that I'd had so much of with Douglas—that, I felt, had been one of our mistakes.

Best were the evenings we spent together, just the two of us, at the Philharmonic, at the opera, at the Bowl. We danced less and less. I savored the evenings we spent alone in our home, reading aloud or running movies in our theater. Ironically, we were so busy we never had time for theater production.

One Hollywood columnist sarcastically tabbed us "the artistic union of two sensitive souls in retreat." Fans besieged us so in New York that we'd sneak out the side door of the Waldorf. This perturbed me, because the fans were my friends. To have a hundred people clutching at my coat, clamoring for autographs, was to me an accolade, but Franchot found this sort of adulation offensive, and my security hinged on him.

I'd have given anything to have saved this marriage, to have kept it on the plane it originally was, both of us reading Shakespeare, singing, talking, appearing on Lux Theater of the Air together twice a year (*Elizabeth the Queen; Mary, Queen of Scots*; etc.). Merely as a woman I might have saved it, but there was another Crawford—the actress. Rumors started again. One writer said, "Is there trouble in the Crawford-Tone home? Sensitive husbands don't like second billing." I don't believe Franchot ever for a moment resented the fact that I was a star. Possibly he resented Hollywood's refusal to let him forget it.

There was never a doubt in my mind that Franchot's talent was greater than mine, and I tried very hard to give him more scenes, to build his ego. It just didn't work. It was no wonder that he gradually broke away, tried to assert himself. He was working in a film, I wasn't. One afternoon I dropped by his dressing room to surprise him. I *did*.

I drove all the way to Carmel that night, drove all night, frightened again, alone again, trying to find a way back. I was in love with Franchot when I went to the studio that day. Now there was no way back—I was no longer in love.

I have the utmost trust in Franchot and regard for him. It took courage for us both to walk away, courage I didn't know I had. Somewhere I'd once read, "Let your courage be as keen but at the same time as polished as your sword." We walked away, we retained a mutual respect. I've always felt that if I were in need, he'd be the first to fly to my side. A few years ago, he did.

Since then, we've done some Sunday broadcasts together and at a recent party at Earl Blackwell's, Franchot arrived with Zsa Zsa Gabor, wearing the diamond studs I'd given him so long ago.

"Dahling, I never saw you wear those!" Zsa Zsa said. "Where do they come from?"

"From my darling," Franchot said, looking across the table to me.

SEVEN

I n *Dancing Lady*, when he finally picks me from a chorus line to play the lead in his revue, Clark Gable says, "Okay, now you're in the top spot where you've got twice as far to fall!"

By 1938 that's where I was for real. For ten lucky years, even if the subject matter wasn't very challenging, my pictures had been top box office. Mr. Mayer always asserted that they'd built Stage 22, Stage 24 and the Irving Thalberg Building brick by brick.

As *Life* magazine summed it up later: "During the thirties she paddled calmly along the stream of success in a golden canoe. Clark Gable, Franchot Tone, Bob Montgomery and Bob Young alternated, often in pairs, as her leading men, and Joan became one of the biggest female draws at the box office, her fans legion."

Then something happened. I'd been a flapper in an age of flappers, a sophisticated lady in an era of sophistication. When you're part of an era, you're not aware of trends at the time. I only knew that I wanted good parts, valid and varied parts, and that I battled constantly to try to get them. To no avail. From *Dancing Lady* on, every picture I made was formula. During 1937 *The Last of Mrs. Cheyney* had movie houses packed to the doors even though it was the remake of a so-so silent. When *The Bride Wore Red* opened at the Capitol, it was ushered in with an enthusiastic demonstration by my fans. But that picture laid the proverbial bomb at the nation's box offices, and a trade paper, *The Independent Film Journal* labeled me box-office poison. I was, at least, in excellent company! Also on the list: Marlene Dietrich, Fred Astaire and Katharine Hepburn.

MGM's answer was a new five-year contract, $1,500,000 a year, three pictures a year.

My answer was *Mannequin,* with Spencer Tracy costarring. Here was a down-to-earth story of a shopgirl who by intelligence and ambition rises from the slums to riches and happiness. Familiar? Yes, but this was a Mankiewicz production, and Joe has a genius for extracting the suds from soap opera. He brings to production an honesty and power of approach. Our story was well told by Katherine Brush, the dialogue was direct, and conflict in the plot between capital and labor added dimension.

I took one look at those poor Delancey Street sets and knew I was back home. I was Jessie—there was no trick in conveying her love, warmth and ambition. And it was inspiring to play opposite Tracy. His is such simplicity of performance, such naturalness and humor. He walks through a scene just as he walks through life. He makes it seem so easy, and working with him I had to learn to underplay. We worked together as a unit, as if we'd worked together for years, yet there was also the extra little fillip of working with a new costar, a powerful costar. No matter how often you rehearse a scene, when the camera starts turning he surprises you with some intonation or timing so that your response is new and immediate.

When we got to the dancing scene the cameraman yelled, "Get closer. Get closer, Joan."

"I can't." I laughed. Spence was as solid as a rock and he wasn't thin. He promptly went on the black-coffee routine.

But most of the time the teasing was initiated by him. *Slug* I called him, from the day he was clowning around and took the stance of a boxer. In the most serious scene, Slug could break me up. As Jessie, I was supposed to be so serious about my life, my job; and as I spoke my lines, he'd watch me slyly, give that half grin of his, and rub his finger along his nose. I'd have to laugh. Take after take. But I learned. From Slug I learned to keep my own identity in a scene, not to be distracted by anything, including Tracy.

Columnists insisted we were feuding. We never had a moment's disharmony. He was considerate of me on the set. He was most solicitous when I became ill with pneumonia. I'd never held up production on a picture ever, but I was working with a temperature of 102 when the doctor stepped in. And even when I was better, Dr. Branch wouldn't sanction my return to work immediately. First I had to grow stronger, inhale some good fresh air.

For maximum oxygen he whisked me out to the polo field where he and Spence practiced every day. They were excellent players. I watched them from the car, with the doors locked. I wouldn't even come out and sit in the stands—that was too close to the thundering herd. My benefactors were not to be deterred. One day after they'd finished a very strenuous game, Dr. Branch suggested that I ride his horse back to the stables. The saddle had been removed and, uncertainly, I mounted, but on the way to the stables I fell in love with that horse, Secret. It figured—Secret was completely worn out from the hard ride the doctor'd given him.

Dr. Branch and Spencer were so delighted with my reaction that Secret was promptly bequeathed to me. And *I* took up polo. I thought if I were playing a game, concentrating on the ball and mallet, I wouldn't have time to fear the four-legged beasts. It worked pretty well. As a matter of fact, I got a little cocky and bought another polo pony and rode them both—though not at the same time.

My enthusiasm for polo was short-lived. Secret threw me one day when I pulled up short, and I did a somersault and landed on my derrière. No horse could do that to me! I climbed back on and rode for forty minutes. The next day I rode again for half an hour. Then I said, "Okay, now sell 'em." You can't just dismiss failure, you build strength by surmounting it. But when you've really given something a good try and find you can't win, it's time to head for other pastures.

I threw myself into work the only way I know how, totally. Once that red light flashed on the set, indicating the camera was in action, nothing else mattered. But there *is* an outside world and in it are not only those who wish to create heroes and heroines, but those who are demolition-bent. The minute I was tagged box-office poison, even though *Mannequin* pleased exhibitors and clicked extremely well at the box office, the fan magazines exhibited a rash of stories: "Is Joan Crawford Slipping?" "Can Joan Crawford Hold On?" "Are Joan's Screen Days Numbered?" Stories that devastated me, stories that made me fighting mad. You don't build a career casually. I'd put my life into this career and loved each second of it. Come hell or high water, I was going to stay in it. The question was, in spite of all these barbed stories and their snide implications—could I?

The studio had shown faith by drawing up my fat new contract. Now I urged Mr. Mayer to purchase for me a play I'd seen in New York, *The Shining Hour*. I also requested stage star Margaret Sullavan to play the young wife who is my rival, and stage star Fay Bainter as our sister-in-law. Mr. Mayer listened to me curiously.

"Joan," he said, "don't you realize that these three women's roles are equal? Those two talented actresses could steal your picture!"

"I'd rather be a supporting player in a good picture than the star of a bad one."

So Maggie and Fay were signed, with Bob Young as the man Maggie and I both love, and Melvyn Douglas as my husband. Maggie and I had never worked together before. The press predicted we'd "fight it out" if it took all winter. We started out tentatively enough. In one scene, where we are discussing her husband who is in love with me, we filmed eighteen takes, and each time, I cried on cue. Each time, Maggie observed as if she were a spectator. Finally, director Frank Borzage said, "Okay, Maggie, that's enough. Let's do the scene!"

"But I'm fascinated. How do you cry on cue?" said Maggie.

And I said, "Let's get the scene, dear, never mind how I do it."

From that moment on, we were friends. I demanded she have top billing with me. Maggie was a fine artist. She charmed me. So did her eighteen-month-old daughter, Brooke Hayward. The baby and I were devoted to each other and I confess I permitted her what I never later permitted a child of my own—she wrote on my dressing room walls with lipstick.

In one scene I had to carry Maggie out of a burning house. Maggie was pregnant, I thought three months, but just before the fire scene, they told me *seven* months. I'd never have guessed. Now that I knew, I was urgently concerned. I carried this girl out of the burning house, trying to watch for falling timbers, trying not to slip on the gravel. I'm strong, heaven knows, but I wasn't strong enough. I fell on the gravel, on my elbows and knees to break the fall, so Maggie wouldn't get hurt. My elbows and knees were bloody, but I didn't know. I was hysterical over Maggie. She had her eyes closed, and they didn't open. "Maggie, dear, are you all right? Maggie!" I screamed. She waited until I was frantic. Then she opened those wide eyes of hers and grinned. She was just fine. She never played jokes unless she adored you—but what a time to show it!

You might think that a play as good as *The Shining Hour,* which received nothing but acclaim from the critics, would have solved my problems and put me back on the high road. But in Hollywood there's a saying that you're as good as your last picture, and my next was *The Ice Follies of 1939.* This was trash. MGM had hired the entire International Ice Follies, they tossed in an old stage play they had sitting on the shelf, *Excess Baggage,* and Jimmy Stewart, Lew Ayres and I kept trying to figure out where we came in. Advertising art showed me on skates but I was no skater. And though I was supposed to be a singer in the picture my three much-touted songs hit the cutting-room floor because they slowed up the skating numbers.

An escapist at heart, I left for New York the day after the dreadful thing was previewed, utterly discouraged. But Grand Central Station was packed with fans. Two press agents, several policemen and my self-appointed guardian, Dore Freeman, managed to get me through to a car. Our clothes were torn, when we arrived at the hotel we found some sizable bruises, but it was worth it!

"Let's go back and do it again," I gasped.

My "interference" laughed. "If there's any going back," they chorused, "you go alone."

Don't think I wasn't tempted! I understand fans because I am one myself. When I go to Hollywood now, I spend days in projection rooms watching all the new pictures. It's felicity to see new talent emerge. In evaluation, no magazine writer could outdo my superlatives. I adore Ingrid Bergman and once wrote her a fan letter. Like millions of others, I have worshipped at the shrine of Katharine Hepburn and Garbo and Judy Garland, Maurice Chevalier, Gable and Boyer. I vote like crazy for the Academy Award candidates and go to premieres for the fun of watching the stars arrive. When people approach me, shyly saying, "I've never asked for an autograph before, but . . . " I can reassure them, I've asked for many, and treasured them!

Such loyalty as the fans showed me after *Ice Follies* was not to be lightly dismissed. I knew how that turkey would fare at the box office.

At this critical moment I set my sights on the part of Crystal, the hard-boiled perfume clerk who uses every wile to catch another woman's husband in *The Women*. I'd seen Clare Boothe's superbly bitter play in New York. It was a frank satire on the feminine sex, and for it, MGM was assembling an imposing cast: Norma Shearer, Roz Russell, Paulette Goddard, Joan Fontaine, Marjorie Main, Mary Boland, Hedda Hopper. Crystal was the heavy. She wasn't too refined, but she was a vital person able to produce violent reactions. Hunt Stromberg said it was too small a part, besides, he said, he thought of me still as a dancing daughter. Mr. Mayer was dubious:

"I don't know that you should play a heavy, Joan. It might hurt your career. You know, I regard you as my youngest daughter, I want the right thing for you. But you're the American girl, the public thinks of you as Cinderella." Then he too mentioned that it was a small part.

"But it's going to be a good picture. And I want a good picture. If I can't have one of my own, let me sneak into someone else's."

I knew I hadn't convinced them, so I turned to George Cukor, who was to direct. No question about it, the idea jolted him too.

"You!" he said. And, remember, he'd merely tolerated me on *No More Ladies,* he'd given me the roughest time I'd ever had. From that had come the beginning of my concentration and projection, for which I've always been grateful to Cukor.

I must have convinced him, for suddenly the part was mine. He is a hard taskmaster, George Cukor, acidulously critical in direction— and if he feels you're closing up because of this, he'll switch, belting you with a humor that's convulsing. I don't know who else could have handled *this* cast. It was a highly competitive picture. I played Crystal hard as nails, asked no sympathy, got none. Even people who didn't like me admitted I had intestinal fortitude, taking my career in both hands and gambling.

The night of the premiere at Grauman's Chinese, while newsboys outside the theater screamed the news that fighting had broken out in Europe, the audience inside rocked with laughter at this other war, the female war. When it came to Norma's and my strident encounter in the fitting room, they applauded so the next scene was lost. I was back in business.

A Clark Gable picture was coming up. That I wanted too.

With Clark in *Strange Cargo,* I eschewed makeup for the first time since *Paid.* There had been cracks about my long eyelashes and exaggerated makeup. As the dance-hall girl who is kicked off a tropical island and falls in with an escaping band of convicts, I used none. For *The Women* I'd had a $40,000 wardrobe, for *Strange Cargo* I had three dresses, worth less than forty dollars all together. The one that saw duty at Pismo Beach was soaked in seawater half the time. Each day I had to look slightly more bedraggled. Each day before I donned the dress, they tore it a little more. For the last day, they soaked the poor shredded gown in the ocean, dragged it through mud, hung it

in the sun to dry, then said, "Now, put it on!" I did. I felt a definite
sense of achievement as Julie, but reviews were mixed. Because of Ian
Hunter's role as a Christlike figure, which he played with consummate simplicity, the picture was banned in Boston and the mystical
theme held up to question elsewhere.

I was in New York after *Strange Cargo* and at a party at Moss
Hart's met Fredric March, who was leaving for the coast to play the
unhappy alcoholic husband in *Susan and God.* How I envied him!
Rachel Crothers' play had scored well on Broadway with Gertrude
Lawrence, and I craved that role of Susan, the rapturous zany who for
most of the script wears her ideals like so much jewelry. But the play
had been purchased for Norma Shearer.

A few days later, my phone rang. Mr. Mayer was calling. Norma
refused to play a mother. George Cukor had *asked* for me—it was
most flattering, Mr. George Cukor asking for *me!*

Mr. Mayer said, "Would you be willing to play a *mother,* Joan?"

"I'd play Wally Beery's grandmother if it's a good part!" I cried
and left that night for the coast. Cukor again led me into a new technique. Thanks to him, the critics called it by all odds, my most important and best executed role. Armed with this assurance, I now asked
Mr. Mayer to buy *A Woman's Face,* the drama of a terribly scarred
woman which Ingrid Bergman had made in Swedish.

Poor Mr. Mayer. He had borne with me as the bitch in *The Women,*
the bleak-looking woman in *Strange Cargo,* the mother of a subdeb
in *Susan,* now he balked at my playing a scarred woman who hated
the world. Luckily George Cukor took up the cudgels for me, and *A
Woman's Face* scored my high point at MGM. I was extolled as the
first lady Lon Chaney, for as Anna Holm, I wore from eye to mouth

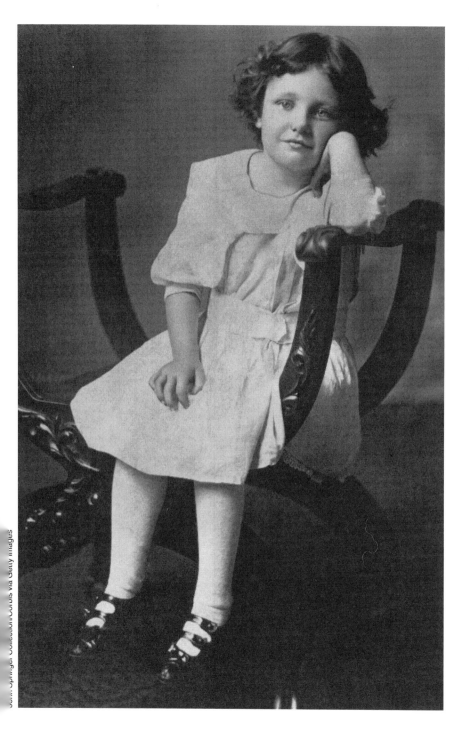

Billie Cassin, age five.

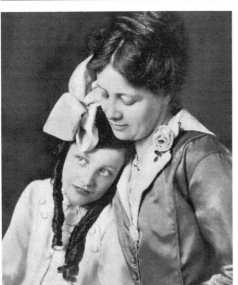

Top: This family picture was taken before I was born. The man in the back row is my father, Thomas LeSeuer. The young woman seated, second from left, is my mother, Anna Bell Johnson LeSeuer, holding my brother, Hal. Seated next to Anna is her mother, Mary Ellen Johnson, holding her daughter, my Aunt Betty; and the gentleman with the moustache is my grandfather, Sylvester Johnson.

Above left: "The little girl across the street" with her mother.

Above right: Mother and I during the St. Agnes Academy days.

Right: Mother, Hal, and I at the time I went to Stephens college.

Below: Mother, my brother, and I in Hollywood, 1932.

Left: As I looked when I arrived in Hollywood. Here I am clearing the hurdles at the University of Southern California. (MGM)

Above: On the set of *Today We Live* in 1932.

Left: Walking arm in arm with Fred Astaire. (Hulton Archive/Getty Images)

Top: Arriving at Southampton with Douglas Fairbanks, Jr.

Above: A widely used picture of me, in the living room of my home shortly after my marriage to Douglas Fairbanks, Jr.

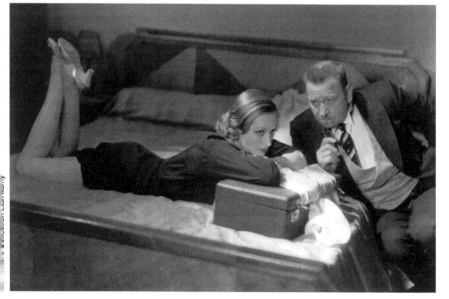

Left: During *Mannequin*, Tracy got me on a horse for the first time since the Tim McCoy pictures. Terrified of horses, I discovered that playing polo was fun! (MGM)

Top: The era of the sophisticated lady got under way when I was teamed with Clark Gable in *Possessed*.

Above: As Flaemmchen, the little stenographer, with Wallace Beery as Preysing, in *Grand Hotel*, the screen classic.

Right: *Forsaking All Others* with Clark Gable and Robert Montgomery.

Below: With John Garfield in *Humoresque*.

Opposite: With Franchot Tone. (George Hurrell/John Kobal Foundation/Getty Images)

Following pages: In *Torch Song* directed by Chuck Walters. My first day on the set was one of the most exciting days of my life. (MGM/Photofest)

Left: With Christina (left), Christopher (bottom), and Cindy & Cathy.

Above: With Alfred Steele in Hollywood after returning from our honeymoon.

Following page: It was a great honor to meet Her Majesty Queen Elizabeth II of England.

on the right side of my face a hideous mass of seared tissue created by Jack Dawn. The studio released no publicity art. They were concerned that my mutilated face would keep people away from the theater. The scar didn't deter me, there are too many beautiful women in pictures anyway.

What worried George Cukor was my emotionalism. He anticipated that wearing a scar could affect me as wearing a cape has been known to affect some actors. To offset the possibility, he rehearsed the very life out of me. Hours of drilling, with camera and lights lined up for the opening sequence in the courtroom, *then* Mr. Cukor had me recite the multiplication table by twos until all emotion was drained and I was totally exhausted, my voice dwindled to a tired monotone.

"*Now,*" Mr. Cukor said. "Now, Anna . . . tell us the story of your life."

I say a prayer for Mr. Cukor every time I think of what *A Woman's Face* did for my career. It fortified me with a measure of self-confidence I'd never had . . . the greatest rave notices I'd ever had . . . the succès d'estime I'd longed for . . . what critics called "the best picture to emerge from Hollywood in a long long time" . . . what others called the best picture, without question, of the year.

It was also my last happy part at MGM and my last good part for a long time. I made three more pictures for Metro, all three contrived, silly and demanding nothing more than that I wear chic clothes. I wanted varied and challenging parts and it was too much of a hassle to get them. I now asked Mr. Mayer to release me from my contract. There were top executives, I knew, who thought me finished. They thought of me as Letty Lynton, they laughed when I asked for pictures like *Random Harvest* and *Madame Curie*. Those went to Greer Garson. If you think I made poor pictures after *A Woman's Face*, you should have seen the ones I went on suspension *not* to make!

What further diminished the value of these pictures was the fact that life had changed—the public had problems to face, we all did, war was a grim reality in 1942. Douglas was in the service, I was getting letters from him "somewhere at sea," Bob Montgomery, Burgess Meredith, Jimmy Stewart, Bill Holden, Gene Raymond and Ty Power were serving. My darling Carole Lombard had been killed in that plane crash while she was selling war bonds. I went to Columbia to take her place in *They All Kissed the Bride,* and donated my salary from that film to the Red Cross, who had found her body. Compared to reality, such pictures as *Reunion in France* and *Above Suspicion* were undiluted hokum, as indigestible as the wax hot dogs served up on meatless Tuesday in a pail of real sauerkraut for a scene in the last named picture.

I certainly wasn't ungrateful to the studio. This is where I'd learned everything I knew. I'd come there as a child and they'd nursed me through school. But there comes a time to grow up. I'd outgrown the rags to riches, I'd proved it, I was sick of fairy tales and so were the people in the audience.

"Life is too full of heartbreak," I told Mr. Mayer. "We can't close our eyes any longer. Put it on the screen, give people the courage to face their own tragedies. And from a selfish point of view, let's keep proving I can act."

But the consensus of opinion among the top brass was that I was all washed up again. A star's career proverbially lasts five years. Ten years was exceptional. Well . . . I'd had it. I was over thirty, as a matter of fact, thirty-four.

"And who says anyone's through because she's past thirty? It's an age when people begin their careers!" I cited Katharine Cornell, Helen Hayes, Fay Bainter, Ethel Barrymore, Tallulah Bankhead.

They just smiled. Not in movies, they said.

"That doesn't prove it can't be done!"

They smiled as if I weren't quite bright.

Carey Wilson, one of my first friends at the studio, asked me to sit in with him producing a short subject, *For Men Only,* which showed hapless gentlemen what transpired in a beauty parlor while they wait hours for wives and sweethearts. He *said* he needed a woman's viewpoint. He knew that the studio had nothing I wanted to do and that the two most difficult words in the language for me always have been "sit" and "wait." Every moment must pay off. I'm let down if it doesn't. Working with Carey, I gave much less than I received, I'm sure, for I bombarded him with questions and the technicians with questions, trying to learn everything I could about production. Who knew where I might go from here?

Years before, Willie Haines had told me that when you start to slide in this business, it's like walking on nothing, the career of no return. I hadn't understood. Now I was walking on nothing.

Mr. Mayer didn't want me to leave. But he realized how unhappy I'd become, and at last, reluctantly, he persuaded Nick Schenck to give me my release.

After seventeen years, I left the studio where Joan Crawford had been born. It was five o'clock in the morning when I gathered up the last of my possessions from my dressing room and left—by the back gate.

EIGHT

had something to go home to—my babies. For that miracle had come to pass, what I had long prayed for, a family.

It's interesting, when you travel the world as I do, to find so many women who envy career women. They feel a career woman *has something.* Yet, exchanging ideas with them, you find that they are compatibly married, they have children, they're surrounded by love, they're living a full, rich woman's life. Does anyone think for a moment that glamour replaces *that?* Since the age of thirteen when I cared for thirty youngsters, washed and scrubbed for them and tucked them into bed at night, I dreamed of having babies of my own. Love is something I had to give. Douglas knew that, Franchot knew that.

My brother's little girl, Joan LeSueur, had been born prematurely in December 1933, only two pounds, but she turned out to be a healthy, dear little thing and I was devoted to her as well as to her mother, Kasha. I raised Joanie-Pants until she was four, then Kasha and Hal divorced and Kasha moved to New York, taking Joanie with her and leaving an emptiness in my life. All my free time away from the studio had been spent with this child. There had been parties for her and for the chauffeur's babies, for Fred MacMurray's children and Margaret Sullavan's children. We had Punch and Judy shows . . . Shetland ponies to ride . . . clowns . . . swimming in the pool . . . and ice-cream parties galore.

When I realized that my marriage to Franchot was breaking, I petitioned an adoption home. After our divorce, I continued petitioning. At that time only thirteen states in the Union would allow an unmarried man or woman to adopt children. I'm told it's even less now—eight. With the vast number of potential parents yearning for children, there is such an inordinate amount of red tape involved that there continue to be homeless babies and childless parents! I can only say I'll be forever grateful for my babies and bless the adoption homes who sent them my way.

I was told originally of five pregnant girls, their backgrounds, their problems. The story of the fourth girl intrigued me. Unknown to this mother, I paid for her confinement and hospital bills, the customary procedure. Then I waited. When the baby was ten days old, she was brought to me—the ugliest little mite I'd ever seen—red-faced, wrinkled, frowning, like all infants at ten days. But she grew into a blue-eyed, blonde-haired doll, typically Scandinavian, and I gave her all my love and attention.

The next year I was given a little boy of French and Irish extraction whom I lost, not through death, but a year and a half later back to his original mother. She had given up the child when he was ten days old, but she'd changed her mind when she read in a published interview where he was—I'd made the mistake of mentioning his birth date and birthplace. From that moment I had no peace. Day after day, she'd show up at my door. She sent threatening letters, demanded money. The situation assumed the aspects of a nightmare. My small son was entitled to *life;* I could not allow his being used as the pawn in a tug-of-war. So I gave him back to the mother who really didn't want him, who promptly sold him. In short order the adoption home stepped in, placing him where he couldn't possibly be found. There is one alleviating note. The people who adopted him knew of me; every Christmas for a few years they sent a card, unsigned, but with his picture on it. It took the agency almost a year to find another little son for me, Christopher.

Meanwhile, the press speculated constantly on romantic possibilities. According to the columns, I was variously about to marry . . . Glenn Ford . . . Jean-Pierre Aumont . . . Cesar Romero . . . Lieutenant Floyd Freeman . . . a handsome rich young man from Florida . . . a rich important man from New York. Never trust rumors. They don't give a woman credit for the ability to be friends with a man, they don't recognize that men and women, particularly professional men and women, have a community of interests, they *can* be friends.

What a loss for any woman not to know this! Women need the stimulus of a masculine point of view. We profit immeasurably by gearing our thought to their broader level. A woman without the friendship of men seems to me terribly limited. You love many people in this life, men, women and children, once you realize that love is no isolated once-in-a-lifetime phenomenon. All love stems from your own capacity. What you learn as you go along is that love and friendship are a matter of giving for the sake of giving—without even necessarily sharing—just for the joy of it. Flowers, not because it's someone's birthday but because those flowers look as if they belong to them. Friendship is like an agate marble taking on a thousand hues as the sun of experience hits it. Ask three of my dear friends—

Frances Spingold, member of the board of directors of FICO finance company . . . bank president Mary Roebling . . . Tobé, professional consultant to major industries and a veritable oracle in the field of fashion trends. Like most businesswomen, they have a large circle of friends, men and women, married and unmarried. I do too, and can't imagine life without them. At least a score of good healthy male friendships are part of my existence.

This was true in 1946 too. Glenn Ford and I had many mutual interests, paramount among which was the artisan side of our business. We'd run his pictures, we'd run mine, studying production techniques, giving each other constructive criticism. Both of us were a little solitary. Our relationship was in the nature of a good aperitif.

"Butch" Romero has been my friend since the night he was introduced to Franchot and me at a cocktail party Walter Chrysler gave for us shortly before our marriage. This divine man asked me to tango. I had to confess I didn't know how. Once on the dance floor, I discovered that with Cesar Romero as partner, you can execute any dance step ever invented. He also has the capacity for long-term friendship.

After the breakup of my marriage with Franchot, Butch was the first to call, the one to say, "Come on, let's go dancing." In every crisis I can talk to him as I could to Adrian and Mr. Mayer, about anything, without mincing words. This is something I've tried to teach my daughters—to be direct. You don't trade on femininity.

In New York I had met a marvelously mature man, one of the best people I've ever known. This man must be nameless because he was never able to get a divorce. He is a business executive and I respect him thoroughly. Again I had to settle for a long and lovely friendship. He taught me to hunt and fish, we used to go on these expeditions with a whole group of men. The first time, I'm sure, their reaction was, oh no, not a dame tagging along! I carried my own gun and my own camera, waded through streams in the vanguard; and at noon when we'd camp, I'd help fix lunch and surprise them with all sorts of snacks packed away in my knapsack just in case they didn't catch any fish. This friend introduced me to politics, to banking, big business and public affairs.

He says I taught him to be brave, to stand up for what he thought was right, to be considerate of other human beings, especially those with whom he was working, and to be generous in giving of himself. I didn't teach him. These were his instincts. He merely needed someone gently to remind him.

This rewarding experience I wouldn't have missed. But his marital situation could not be altered, and when I left for California I knew I might not see him again in years, if ever. In his position, he could not afford the publicity of being associated with *any* woman. I understood. Why risk hurting him? What I'd fought all my life for, this career, this name, made it impossible to be anonymous.

Turning your back on love spells loneliness. I cared for the babies and the days were busy, but when they were safely tucked into their cribs, I'd wonder why God had made me like this—warm, loving and so alone. I wasn't interested in the quick romance—there's no satisfaction in that. I wanted to marry, give my children a father, market for groceries, be part of the human race. I read poetry. I even wrote poetry:

Where are you?
My heart cries out in agony,
In my extended hands
I give my heart with

All its cries—its songs—its love,
But it's too late.
You are not here to see its sorrow
Or hear its throbbing of your name
Perhaps it's better that way
You who love laughter—
Did you ever know I love laughter too?
Oh my beloved
Where are you?

But I had married—twice—and twice experienced the fiasco of divorce. It seemed unlikely to me that I'd ever marry again, that I'd ever have the courage.

One Sunday, press agent Harry Mines asked if he might bring Phillip Terry to dinner. Phillip was a reserved, bespectacled young man, tall, dark and slender, an actor under contract at MGM. We'd met casually before through Harry. This Sunday they came over for a swim, stayed to dinner. I remember the candlelight, and blonde Christina in her high chair, and the deep tenor of Phillip's voice.

You had to ask questions to discover that this quiet man was a native San Franciscan, an alumnus of Stanford, that he'd studied at the Royal Academy of Dramatic Art in London. Despite five years in show business there was nothing of the Hollywood actor about Phillip, nothing of the exhibitionist. Poised, yes, but that he was reserved and rather shy was apparent to me, perhaps because poise is something I wear like a cloak over my own shyness. The next night he took me to dinner and later we read my new script, *Reunion in France*.

We dined, read, checked the nursery to be sure all was well. Evening after evening Phillip and I would dine quietly at home. His very presence was an anodyne, comfortable and comforting. I wasn't alone. Someone was content just to be with me and the baby. Strange. The men who'd attracted me before were passionate, volatile. The man in New York was a dynamo. But I couldn't have him, and here was his antithesis, an easy-going, unpretentious man who seemed to adore me, who was calm and absolutely uncomplicated. No one even knew we were dating, and we wanted it that way. I've never really known why I married Phillip. I guess I mistook peace of mind for love, and at the time believed in it with all my heart. July 20, 1942, six weeks after our first date, we were married, at the home of my attorney, Neil McCarthy, in Hidden Valley.

Our marriage license was granted on Friday under our legal names, Lucille Tone and Frederick Kormann, and Judge Flynn married us at a moment past midnight on Sunday, fulfilling the three-day waiting period required by California law. At 2 a.m. Phillip and I were back home, sitting in the kitchen drinking milk. At 8 a.m. I was on the set ready for filming. By noon, word of our marriage had circulated around the studio.

Mr. Mayer, Eddie Mannix and Joe Mankiewicz all came to the set to congratulate us . . . Mrs. Ray Milland was on the phone planning a wedding reception . . . my friend Ruth Waterbury was writing the story . . . Judy Garland, jubilant, was running back and forth from the set of *For Me and My Gal*. It was a scene of pleasant bedlam. My friend Katherine Albert was the one assured person. Her complete self-confidence I had always linked with the fact that she was happily married. Now perhaps I too would be confident. A wedding cake was conjured up, ice cream was served. Phillip and I were photographed cutting the cake, showing off our wide gold wedding bands.

Six months later I left MGM, and for the first and only time in my life since I'd started working at St. Agnes Academy, I was without a job. Phillip wasn't employed either, but how we *worked*. We had the new baby boy, adopted in November, another Scandinavian blue-eyed blond infant. We lost our cook to a defense factory, the children's nurse to the WAVES, and the local diaper laundry burned down. You couldn't get help, everyone was off to the aircraft factories—Phillip too after a while, with his lunch pail. We closed down part of our twenty-seven-room house. Since gasoline was rationed, we had a motorcycle, and I rode it to the grocery with Christina and Christopher tied in the little sidecar.

I cooked, cleaned, cared for the babies and worked in the victory garden that covered the front lawn. We had tomatoes, beans, carrots, radishes, corn. Phillip worked in the garden weekends. He'd mend fences, sand and paint garden furniture, stake up tomatoes. My friends Helen Fullerton and Betty Barker found out what was going on and they'd don jeans and come out over the weekends to help. Phillip was quite at home with them. He'd cart them along to shop at the Farmer's Market, take them to the bus line when it was time to go home. They adored Phillip because he was as "easy as an old shoe" and enjoyed all the little things. To them, ours seemed like a tranquil happy life, the gardening, the sewing, the quiet. Heaven knows I tried to like it, tried to fill it with meaning.

Monday nights we worked at the Hollywood Canteen. I served behind the snack bar and wrote postcards—hundreds of postcards. "Dear So and So, Joe (or Frank or Fred) is at the Hollywood Canteen tonight and misses you very much. Joan Crawford." There was work for Allied Relief, for the Red Cross, and recordings for the boys overseas—"Words and Music."

I had never had a speech lesson, so for these poetry recordings I worked with Gertrude Fogler, a delightful woman with the softest speech you've ever heard. I love poetry; with her, I read new poetry, she taught me how to read verse conversationally.

War work was what mattered. I was up to my ears, organizing a day nursery for fifty youngsters whose mothers were working in war plants. In the papers you read constantly of children "abandoned" in cars while their mothers worked. I thought of my three-year-old Tina and her year-old brother locked in an automobile sobbing, and promptly joined the American Women's Voluntary Services, uniform and all. The Board of Education supplied a principal and assistant teachers and we had a wealth of volunteer workers. We found an old house near the aircraft factories and the volunteer workers and I scrubbed it from top to bottom. It took us a week to get it in shape, then we were ready for the children. This type of project is something I've been interested in ever since. Recently I went to Las Vegas to help Tent 39 of Variety (of which I'm a member) raise money for their nursery school for working mothers. Two hundred nursery and kindergarten children are watched over so their mothers can work with free hearts.

During the war years, I cooked the meals, took care of the children. While they slept I scrubbed floors, washed diapers, lined shelves with paper, scrubbed cupboards and still wasn't tired. Alongside the house was a line of huge eucalyptus trees. I helped cut down those trees, thirty-six of them. And still I wasn't tired. Outsiders writing of Phillip and me described these years as the most serene of my life. They were the most difficult. Frankly I was bored because the actress is half of this woman and the actress had no outlet.

It was three years before I found work, before I could find a story I believed in and a producer to believe in me. Warner Brothers had put me under contract two days after I left Metro, for two pictures a year, at one-third the salary I'd received at MGM. But the scripts submitted were not suitable, in my opinion, and one mistake I wasn't going to make—I wasn't going to start off at a new studio in the familiar rut of stories that were stereotyped. All I did in two years was a guest appearance in *Hollywood Canteen,* in which all Warner's stars appeared, including Trigger, the horse. When they offered me a part that called for an ingénue, I told them candidly they'd tabbed the wrong Joan, the part was for young Joan Leslie who'd scored as one of the Cohans in *Yankee Doodle Dandy.* I also asked to be taken off salary.

"What does she mean, *off salary?* Nobody's ever asked to be taken off salary," Mr. Warner said. "She must *want* something."

I did.

I wanted a good picture. Since I wasn't making one, I didn't feel justified in taking the salary.

During those difficult years, it was Lew Wasserman, then an agent, now president of MCA Artists, who bought my contract from my unenthusiastic agent and told me I was *not* through. While I kept my house and babies bright and shining, Lew Wasserman kept my faith bright and shining.

And Producer Jerry Wald at Warners didn't think I was box-office poison either. It was Jerry who found *Mildred Pierce.*

Mildred was a meaty James M. Cain story. Warner Brothers' star Bette Davis had turned it down. Director Michael Curtiz wanted Barbara Stanwyck, who attained such a triumph in Cain's *Double Indemnity.* Jerry Wald fought for me. I heard what Curtiz said: "Her and her damned shoulder pads!" But when he broke down and cried, watching my test scene, I knew he'd support me and he did. I asked to test with each potential member of the cast—a task usually relegated to a stock actress—but I'd been away from the cameras so long . . . and I was eager to get to work, and not in the garden or the kitchen for a change. It took six weeks of testing to select our cast: Ann Blyth, Jack Carson, Zachary Scott and Bruce Bennett.

For my early scenes, the studio designed some cotton frocks. Mr. Curtiz said NO, they looked too smart. I went down to Sears Roebuck on my own and bought the kind of housedresses I thought Mildred would wear. When I arrived on the set for wardrobe tests, Mr. Curtiz walked over to me, shouting, "You and your damned Adrian shoulder pads. This stinks!" And he ripped the dress from neck to hem.

"Mr. Curtiz," I sobbed, "I bought this dress this morning for two dollars and ninety-eight cents, there are no shoulder pads," and I rushed to my dressing room in tears.

The assistant director followed me. "Don't let him hurt you, Joan. This is the way he likes to start a picture, he'll needle you if you'll let him. Don't let him." An actress friend told me the same thing— she'd just finished a picture with Curtiz and was a nervous wreck. We had no more arguments about clothes. I didn't care *what* I wore, I sailed into Mildred with all the gusto I'd been saving for three years, not a Crawford mannerism, not a trace of my own personality. After they saw the first rough cut, Jack Warner gave a luncheon for me and Mike Curtiz made a speech:

"When I started the tests for *Mildred Pierce,* I heard my star was very deefeecult. So I say, okay, Crawford, Curtiz will be more deefeecult. She took it. Like a trouper. We have now finished the picture and I see she is one swell actress. We get along fine on the picture. I luff her."

My gift to Mr. Curtiz—a pair of Adrian's supersize shoulder pads. He is a master director, but you have to be a mistress of comedy to get along with him.

I was going through as much at home as Mildred was at the studio. I had never really known Phillip, I realized that. I had not really loved him. Peace of mind may have resembled love, but it *wasn't*. It wasn't peace of mind either. I don't like pauses, and this pause ended in divorce. Never marry out of loneliness. I owed him an apology from the first.

This time I was almost destroyed financially, but I was not destroyed emotionally, and I had no time for bitterness. I had two children to care for. By the grace of God I'd recaptured the means of caring for them. *Mildred Pierce* grossed the studio five million dollars. A happy ending to a big gamble. How I wish I'd had a percentage!

In March 1946, after having almost been out of the business, I was nominated for an Academy Award.

On the night of the Awards, I was running a temperature of 104. I'd been suffering with flu for the past week, filming *Humoresque*. The picture could not be delayed. Flu coupled with the nervous tension of being eligible for an Oscar had me shaking with chills and fever. Although I was dressed to go, Dr. Bill Branch stepped in. "Over my dead body," he said. He put me back to bed and sat there to make sure that I stayed.

As early as six o'clock, cameramen started arriving at the house *just in case* I won. We turned on the radio to hear the proceedings from Grauman's Chinese Theater. I'll never forget it! Best supporting actress, Anne Revere for *National Velvet* . . . best supporting actor, James Dunn for *A Tree Grows in Brooklyn* . . . best screenplay, *The*

Lost Weekend . . . best director, Billy Wilder, *The Lost Weekend* . . . best actor, Ray Milland, *The Lost Weekend* . . . best picture, *The Lost Weekend* . . . best actress . . . it took so long to open that envelope . . . Joan Crawford! I'd made it! I thought of the other nominees: Ingrid Bergman, Jennifer Jones, Gene Tierney, Greer Garson—but only for a little minute. Mike Curtiz was accepting on my behalf. I was crying.

Almost before the broadcast concluded, Van Johnson came bursting into my house. He was more feverish than I, that Van, he was a charter member of my fan club! Now, Dr. Branch relented. He said I might go downstairs, in a flannel nightgown, heavy robe, and with a scarf wrapped around my neck. Within minutes, a bevy of people had the place jumping. There was no help, no food; we feasted on effervescence that night, and I was so overheated, the fever broke.

My gamble on abandoning straight-line glamour girls had paid off, but you don't stop there. A star has to keep in the race every minute. Oscar's not the end, he's a new beginning; with him gleaming in a little shrine at the foot of the stairs, I turned to *Humoresque*. One day I'd been chatting on the phone with Connie and Jerry Wald.

"Jerry, what are you doing?"

"Reading a script."

"Is there a part for me?"

"It's the story of a young violinist for John Garfield," he said, "but let me read you this scene between the violinist and this nymphomaniac, alcoholic woman." It was exquisite, the way Clifford Odets and Zachary Gold can write.

"Jerry, she sounds interesting," I said. "Let me play her."

"There are only three scenes for this woman, Joan."

"I don't care. Please, Jerry, at least let me read the script."

Of course, I fell in love with Helen, the woman who drinks too much, has too much time on her hands, too much love in her heart. The studio felt the part wasn't big enough, the answer was no. I kept phoning Jerry every day. Then one day, Jerry phoned me. Johnny Garfield had just flown back to New York—he couldn't stand the leading lady. Jerry loved Johnny, hated to see him suspended and knew how rebellious Johnny could be. And he hated to ask me to do only three scenes, but . . .

I said, "Jerry, I'm thoroughly selfish about this. I *want* the part!"

He contacted Johnny in New York, spoke to Jack Warner and phoned me right back. "Johnny's catching the first plane west before you change your mind," Jerry said. "Matter of fact, he may fly on his own, he may not bother with a plane."

It was glorious working with Johnny and with director Jean Negulesco. Here, brilliantly coordinated, was the work of scriptwriters, director, camera, cast and music. Franz Waxman conducted the hundred and fifteen piece symphony orchestra, Isaac Stem dubbed in for Johnny on the violin, Oscar Levant played his own piano, balancing Paganini, Mendelssohn, Beethoven and Gershwin with his own light fresh brand of humor. Initially, there may have been scant sympathy for this dipsomaniac married woman, but when she walks at last into the sea with her lover's violin playing "Liebestod," backed by full orchestra, it was uncompromisingly dramatic.

Warners promptly signed me to a seven-year contract at $200,000 a picture. As *Variety* put it: "Crawford's Back and Metro Hasn't Got Her."

I went on to an even more difficult part in *Possessed,* the part of a schizophrenic, a woman going insane from unrequited love. The role of Louise was violent and fearful and required medical accuracy.

I spent six weeks in hospitals watching schizophrenics, seeing how sodium pentothal and sodium amytal restores them to memory for a few brief moments—six weeks at L. A. General Hospital, and many sanatoriums. Even the critic who disliked me most called me "Hollywood's great sufferer Academy style." Mr. Mayer ran *Mildred Pierce, Humoresque* and *Possessed* and made his MGM producers look at them each three times.

"She's through, is she?" he said. "Why couldn't we have done this here? Every one of them is Academy timber!" He was right, I was again nominated for an award.

I didn't win the Oscar, but I got something more wonderful—my twins, Cynthia and Cathy, darling babies two months old, still in incubators. The authorities at the adoption home didn't want anyone to have those babies, they loved them so much themselves. For several months they checked our home carefully, saw how Christina and Christopher were being raised, the air of security in our home, the competence of Mrs. Howe, the nurse, when I wasn't there.

We waited impatiently. We thought it took forever. Can you imagine the thrill the day the phone call did come and a voice said:

"Miss Crawford, we have checked many homes and we feel that yours is the home the twins should have. Will you meet the plane tomorrow at ten?"

Would I? I *flew.*

NINE

C an you imagine what it meant to me to be surrounded by four warm young lives? To come home to their confidence and love, their chorus of "Hi, Mummie-dearest!" (Until Tina and Chris were in the fifth grade, they didn't know that Mummie and dearest were two separate words.) Four little faces, changing daily as they responded to each new filament and fragment of living. Four pairs of hands reaching to clasp mine. They changed my life, these children, gave me a whole new world—not all at once, but little by little as I saw I could help them to grow and flourish.

Being a mother is a full-time job and like all mothers when something goes wrong, I'm heartsick. I ask myself, as most mothers do, how did I fail? There are plenty of people who have thought me too loving, others have criticized me for being too severe. They've warned me that a child thinks anyone who disciplines them is agin 'em.

In my opinion, you have to give a child a line to follow, show him you love him but make him follow it. Discipline is part of a child's security. If the adults he believes in fail to punish him for wrongdoing, he ultimately loses confidence in those adults. Obviously, I've tried to provide my children with what I didn't have: constructive discipline, a sense of security, a sense of sharing.

My twins are at school in upstate New York. We just spent a joyous summer together at Westhampton. We had a dear little house more than two hundred and fifty years old, as snug and compact as a salt box, with lovely green lawns, with apple trees and a privet hedge. The girls biked, we shopped, swam and kept house together. They are the dearest companions I've ever had. Every day, wherever I am, they phone me, or I them. It's a ritual, a quarter to six, the children's hour. And they write. . . .

French is part of the curriculum. My most recent letter from Cathy was signed, "Je aime vous bien. Lots de aime, Cathy." (In a hurry they'll sign themselves "Ci" and "Ca.") They've drawn lots, their soccer team will be the Invincibles, to be pitted against the Defenders, last year's champions. Now that Cindy's on the Invincibles, Cathy's certain they'll win. Cindy is a well-coordinated athlete. High scorer in her basketball league last year, she scored forty-two baskets in a game her team won 89–86. She's on the baseball team. Her idea of heaven is wherever the Dodgers play and there are autographed baseballs for breakfast.

Cathy adores her sister and her sister's prowess. She herself doesn't care about competitive sports. She is Honorary Representative of her class and is studying Special Arts. She loves horses, rides them, draws them—one dear pastel of a mother horse kissing her colt. At fourteen, the girls are developing into beautiful young ladies. I watched them graduate from Marymount, June 1960, with such pride—tremulous as if I were the one faced with the necessity of making a graceful entrance on that stage in first high heels. They looked so poised and were inwardly so quaking I cried as I had when Christina was graduated from eighth grade. These were the first commencement exercises I'd ever witnessed. I never attended any school long enough to graduate!

The twins' graduation gift was a trip with me aboard the S.S. *Brasil* to South America. They embarked, two demure little girls, and returned with new poise and assurance. Cindy, the more reserved, promptly fell in love with the captain! I don't know whether this metamorphosis had to do with sun and sea air, or with the fact that we had had each other for the last year only on weekends or school holidays, and now for a whole wonderful summer we were as close as a mother bird and two fledglings. Three of us in one little stateroom—I sometimes thought one of us would go out the porthole. They had a chance to express their views, and discover who they are. They're not identical twins and their personalities are quite diverse.

Cindy has always been the cowboy with a penchant for trouble. Sometimes I've wondered if she gets into jams just so she can confess, be scolded and then be loved and forgiven. She craves affection as I always have. So does Cathy, but she is more docile. She was a coquette at two, with black velvet eyes. When she was a baby, she had tantrums that resulted in convulsions. She'd hold her breath, turn black, I'd grab her while the nurse stood pale and paralyzed.

"Breathe!" I'd shout. "Breathe, breathe!" as I swatted her little bottom.

Every nurse we had, left. Three of them diagnosed these convulsions as epilepsy and refused to handle an epileptic child. When Cathy was a year and three months old, I took her to the hospital for a checkup.

"To allay your fears, Joan?" asked the doctor.

"No, damn it, to prove something to those nurses. I want you to examine this baby, then put it in writing and sign it. Show these nurses they're wrong!"

They *were* wrong, the tantrums were outgrown, the twins were and are adorable, they simply charm everyone, including me. And they know it. I'd never withhold love from my children. That's why I wanted them, to give them love.

And what happy times we've had! When Christopher and Christina were little, I'd charter an entire car on the train, for the two of them, myself and a nurse. I'd sleep with the children and cuddle them every time the train rocked or jerked.

Once, because they'd never seen snow, I chartered a car on the train and we went racing away to New York for Christmas. I'd called ahead, rented a house at Bedford, a small town just north of the city, and en route I embroidered fantasies of white Christmases and snow. Sure enough, when we reached Bedford, snow was whirling down like duck feathers, but the next morning it was raining and rain washed the snow away. The children were so disappointed. Then on Christmas Eve, the weather grew colder, big soft fluffy snow began whirling down. Christmas was saved!

I never left home without them. Our vacations were all family style. One year I drove them up the coast, through the redwoods, to see the salmon run in Oregon, and home through the mountains, all of us playing word games. Can you imagine me, taking four kids alone through the mountains? Three or four times a year we went to Alisal Ranch, up near Santa Barbara. Easter vacations were spent at Palm Springs. We went to Lake Arrowhead to see the snow, and always, once a year, visited Monterey and Carmel. Christina still remembers our long walks along the sea, how we talked and read poetry.

She was a bright little girl, very definite, very poised. I remember her on the set of *When Ladies Meet,* aged two, in her yellow Lily Daché bonnet with one tiny ostrich feather. She was brought to the set every day after her nap and sat there watching, round-eyed, quiet as a mouse. This particular day, during a scene, someone walked by with a roll of cotton and she screamed her delight, for a lump of cotton happened to be her favorite plaything. Director Bob Leonard called "Cut!" and presented my daughter with a whole lovely wad of cotton, which kept her quiet from then on. Christina today says that when she walked on a sound stage for the first time as an actress, it was like coming home.

What pictures you keep in your heart! Christina's first bath . . . Christina trying to dance . . . both of us recording "Three Blind Mice" . . . her childish printing that wobbled across the page to say, "Dear fairies and brownies, here is my tooth" . . . my children and the neighborhood children listening enthralled to my recording of "The Littlest Stork" . . . and later the breakfast and moonlight rides at Alisal Ranch.

I never wanted the children to know how I felt about horses. We rode. One day Tina said, "Poor Mommie, you're not having a good time, are you?"

"Well, of course I am!"

Tina knew better. "You're a good sport, Mommie!"

None of them have had my fears inflicted on them. What I *fear* has nothing to do with what I've allowed the children to *do.* You can't rein in youngsters any more than you can rein a polo pony. Each of them started swimming when still tiny. I gave the first lessons; later there were lessons with Captain Paul Nast; and the twins had Crystal Scarborough. At four they were each able to swim the sixty-five-foot length of the pool and dive into twelve feet of water. Tina and Chris developed into excellent swimmers and brought home ribbons. Tina was jumping in a horse show once when she went sailing. . . .

"Are you hurt, Tina? *Are you hurt?*"

"I don't know," she muttered, "but I'm awfully embarrassed."

None of the teenage problems can change the essence of what we had when we were all together, Tina and Chris home for the weekends and the twins toddling to meet them; they'd jump up and wrap their legs around their brother and sister like little cubs. We all ate together, one child saying grace and all chorusing, "Thank you, God, for everything." There was never a day without Judge Hardy sessions.

In my own childhood there were so many things unexplained that I've been careful *to* explain. There were times when they weren't actually qualified to understand, they were too young, but a child is never too young to start forming opinions and each facet of my life that involved them was explained by me before they heard of it via television, radio or newspapers, or from their friends at school.

There was never a day without tasks performed together. The twins still follow this pattern. When we're together, we do everything together. They assist me cooking and serving, we all make our beds, dust our rooms and tidy up, wash our undies and hose. My three girls were taught to wash and iron, all the children learned to take their soiled clothes to the laundry room after baths as soon as they could walk. When they were old enough, they dusted and vacuumed their own rooms. A room not properly taken care of—no television. Sloppiness has never been tolerated in our home, nor has rudeness.

I once broke my toe, chasing seven-year-old Cindy to give her a wallop when I caught her jumping up and down on Cathy, who had the flu and a high fever. "You kids are going to grow up to be considerate of others if I have to break my other nine toes," I vowed. "You have to learn to live with people!"

Mary Margaret McBride was so surprised when she heard about my children's self-help program. "I never dreamed you'd be like this," she said, "with all the servants you can afford to give them."

But our house has never been *staffed* with servants, because I wanted the children to be prepared for life. Not my life—theirs. They're going into a world that isn't easy, a world where unless you are self-sufficient and strong, you can be destroyed. Tina and Chris each started boarding school at the age of ten. There were three reasons for sending them. 1) Tina was sent when she began being catered to because we had a swimming pool, and because, as she once said herself, "Mommie, I'm so glad you're a star. When we're choosing up sides for a game, I'm almost always captain!" 2) I was giving the two older children so much individual attention the older they grew, that the younger ones weren't getting enough. 3) This was because in public school, Tina and Chris made few friends. Our neighborhood was a far-flung one; after school, the children scattered to their homes. At boarding school there were other children their age to live with, adjust to, with whom they could make friends. Christopher had a chance to be with boys rather than under his older sister's thumb.

My first concern has always been to help them prepare for a full, normal life, and my severest critics can't say I ever *played* at motherhood. There is a certain public dubiety about actress-mothers. Have they time? And do they care? The children's bedrooms adjoined mine and I did all the normal, routine things. When they were ill in the night, I was up with them, checking temperatures, sponging with warm alcohol, changing damp nighties. I walked the floor with every baby, kept in touch with all crises during the day by telephone from the studio when I was working, drove them to the dentist and the doctor's, planned their menus, checked their school papers daily (still do), enrolled them in their schools, picked Tina and Chris up on Fridays and delivered them back to Chadwick School Sunday nights myself. On the weekends I accompanied them to baseball games and matinees, to the beach, to the Ice Follies and checked all details of clothing, eating habits, cleanliness and school necessities. In homes where there are numerous domestics, perhaps these details are relegated to others. Not so in ours. I waited too long for motherhood to evade its responsibilities.

The one worry that seems to haunt every adopted parent is—will the child feel he is given enough affection if he's told he's adopted. Some years ago, when Christina was fourteen, Christopher eleven, a friend with adopted children asked me if she should tell them they were adopted.

"Talk to my older children," I said. "Let them answer your question."

First she asked Christopher. What did adoption mean to him? He thought a minute.

"Why it means I was wanted more than any other boy. Mother chose me."

Then she asked Tina. "I was hand-picked," Christina said. "Mother says that some women just find themselves pregnant without especially wanting children, but those who adopt them want them terribly. You know something? I think that people who adopt a child feel a need for security just as much as the child feels that need."

This fourteen-year-old had summed up the very essence of every adopting parent.

Once I asked her if she ever worried or wondered who her original parents were. She looked at me with complete trust.

"Why, no, Mother, I've never even thought about it."

For ten years, fans and many friends asked the question—wouldn't I marry again to give the children a father? The answer? No. I wished my children to have a father, but I'd never marry just to provide them with a parent. The lack of a man in the household was something I was aware of many times, and once Christopher's teacher told me he had mentioned it.

When I drove him back to school after the weekend, I said, "Chris, honey, have you been wondering why you don't have a father?"

He gave me his how-did-you-know-that look.

"It's a normal, natural thing to wonder. Let me try to explain. The easiest thing in the world would be to get a man for you to call Father, but I might not love him. Or I could fall in love and he might be a man who disliked children. I've known men like that."

His face was something to see, like a blond athletic angel's. He wriggled closer to me.

"Are you sure that the boys you like at school, Chris, all have mothers and daddies? Do they have a happy and serene home as we have?"

"Gee," he said, "I never thought of it that way. Let's stay just as we are."

What a dear little boy he was. How sad I am that the child who started out a Huck Finn wasn't able to make an easier transition to reliable young manhood. I thought and prayed he would. He loved adventure, but some boys who love adventure grow up to be jet pilots or navy men, adventuring the sky or sea. My son was rebellious.

It isn't easy to cope with a problem child. In the hearing at a New York court, four years ago, the Judge made that very clear. Christopher was sentenced to a school where he had the advantage of excellent psychiatric care. As this is being written, he is nineteen, he's married and has a darling infant girl.

And Christina is in Hollywood, working in films. She is twenty-one, a beautiful, ambitious young actress fighting her way up. Columnist Hy Gardner recently asked me: "Joan, why are you against Tina's career as an actress?"

If she weren't an actress, Hy, I'd be the most disappointed woman in the world. It's been her ambition since she played the lead in her school production of *H.M.S. Pinafore,* and what could gratify a mother more than for a child to share her dream and follow it? I'll admit I had two weeks of disappointment when she refused to finish college, when she left Carnegie Tech in favor of the theater. I wanted her first to have the education that I felt she'd need for her future. But this is Tina's life; and by the way, I've opened for her every stage and film door at my command, you know that. Every producer, every director I know, in Hollywood or New York. Against her career as an actress? What a strange contradiction that would be!

I am only filled with sorrow and compassion for my daughter because she's paying too much for whatever it is she wants. I certainly understand ambition, but you can't afford to throw away people, especially the people who love you—and you can't afford to use them. Mother-and-daughter feuds make for reams of print; they also make for reams of inaccuracies:

. . . that, for example, she has never known her birth date or her parents' names! The first time we went to Switzerland, seven years ago, I gave Christina her passport and her birth certificate with all the pertinent data on her birth date—which we'd always celebrated—and the names of her original father and mother, even her little heel print.

. . . that—another example of inaccuracy—when I objected to her leaving college after *one* year (the articles usually say *two)*, my daughter thought it wise to leave the penthouse apartment where Alfred and I lived and find a small furnished apartment for herself in order to escape my displeasure. Since Christina had never lived with us—she'd been in school—she simply took an apartment and my displeasure had nothing to do with it. My displeasure concerned her decision, to drop further formal education, but once she'd made that decision and left school, my attitude was that if she wished to tackle the adult world, more power to her.

. . . it has also been stated that I asked her to change her name for theatrical purposes! When Christina appeared in her first Off-Broadway show, a huge placard announced her as "Joan Crawford's daughter, Christina Crawford." No actress profits from this type of billing, it detracts from her own personality. I told Tina that if I were she and the theater refused to bill me in my own right and insisted on the "Joan Crawford's daughter" bit, I'd change my name.

But the greatest inaccuracy is the feud itself. It takes two to feud and I'm not one of them. I wish only the best for Tina.

It is impossible not to wonder occasionally, when rumor and gossip fan up brush fires about my relationship with my children, whether or not the special circumstances of our lives have any effect on our problems. But I know that there is difficulty in communication between parents and children, when the children are experiencing growing pains in the most typical home, with a full complement of both parents whose children were born to them; where the mother has never worked, and where there has been no prod of publicity to make things more difficult. It seems to come natural to many young people to rebel in all circumstances. Most teenagers find it difficult to listen to the voice of experience. It is only later, when they are grappling with the problems of adults, that they wish they could have listened.

I used to think environment obliterated heredity. I was wrong. Unlike Christina and Christopher, the twins don't resent my life, they're pliant, joyous, they link arms with me and off we march into whatever life may offer, sometimes great crowds of people, situations trying for children their age, into a sea of adult conversation, adult manners, sometimes regal formality. They have learned readily from everything, these two. We are so close, in such accord, we all reinforce each other.

They've developed a beautiful self-reliance. Once I married Alfred Steele and started traveling the world, they became accustomed to crossing the country alone or with Mrs. Howe, their governess since infancy, coming to us at Christmas, Easter and on vacations. Now they travel back and forth to school by train. My trust in them is implicit.

How proud they were the night they were on the Maurice Chevalier show. I'd told them to look at Uncle Maurice, enunciate distinctly, sit up straight, and share the magic this man generates in a performance. I did not go to rehearsals with them, I was at the Pepsi-Cola Convention at the Waldorf and they were living at the hotel with me. On their first appearance before the camera, they were on their own, and they were all you could ask. The night the Chevalier spectacular was to be shown on television, they taped the Jack Paar show and we had dinner and saw both TV programs at Twenty One.

Then we came home, unzipped each other's dresses, and got into pei-
gnoirs, chatting like girls in a dorm. Nothing could be more gratifying to a mother than the moment when her children start sharing her
world, when they begin to understand that she's a human being and
that they can be friends.

I believe the most important thing a parent can give children is
the ability to stand on their own feet, achieve their own personality, slug it out with tire world if necessary, and still not lose dignity,
integrity or a sense of humor. You don't try to keep them children.
You keep giving responsibilities, preparing them for an adult world.

My children owe me nothing but love and respect. They have
given me from the beginning a tremendous emotional experience I
wouldn't have missed for the world. I hope only that they will walk
in happiness and dignity.

TEN

I t has been said that on screen I have personified the American woman. This is probably because from the time of *Mildred Pierce* I was cast, in picture after picture, as all varieties of her . . . the woman tremulously mature . . . sometimes so bruised by love she sinks into the psychotic, as in *Possessed* and *Humoresque* . . . sometimes bruised but victorious as the fashion illustrator in *Daisy Kenyon* and the waitress in *Flamingo Road* . . . and on occasion, her own worst enemy as in *The Damned Don't Cry* and the predatory *Harriet Craig*.

The *New Yorker* said of this one: "As Mr. (George) Kelly originally had it, Mr. Craig's wife was a cold one. As we have it here with Joan Crawford, she is villainous but torrid which should make for some sense."

It was the last good word that could be said of my pictures for a while. We were running into script difficulties again, the pickings were slim. *Goodbye My Fancy* had scored on Broadway, but it got dulled down when they edited all political angles for the screen. Incidentally, this cast included a young girl named Janice Rule whose personality definitely clashed with mine. I felt she was nonprofessional in her attitude, that she regarded movie work as something less than slumming and one day I told her so. "Miss Rule," I said, "you'd better enjoy making films while you can, I doubt that you'll be with us long!"

On shipboard last summer, I sat watching *The Subterraneans,* absolutely rapt over the performance of an actress who dances brilliantly, who has a flair for drama, for comedy. "Who is this girl? She's fantastic!" I said. Well, the girl was Janice Rule. I've since seen her on TV and I can only add superlatives. Miss Rule, my apologies, I think you're going to be with us a long long time.

But *Goodbye My Fancy* did nothing for any of us. As soon as the picture was finished, I took the children and went to Carmel. It was summer, we'd swim, and play on the beach. After they went to bed I'd read scripts, novels, everything available, hunting for a great story. I needed one and I needed it now! After I drove the children down to Los Angeles and put them in school, I picked up another armload of books and headed back to Carmel. I'd read all night, but none of those properties were for me. They offered characters too similar to those I'd played, backgrounds too reminiscent.

Then one midnight I started a book and couldn't put it down until I read the last page at 4 a.m. Sleep was out of the question. I arose and walked along the sea. By daybreak I had *Sudden Fear* shot and ready for release! I watched the clock. At seven I phoned Arthur Park of MCA and urged him to buy this book at once. At 8 p.m. Lew Wasserman called. *Sudden Fear* was not for sale. It belonged to a man named Joe Kaufman who'd brought it to Lew months before for *me!*

"But I explained, dear, that you're all tied up at Warner Brothers," Lew said.

"Where is Kaufman? I'll leave Warners. Find Joe Kaufman!"

At a moment when I needed a blockbuster, my next picture was one that could easily have been my swan song, *This Woman Is Dangerous*. It was the type of improbable corn that had gone out with Adrian shoulder pads.

At my request Lew Wasserman now obtained my release. I left my perfectly good safe contract at Warners to take a gamble on *Sudden Fear*. Almost a year from the night I'd read the book, we located Joe Kaufman in Spain where he was filming *The Flying Dutchman*. He flew to California. I accepted his offer to star in the picture without a salary, but at a percentage of the profits.

I asked for director David Miller. David and I had grown up together at MGM, where he'd first been a film *cutter,* and I knew how valuable he'd be to an independent production where budget counts. Mentally he cuts as he shoots, and wasted angles and film are at a minimum. Even with David, ours was a major undertaking. We had to have the right casting, the right script—and it took us almost another year to accomplish that.

Storywise, it was one of the most harrowing experiences I've ever had. I'd been trapped before, but never like this—as the successful playwright who marries for love only to discover that *he* has married for murder. It was an actress' field day, and director David Miller scored a triumph.

Every director has his own interpretation of a script, so does actor, producer and writer. So does the cameraman for that matter! It's as important to cast your producer, director and writer as it is to cast your star. Whatever I can contribute technically to characterization I learned through the years working with Joe Mankiewicz. He was first a writer, then producer-writer, and beginning with *The Gorgeous*

Hussy we worked together on seven pictures. It was one of the happiest times of my professional life. As we worked on new scripts I was allowed to sit day after day during writer-director-producer discussions, listening to each new facet of characterization. Sometimes I'd ask a question. "How do you think she would react in this instance?"

Often I'd get three different answers. Paramount to your picture is consistency in character development and you profit immeasurably from hearing what producer, director and writer have in mind and by coming to agreement with them on a line of action. Sometimes you can't agree.

After *Sudden Fear,* months passed while the cameraman, the crew and I sat on the Paramount lot awaiting action on *Lisbon.* The script wouldn't jell, despite all that scriptwriters, producer and director could do. I was so disappointed, this was my one chance to work with designer Edith Head.

Then March 1953, Benny Thau, one of the gentlemen at MGM who had thought me all washed up ten years before, sent me a script, strictly undercover. When I got as far as page forty-five, I picked up the phone and said, "When do we start?" I wanted to do *Torch Song,* I wanted to go back to MGM more than anything in the world. Also, I'd seen Chuck Walters' delightful *Lili,* and if I were to achieve *Torch Song,* I felt he was the director for me.

He *was* the director, there was a dressing room filled with flowers, everyone came on the set to welcome me, from Dore Schary to the propmen and waitresses from the commissary. There was a giant-size market basket of chocolates from Clark Gable, a basket of roses from Fred Astaire, a bunch of violets from one of the grips, dozens and dozens of orchids . . . one of the most exciting days of my life. Chuck Walters took me by the hand, led me out onto the stage, and we started the first dance number, "Follow Me." Chuck originally was a dance director, became a top choreographer, and he danced this first number with me, I'm sure, to put me at my ease. His is a touch, a delicacy I've never seen in anyone else.

To me this picture meant much more than just a triumphant homecoming. *Torch Song* was my first Technicolor picture, my first dancing picture in eleven years and a new approach to moviemaking—wide screen. There were moments when I thought I'd bitten off more than I could chew. You can't stay away from dancing as long as that and get back in training without muscle-wracking work. While we were rehearsing the big dance number, "Two-Faced Woman," I asked Willie Haines to come to the set and tell me the truth. How was I doing? He watched for a while, then picked up a paper and started to read. My heart sank. That night, with diffidence, I phoned Willie.

"Cranberry," he said, "you amaze me!"

I breathed again. "God must have his hand on my shoulder, Willie."

"I don't know about the shoulder, Cranberry. But only God could get your legs up that high."

Luckily dancing is like swimming, you never forget, but was I muscle-bound that first week! And there was makeup to devise for Technicolor and for the glamorous high-yellow number, fifteen costumes to fit, and photographs constantly being taken without makeup by *Colliers'* skillful Sanford Roth. *And* we had a shooting schedule of twenty-four days, including production numbers! We made it.

There is an amazing discipline you acquire when you're raised in the business, that you *have* to acquire, the exact measure of all the details. There are no pauses. Between scenes are conferences with director and assistant director, conferences with producers and writers, discussions with wardrobe people, the constant exigencies of grooming. A whole fresh makeup at noon. How can you face a camera closeup late in the afternoon with makeup from 6 a.m.?

Flats are my footwear until I'm ready to go into a scene, then high heels, not from wardrobe either, always my own shoes with the crossed ankle straps and open heels and toes that mold to my foot. Jerry Wald has an absolute fetish about those ankle straps and for his sake I had them made of plastic which fails to photograph. What Jerry doesn't know is that I've broken ankles three different times, I've sprained them three times and I need those straps for support. In a pump there's no security for your ankles.

Most comfortable of all is to be surrounded on the set by people who are not only familiar co-workers but old friends. My fellow workers have been with me for years, they are as keyed up as I am and as critical as any director. They don't *yes* me. Costumer Elva Martien who's been with me sixteen years, will walk into a scene just between rehearsal and take, ostensibly to fix my collar and straighten my jacket, but as she does so, she'll whisper, "You were so tense, darling, you were slouching a little. That's not like you, Joan."

When the costumers presented me last year with their handsome golden Figleaf Award for having worn costumes glamorously through the years, I insisted Elva share the spotlight. She'd earned the right. Elva, Eddie Allen, the makeup man; Nora Brown, body makeup; Peggy Shannon, hairdresser and Sylvia Lamarr, my stand-in and double for nineteen years, have all given far and above the call of duty. So has brilliant cameraman Charles Lang who worked with me first in *Sudden Fear.*

You're married to everyone on the set for the duration of a picture. These skilled people know what I need, what I want, and every requirement of the director. They're the best in their jobs in the industry. I love having them with me.

I also love the stream of visitors who come and go. My sets have never been closed, except for a difficult scene, such as the one with the sound scriber in *Sudden Fear,* or when a director has felt visitors were distracting to *him.* Friends dropping by give me confidence and incentive–talent can't grow without this.

At MGM, while our set was being lighted, Clark and I would go over to Spencer Tracy's set to watch him work. He'd visit us. So would Bob Taylor, Bob Young and Bob Montgomery. We'd all visit back and forth. This interest we had in each other's performance created an invigorating atmosphere. You work twice as hard, give twice as much when your audience includes great pros.

On *Torch Song* I was under tremendous pressure because of the dancing; going home at night was a mistake. At home I'd find myself checking cooking supplies, scouring stainless steel, romping in the nursery with Cathy and Cindy, listening to their first-grade problems, coping with household crises until I was so tense I couldn't sleep. I was afraid my tenseness would communicate itself to the children. This is something every working mother and father has to face—the times of business tension we don't want to impose on our families. My children always knew that in any crisis I'd leave the studio for them at once.

But after the first few days of *Torch Song,* I knew I was bringing my worries home. Better to leave the twins to their busy days at school, their competent nurse at home, and for me to stay right at the studio in my dressing room—except, of course, for weekends. I talked with all four children every night and our talks were calm and loving as they should be, not a distraught mother rushing in and out disturbing the very order she has established.

This way, when we'd stop shooting at six, I could see the rushes, go back to my dressing room, talk over the next day's scenes with Chuck Walters and the cast. We'd eat peanut butter and crackers, have a drink and talk.

This is a pattern I've followed ever since when making a picture. After my cohorts leave I'm locked in that dressing room at night with my script, getting ready for the next day, evaluating all that we've discussed. Sometimes I go over to the empty set and walk it, rehearsing. One of the most wondrous places in the world is the night studio, quiet, shadowed, the vast equipment standing idle, the city of a million fantasies and as many combined talents, ready to spring into being at daybreak. Try to sleep!

And I'm awakened each morning at five thirty by the arrival of Elva, Nora, Peggy and Eddie. At the start of a picture I order breakfast for all of us for the duration. Scrambled eggs, crisp bacon, sausage, coffee cakes stuffed with apples. While I eat, my hair is being done. We're due on the set at nine, but my first requisite is peace of mind, and that doesn't include hurry at the beginning of the day. Once you yourself are adjusted, then you can be as upset in "character" as need be. The girls and Eddie share my moods, they know the script as well as I do, they know when I'm about to face an arduous scene.

In *Sudden Fear* I went through nine solid days of hysteria. For those nine days my crew maintained absolute quiet. Eddie would just hand me a lipstick, Elva would just straighten my hem, each of them quietly attended to the details, so deftly I was not aware. While lights are being adjusted there is usually kidding and lighthearted banter on a set, but now Sylvia stood mutely in my place until we were ready to shoot; and the electrical crew, when they saw that a take was final, would change lenses quickly to get into the closeup or medium shot while the mood was still sustained. No one asked these people for silence, they simply were with me.

On one Zane Grey Theatre presentation, I was cast as a woman with a split personality, but the audience must accept her as *two* women, sisters, one with the disposition of a witch, the other, mild, sweet and cruelly frustrated. This would be a large order on *full-size* screen with an eight-week shooting schedule; and Aaron Spelling, writer-producer, studied me curiously when I suggested playing the dual role without any change in makeup. "In thirty minutes . . . on that little box?" he said. "Do you realize we shoot the whole thing in three days? Isn't it dramatically cutting your own throat?" But I held out against any makeup change differentiating the characters—that would render the split personality phony.

Incidentally, when I'm working for Zane Grey out at Republic, my dear Jackie and Jack Webb take me under their wings and I houseguest in their beautiful apartment on the lot. I can't imagine anyone else's hospitality I could accept when working, but Jack and Jackie understand the rigors of fast TV shooting, the long hours involved. They respect my need for sleep, my need to rise at five. They send dinner to me when we're working late. If Jack is working, he goes on to bed, but Jackie stays up to cue me on my lines for the next day. They know that every night of my working life I study script.

How can an actor or actress walk on a set not knowing the dialogue, or fail to study the rushes every day? Most professional actors are instinctively prepared *and* punctual. To any job you value, you give value.

Most actors want to spark each other, that's part of the fun. I've always insisted on talented actors; you're only as good as the script you work from and the cast you work with. Talent is something to revere. New talent is something to seek out, it's thrilling to watch a Diane Baker, a Katherine Crowley, a Sandra Dee, a Carolyn Jones, a Shirley Jones, a Shirley MacLaine, a Lee Remick, a Madlyn Rhue, a Natalie Wood.

Recently when a group of exhibitors honored Janet Leigh, their master of ceremonies said, "Tell Hollywood to give us pictures with stars, stars, *stars!*" "Isn't it strange," was Janet's answer, "three years ago you said you wanted new faces." As anyone who respects the industry knows—it takes the one to produce the other. Actors and actresses don't resent other actors, you depend on them!

I've been quoted as saying that if there's no excitement on the set, I'll produce it. But I mean *creative* excitement, not chaos. The last thing any professional actor wants is turmoil or crisis which imposes a strain on the individual, impedes concentration, ruins teamwork.

On *Johnny Guitar* we had in the cast an actress who hadn't worked in ten years, an excellent actress but a rabble-rouser. She was perfectly cast in the picture, but she played her part offstage as well. Her delight was to create friction. "Did you hear what *he* said about *you?*" she'd tell me. "And in front of a group of people!" I couldn't believe it. I thought I'd known that actor so well . . . I couldn't help showing my hurt.

The picture became a nightmare. She would finish a scene, walk to the phone on the set and call one of the columnists to report my "incivilities." I was as civil as I knew how to be. I took complete makeup tests with her, color tests, wardrobe tests, asked her to my dressing room for tea, asked her to cocktails, until my good friend

Harrison Carroll called me up one day to ask my version of this tug-of-war. I assured him the whole thing was weird and would he be an angel and lay off, we'd built up enough tension on that sultry desert location near Sedona, Arizona.

At that moment, director Nick Ray walked into my dressing room, grabbed the phone and yelled, "Keep it going, Harrison, it's good for the picture!" *Good* for the picture! She had us all at swords-points, and as if that weren't enough, she also had a friend in camp, an actor with an equally dubious reputation.

Shortly after *Johnny Guitar,* the Los Angeles *Mirror* ran a series of scathing articles about me, written by a man named Roby Heard, and quoting my fellow actors from that picture bitterly: I was a tyrant tortured by my own ambitions.

Since *Johnny* was my seventieth picture, and since I had worked with literally thousands of people during those years in Hollywood, if I were as "tyrannical" as those articles described me, I would certainly have been exposed long before. I'm *not* indestructible, I was crushed by those stories. The one extenuating factor was the fierce loyalty of friends and public who flooded the paper, the editor, and me with letters. Words of protest came from stars and directors, electricians and propmen who've worked with me, from people flatly contradicting statements to which they'd been eyewitnesses, from moviegoers and press who'd never particularly been my friends but were now. Among the letters and wires were those from newspaper editors who had subscribed to the syndicated series thinking it a life story.

"I've seen a lot of CHEAP CRUEL TRASH," wrote Lily May Caldwell of the Birmingham *News,* "but, I'll give you my word, THIS IS THE WORST. I am proud of my profession and I resent and have contempt for a person who will defile that profession by turning out this kind of copy. . . . I'm convinced it will boomerang and will serve only to win the sympathy and affection of the public and the decent newspaper people for you. Were you one of my friends, I might be accused of prejudice. But you happen to be someone I have never even seen in person. My indignation is for a principle, for a person I feel has been the subject of a cruel attack. Please accept my sympathy, regrets, and assurance that this story is going to affect a lot of people the way it did me."

Criticism, of course, is a concomitant of an actress' life. It's the price you pay for assuming so many personalities, and believing in them so much. There are those who cannot find a line of demarcation between the actress and the woman and suspect an element of pose in your most valid relationships. When we were making *Sudden Fear,* Jack Palance would never say good morning to me. I would walk on the set, greet him; he'd turn away. I went to Joe Kaufman in tears to ask why Jack didn't like me. I didn't find out why until very recently, when Jane Ardmore interviewed Jack as she's interviewed hundreds of people whose lives have touched mine. Jack explained how I arrived on the set every morning with my "entourage" (the job of hairdresser, costumer, et cetera, is constantly to *be* with the star to whom they're assigned, "entourage" indeed!), and, as we came in I uttered my "Good morning," "Good morning," "Good morning" to the men working high up on the lights, the set decorators, the camera crew, the man adjusting the boom. To Jack Palance, the *good mornings* were a "performance," "so artificial it turned my stomach," he said.

Well, I meant those *good mornings,* every one of them. Coming on a set each day is a homecoming to me, it's where I'm part of a team. What a pity Mr. Palance has never experienced being part of a team.

They've said I worked with the diligence of a ditch-digger being the great star. They're right. I've worked with the diligence of a ditch digger period. They say I'm too emotional and that's true—I've hated with a vengeance and loved with a passion. Criticism is a whip that forces us to analyze ourselves deeply for justice and injustice. I have yet to know an intelligent person who doesn't profit from the resultant self-knowledge.

In this business, columns and the people who write them are an essential element. If your name isn't in the columns, you're dead professionally. If your name is in, you're often dead personally. Don't believe for a moment that actors are lined up against columnists or columnists against actors. Columnists can be good friends, and living proof of that are, alphabetically speaking: Army Archerd, Harrison Carroll, Mike Connolly, Hy Gardner, Radie Harris, Irv Kupcinet, Hedda Hopper, Leonard Lyons, Louella Parsons, Earl Wilson, Walter Winchell and others.

Don't believe for a moment, either, that actresses can't be friends. I have found to the contrary—they grasp each other's problems and admire each other's talent. We're not the kind of women who have time for canasta, bridge, gossip over long luncheons or tea, however, and our lives carry us in different directions. Picture-making and theater engagements take my friends all over the world. I haven't seen Claudette Colbert or Barbara Stanwyck for a long while. Helen Hayes and I are staunch friends, sometimes only by letter. Hedda Hopper, Virginia Grey, Liza Wilson, Jan Sterling, Mary Martin, Jean Dixon, Margaret Sullavan—as long as she lived—these are friendships constant through time and space. Crowded as time is, and new people constantly added, it is important to keep in touch with valued friends.

It is a deep thrill to spend an evening with Cole Porter. I'm still friends with my first beau, Ray Sterling. I keep in touch with Johnny Arnold, Eddie Mannix, Sidney Guilaroff, many of the people I worked with at MGM. The one lost friendship that grieves me is that of Katherine Albert. She and her husband named their daughter Joan, and she grew into the talented and lovely Joan Evans, whose career as an actress was promising.

But Joan fell in love with Kirby Weatherly, and the only world she wanted was with him. Katherine couldn't sanction it. She asked them to wait until Joan was eighteen. They waited. They waited quite a bit longer. Joan and Kirby had had their marriage license for months when they dropped by my house one evening to discuss their problems.

Katherine thought I wanted to play the almighty Cupid. I didn't. It was for Katherine's sake as much as for my namesake's that I wanted these youngsters to be married in a home setting with someone close, rather than have them take off for a marriage mill in Reno. I called a judge, called Katherine, and Joan and Kirby were married that evening in my living room. It has been a good marriage, they have two darling babies. But Katherine has never forgiven me, and that's sad, because I've missed her.

But I must be grateful for the friendships I have kept. Many of them started with a fan letter and have continued through the years. It's natural when you become successful that you're sought out by people who would never notice you otherwise. You accept that. What compensates is the reaction of a public at large who recognizes you but doesn't intrude on that.

A group of teenagers used to follow me everywhere I went in New York. Their fun was in guessing where I'd go. Whenever my escort and I would emerge from my hotel, the group would be waiting.

They'd leap into six cabs, crying, "Follow that car!" They'd be there ahead of us to welcome me, and when we'd leave the theater or nightclub, our car would be waiting, the first one at the curb, with a path clear to it guarded by this group of fans.

Some of my escorts loathed this attention, some were annoyed by it, some basked in it. But the loyalty and faith of these friends bolstered my ego. It still does. Tremendously . . . because they're *givers* not *takers*. They know that I'm human, that I get tired, that my life is not all glamorous, not all easy; and they've been trying to help and protect me, from the first.

Whenever I come into New York today, five members of that original group are on hand to greet me. These girls all hold down responsible jobs. One is teaching school and doing remarkable work with retarded children, but at night and on weekends, they follow my activities. When I'm in need of extra secretarial help, aid in shopping, when I'm packing for a trip or desperately in need of someone to answer phones, they're always on hand.

In Los Angeles, another group: Milderene Muse, Helen Fullerton, Florence MacDonald, Dore Freeman, they are now mature, thoughtful friends who never intrude on my time—they give theirs. So does Dorothy Cochrane whom I met when she was dancing in the line at Earl Carroll's Theater Restaurant. Hymie Fink, one of the Hollywood photographers who was so kind to me, discovered pretty Dorothy was my fan and saw that we met. She has given me loyalty, friendship and one hundred and three scrapbooks carefully annotating my life and career.

Betty Barker, whom I've mentioned, is one of the most wonderful people in my world. She is today my full-time secretary and has traveled all over the world with me. Bettina has a life and interests of her own. Her love, understanding and faith I depend on religiously. And there is Gerrie Greuner whom I met through the fan club. Gerrie, too, has a life of her own in Hartford, Connecticut, a husband and child; but from time to time she comes to New York when she knows I'm bogged down with an unending amount of work. Gerrie asks nothing of me. She answers phones, takes dictation, all so quietly, so calmly, I call her "Quiet Girl."

All these people, an integral part of my life, came to me because of my career. So did these three outstanding men: Pete Smith, Carey Wilson, Frank Whitbeck, mentors of mine at MGM. I love them not just because they helped bring me up but because they have what men should have—guts. And I don't mean this in a vulgar sense. I mean intellectual, physical and mental vitality. When I asked a question, these gentlemen always *explained;* they told me truths that in my youth and inexperience I found it hard to accept at the time, but I learned.

Unfortunately, everything we learn from life comes slowly, wisdom especially, and yet wisdom is the only thing that gives beauty or depth of character. I agree with Daddy Wood that schooling is not the end and all of education—you have to keep developing the curiosity and the ability to learn. He envisaged a college for women forty and over; by that age, he said, they have developed the capacity and desire for learning. For example, Grandma Moses!

Nothing could be more pathetic than those who fear age instead of looking forward to maturity. I believe if you live day by day for each God-given hour, you are preparing for the future and a good one. You must be grateful for what you have, discontent with what you've achieved; I've always wanted the woman I am to be the foundation for the woman I can be.

My friend June Taylor had some suggestions about what should be included in this autobiography. "I want to know where that iron strength of yours comes from," she said. "You must have had heartbreak. I want to know about it. I want to know how you survived and overcame it. So does every other woman. What's the secret?"

The answer to that—a capacity for living develops through a determination to grow with each experience, happy or otherwise. Enemies have value, sometimes you can turn them into friends. Mistakes can be valuable too. The point is not to let mistakes destroy you, get rid of the guilt. Say, "I'm wrong, I'm sorry," then try never to make the same mistake again. There'll be plenty of new ones, heaven knows. Everyone wants to be right. Since that's impossible let's just settle for being human. I've nothing to be ashamed of except my personal limitations.

The actress craves a challenge. The woman does also, but her challenge is love, her challenge is security and peace of mind. The woman is concerned with every facet of living, a love of life, a love of love; the woman in me doesn't deviate, she's always known what she wanted.

Certainly there was heartbreak. In the ten years I was alone, I was terribly lonely. I dated—in ten years there have to be some men to whom you look like a woman—but unfortunately an actress often attracts men who see her as a glamour symbol but have no wish to be involved with a long-term relationship. And the casual affair is not for me.

I filled my life with work, with the children, and gradually with faith. It took me a long while to stop fighting frantically and let Him help, but I learned. No one goes the long road alone. God is an inexhaustible source. This I know, but sometimes I get in His way.

What has always bored me is the harping of the length of my career and my damned durability. So I've had the longest career in Hollywood. Mine was an early start, personal unhappiness and good health. As early as 1954 they were calling me "The Last Movie Queen." I'm no queen. I started as a hoofer in a chorus line and by hard work and good breaks became, I hope, an actress. More than that—again I hope—I've become a woman, learning and growing. I believe in *now*. Looking backward is negative and I like to think of myself as affirmative, with God's help a flier, not a pedestrian.

ELEVEN

On the eve of New Year 1955 we were shooting *Female on the Beach* at Universal. At 1:30 p.m. production stopped and we gathered on stage twelve for a buffet luncheon. In Hollywood on the day before Christmas and New Year's, shooting always stops at this time. Each person is permitted only one drink and by three o'clock everyone who is leaving the lot is asked to be on his way to insure safe driving. Director Joe Pevney, cameraman Charles Lang, Jeff Chandler, Jan Sterling and I toasted the new year and each other, had our lunch, now they had gone.

I went to my dressing room, dictated into my sound scriber, studied my script, the day flew. Far too tired to essay the trip home to Brentwood through holiday traffic, I ordered dinner sent in and phoned the children. They were in their pajamas already, eager for tomorrow's festivities. I explained that it was now dark, people were on the road after cocktail parties and I didn't want to drive at such a time. They understood and I promised to be home early in the morning, in time for breakfast.

Night swept across the empty studio, blotting out the village of tiny houses, swallowing the great sound stages. My dinner eaten, the dishes removed, I dictated additional letters into the sound scriber. Finally it was time to curl up with a stack of newspapers and await the new year. When the phone rang, it created a shocking clatter. Earl Blackwell was calling from Las Vegas, he was with a party of friends, they sounded very convivial as each one came on to speak with me.

"This is Al Steele," said a quiet male voice. "Happy New Year, dear."

I'd known Alfred and his wife, Lillian, casually for five years. They were friends of the Werblins and we'd met in New York at dinner parties. Alfred was a most attractive man, president of Pepsi-Cola. He'd been a football player and he looked it, solidly built, heavy-muscled but graceful, with salt-and-pepper hair, a quick grin and merry blue eyes. What had impressed me was the sense of power he conveyed so quietly, the tenor of his conversation. He was one of the best-informed men I'd ever met, tuned to the world's turning. Exciting, but quiet, almost, for some reason, subdued.

"Where are you, Joan?" he was saying. "What party?"

"I'm in my dressing room."

"*Where?*"

"In my dressing room . . . at the studio."

"Alone?"

"Yes."

There was dead silence, then he shouted, "For heaven's sake, girl, why?"

"Why kick up a storm unless there's someone you really want to kick up a storm with?" I laughed. "I don't particularly like New Year's Eve parties. I've been living here at the studio for weeks. To me, tonight is just another night."

We chatted briefly about his flying west on business, I said I hoped to see him and his wife. Only a few days later I read of trouble in the Steele household and in short order, news of a divorce action. Some strange little shiver of anticipation accompanied that news. If it's right, I thought, we'll meet again.

We did, eventually. First I had to live through the fright and fulfillment of *Female on the Beach*. Then I launched into the drama of a thoroughly selfish bitch, *Queen Bee*. Columbia had purchased the Edna Lee novel, and Randy MacDougall, who had written *Mildred Pierce* and who had always wanted a crack at directing, was signed at my request as writer-director. Jerry Wald produced. This is the picture where two men and the entire audience want to murder me, for the character I portray.

Sonny and Leah Ray Werblin came west, and one evening there was a party in their honor at Joseph Cotten's. There would be just six of us . . . would I come? I almost didn't accept the invitation because working so arduously, I didn't see how I could make it by six thirty. But *he* was going to be there. I wore a white chiffon dress, a white mink stole and made it by six thirty-five. Alfred was waiting. It was as if he'd been waiting a long while. He gave me the dearest look I have ever seen on a man's face, took my hand and never let it go. A good friend of ours, Alfred's masseur, Gunnar Ohberg, once said that the flintiest of souls couldn't help but respond when Alfred turned his heart's warmth on them, his was the art of breaking down all the barriers that keep human beings shut within walls of self.

I remember every moment of that evening and that heart's warmth. At dinner we talked of his travels, the world he was conquering for Pepsi like Marco Polo. There were new bottling plants in Iraq, in South Africa and the Belgian Congo, and he was dreaming further. I'd never met anyone quite like him, a man who invested big business with a romantic challenge, a buccaneer in French cuffs. He was not only strong, he was gentle, his was a boyish quality very charming in a high-powered executive.

After dinner he got out a map and indicated all the farflung places he had been. He showed me Caracas seven thousand miles away, he was embarking by air for Caracas in a few days.

"It must be exhilarating to travel," I said, and he answered:

"We will. We'll see a world you never knew existed, Joan."

I found myself *longing* to travel. For years I'd been reluctant to leave Hollywood for one minute—they might forget me, I might miss a good script, a *Mildred Pierce* might come along and I'd not be there. Now I was eager to travel and I was afraid of many things, of planes, for example.

"Planes! I've been known to walk fourteen flights of stairs to avoid elevators," I told Alfred.

He just smiled, showing me the map, and told me how many hours it took to fly from Caracas to Los Angeles. He'd return to see me, he said, he'd have twenty hours before flying back to New York for a Monday morning conference. Seven thousand miles for twenty *hours?* I thought. But you knew that whatever this man said he'd do, he'd do. He arrived back in Hollywood on a Saturday and spent the day on the set watching us shoot. It seemed unfair for him to sit on a sound stage, this active man!

At dinner that night he said, "Joan, I'm going to marry you." He never did get around to *asking* me. Just "I'm going to marry you," and a few hours later, he was gone. But there was never a question, never a reservation in his mind or mine, I was going to be his wife.

The chemistry was right and beyond chemistry, a breath-taking premonition of new horizons, a way of life.

On his next visit Alfred spent most of the time at our house so the children could become acquainted with him. He had two children of his own, grown-up Sally by one marriage and seven-year-old Sonny by another. Devoted to them, he understood how I felt about my children and never for a moment either patronized them or relegated them to the background as some suitors have. He talked to their comprehension, not only to that of the older children but to that of Cindy and Cathy, who were only eight.

One Sunday morning the twins, Alfred, and I were having brunch at our house, and when we had finished, Alfred lit a cigarette and handed it to me across the table. Two amazed pairs of eyes, round as dollars, followed this transaction.

Cathy said, "You must like him very much, Mummie, to do that."

"I do, darling. I *love* him very much."

Two knives and two forks dropped. They've heard me speak of love all their lives, "I love you" every day of the world to them and to their sister and brother; but this was the first time they had ever heard me apply the word to a man. Alfred was darling. He said:

"I'm going to marry your mother, do you mind?"

Cathy said, "I don't know."

Cindy said, "I'm glad. Now we can have another baby."

"Darlings," I said, "we've had all the babies we're going to have in this family. The next one'll be yours."

"I think we'll all have a baby," insisted Cindy, and she was right in a way. The baby was Sonny. He and the twins were just heaven together. But that came later.

On his next visit to Los Angeles, Alfred brought along his own lit-tle plane, the Pepsi Lodestar, "just in case you want to take a ride. I'll never force you, darling, but if you should want to just taxi out to Santa Monica or Palm Springs or Las Vegas . . ." He didn't mention it again.

Our wedding was planned for May 24. The Werblins were going to give us a glamorous garden wedding at their home in New Jersey. Then we'd sail on the twenty-sixth for Europe. My wedding ring of tapered baguettes in a platinum sheath was being made by Ruser, the diamonds had been cut in Antwerp, Jean Louis had designed my trousseau, including a white satin wedding dress and coat trimmed in swirls of silver beads. There were my clothes from *Queen Bee*, which I bought, and cruise clothes, and dozens of hats from Rex and the most luscious embroidered lingerie you can imagine. Alfred had four enormous trunks designed for me so that nothing need be folded, plus several boxes to carry hats, shoes and cosmetics.

About now we discovered that the guest list for our wedding party had grown to five hundred!

On the evening of May 9 we were having dinner at Romanoff's when Alfred suddenly leaned toward me and whispered:

"Let's fly to Las Vegas and be married, Joan, right now."

And I said, "All right, darling."

"Or do you want the big garden party?"

"Who *me?*"

"I'll phone Luke (pilot Luke Moseley) and tell him to warm up the plane."

He left the table to phone while I sat wondering if I would really be able to fly. Would I find myself at the airport, a grown woman sud-denly reduced to the panic of a child? Alfred returned. Luke, he said, had not been too surprised, but copilot John Hughes was at a movie. We kidded him ever after. "Seen any good movies lately, John?"

There were a number of us at dinner that night, but no one was aware of our plan except my good friends, the Andrew Fullers, who were visiting from Texas. I spirited Gerrie Fuller to the powder room, Alfred got word to Andy, we four disappeared right from under the noses of eight Pepsi executives who were flying out that night by commercial plane to New York.

"See you in New York day after tomorrow," they called to Alfred. By the time they arrived in New York and picked up the papers, we were married.

For fly I certainly did. Alfred led me into the plane, kept my hand warm in his and I found myself rising into the air without the slightest trepidation. Over the San Gabriel mountains he held me in his arms while moonlight shone silver on our wings.

"We're up eleven thousand feet, Joan, we're going higher, the mountains will grow smaller and smaller." Alfred kept describing the terrain, the cloud formations, he explained about weather, what caused air pockets. He had chosen, of course, a night that flowed past us like dark silk. At midnight we circled Las Vegas three times and glided gently to earth.

For the next month he told everyone we met, "You should see my girl fly."

When he'd phoned Luke, Alfred had also phoned Ben and Dottie Goffstein in Las Vegas and those dear people managed all arrangements as if they'd had two months rather than two hours. They were waiting at the airport, took us to the courthouse where our license was waiting to be signed, then whisked us to their handsome penthouse at the Flamingo Hotel where Municipal Judge Ben Mendoza married us at 2:10 a.m., May 10. No photographers, no reporters, no TV cameras. Dottie loaned me her wedding ring, Bert Knighton stood up with Alfred as best man, but he didn't have to support my fella—I never saw a man with such ease and when I said so, he laughed. He'd spent his whole life preparing for just this, he said.

Everyone was sympathetically radiant . . . the suite filled with flowers . . . the elaborate wedding cake . . . phone calls . . . I called the older children to tell them of our marriage, at six when I knew they'd be getting up at school . . . called the twins at seven—they were delighted . . . and all the while Alfred looked at me as if he were the boy from Nashville who'd finally found love.

He'd found love all right, but my Alfred was no boy from Nashville. He was dynamic, a titan in his way, slow to anger, thoughtful, a stubborn man who had complete confidence in himself, a man of immense talents and in a burning hurry to use all of them, a man who made $150,000 a year and knew if he lost that, he'd go across the street and make $175,000. I didn't assess Alfred's business acumen when I married him. I recognized it later as we worked together and had time together.

We sailed on the twenty-sixth on the *United States* for a honeymoon that turned into a battle royal. We were madly in love, yes, but we were also a strong mature man and woman, each used to his own way and not about to relinquish it. Alfred had evidently been warned by countless associates that a movie star is self-centered and just naturally annihilates men, that he'd have to subdue me and show me from the beginning who was boss. This I was not prepared for. He'd been a persuasive wooer, a passionate bridegroom, now I met a streak of bullheaded obstinacy that frightened me. I had longed all my life for a strong lover, but I wouldn't be bullied. And I wasn't going to play a part I couldn't maintain. I'd done that before.

What Alfred didn't realize was that movie star or no, I was a woman and needed reassurance.

What I didn't realize about Alfred was that he not only loved business, he lived, ate, slept and breathed it, and his business associates were literally his family. His social life and business life were one and the same. All the Pepsi people are hand-picked men, intimate as brothers. Most of them were happy in Alfred's romance and marriage, but a few of them weren't buying. I was Hollywood, they thought, and how would Wall Street react to that? They probably thought I'd spirit him away, that with me he'd spend his life lolling about a west-coast swimming pool. Sensing the lack of enthusiasm among these few, I didn't *let* them know me. To them, the company was the most important thing in the world, a holy grail. To me, our marriage was.

I found myself in a whole new world, a world where you couldn't plan. Oh, you *might* plan, three for dinner, let's say, and at the last minute find yourself confronted with forty-five. I had to learn to play it by ear. Within a year, as Alfred's cohorts discovered I'd made him a happy man, that his happiness was reflected a thousand-fold in his business prowess, they came not only to accept me but to share with me the magnificent warmth they felt for him. It just took a little *time*. It took *us* time too.

How often Alfred and I laughed about our honeymoon. We spent it at my friend Bob Hornstein's lovely villa in Capri, and before we left, Alfred bought me a superb diamond plume, the coat of arms of a noble Capri family. He always said I'd earned those diamonds, they were my service stripes. We'd pitted strength against strength at Capri. It was an impasse.

We came back to this country, Alfred to Pepsi, I to fulfill my picture commitment at Columbia. The film was *Autumn Leaves,* with Bob Aldrich as director. I must say that I was glad to get back to work, back to a world with which I was familiar. I had a lot of suffering to do in this picture. It was easy. I was suffering over the uneasiness of my marriage.

When Alfred came west he found me living in my little eight-by-ten dressing room, as I do when I'm filming—but as a brand-new bride shouldn't. I began to change in his eyes from a pampered darling in chiffon to a woman who worked as hard as he did. When he understood my dedication to my profession, he began talking about *his.* He was full of plans for the Pepsi convention at the Fontainebleau in Florida. When I understood how important this was to him, I made it a stipulation in my contract to the studio—I'd go out on tour to plug *Queen Bee* on condition that I could have one week off to join Alfred at convention time in Florida.

And this, in reality, was our honeymoon. Not Capri where we had the most romantic setting in the world, but the Pepsi convention where we were surrounded by hundreds of bottlers and their families and I was accepted finally into Alfred's world.

I listened eagerly at this convention. I attended every session. I realized that what Alfred had accomplished in five years could not even begin to be evaluated. New plants, new trucks, equipment and material, increase in stock value, earnings, credit, and taxes paid—but more important, the bringing together of a group of men who could work alongside him in complete harmony, new jobs that had been created where none had existed, jobs that were the backbone of numerous families. Who could measure the community of people whose livelihood and happiness stemmed from him and his stubborn belief that people *can* work together as a team? This was something I thoroughly understood.

I found myself falling in love with this great family and they saw that we *were* a team. I gave myself to Alfred irrevocably at that convention, and he discovered that when a career woman lets her hair down and opens her heart, she's the biggest clinging vine in history—not excepting Juliet. I opened my heart completely because I discovered he *needed* me. Tough as he was, strong and professional, this man needed a wife; and from that moment, Alfred Steele was the tenderest of men and I the gentlest of women. We not only loved each other, we watched over each other, we were able to lean a little and share a lot.

At Christmas that first year, Alfred took the four children and me to Switzerland to St. Moritz. It was strictly *Please Don't Eat the Daisies*. Christina and Christopher skied all day, ate lunch four thousand feet above us at the ski club, and were exhausted by teatime. The twins didn't understand about altitude at all and were sleepy and irritable. At four thirty we'd have tea or bouillon and try to get everyone rested for dinner. Alfred never complained, but he kept explaining to me why the children were so weary, and I gradually perceived that he was weary too, that altitude did not agree with him. Next time we went to Switzerland, I insisted we go to Gstaad—with a lower altitude. I knew how hard he was working, I wanted him to have peace and comfort on these rare vacations. And he insisted we take the twins—he wanted me to have the joy of my twins. I worried about his need for *his* children, especially young Sonny.

Our marriage had been a surprise to Sonny, he hadn't been prepared, and it was a year before we had the privilege of having him with us for a three-week vacation in California. Alfred had arranged for us to fly west. But another thought occurred to me.

"Alfred, we've been married a whole year, darling, and I've never met this little boy. Let's go by train, please. Give us two days and three nights on the train, let Sonny get used to me first and let me prepare him for the twins and the other life in California." And it worked, oh, how well it worked. This is a most responsive boy, so like his father it was startling! Alfred marveled at our closeness, the way the child would say, "Please say my prayers with me, Joan, the way you do with Cindy and Cathy." Sonny, Cindy and Cathy were like pixies together, and he was with us three times, once for a whole summer in Europe.

Alfred's daughter Sally we met in Paris when we were on our honeymoon. She was traveling with three other girls in a Volkswagen that summer. I got to know her better when she, her husband, John Comer, and their seven-month-old baby came to visit us in California. Sonny was with us at the time, the Comers stayed nearby, and we were a family for three weeks. There was softball in the garden and a trip to Disneyland. How Alfred enjoyed the hippo going up the Amazon River! Alfred loved Sally and really believed he had raised her, but the fact is, he hadn't been home much and she'd been a rather lonely little girl, something I can spot at twenty paces. We were able to bolster each other's thinking, Alfred and I.

We worked together like two human beings should. In California, he learned to bring his business to our home, the first time he had ever essayed such a program, and he found it most effective. It was as if my home had been planned for just such use, and in a way it had. There were areas for work, for activity and for quiet. When I had to concentrate I had always used the garden or the theater, they were for me a world apart. Alfred could work quietly in the garden with one man or twenty, work the whole morning, interrupted only when I'd announce lunch.

Afternoons, he'd meet a second group in the theater and brief them on what had transpired in the morning. The only interruption, cocktails and dinner.

When we returned from California to New York, he was longing to repeat this pattern, and I was longing to have him repeat it. Indeed, this became our way of life. My joy was to have a home where Alfred could entertain national and international business executives—he needed an atmosphere of relaxation to ease some of the pressure from his frantic schedule—and my job was to transfer to New York the peaceful atmosphere he'd enjoyed in California.

He'd call at four thirty to ask could he bring his five o'clock conference home and there'd be another group at six and perhaps another at seven. *Could* he! I'd have tea waiting in the den. When the six o'clock group appeared, I would serve them in the living room until Alfred was free and could take over. At seven, a new group. Alfred would insist on my joining them. He knew I wanted to learn more about the business. Besides, he wanted to have me see him in action. There was a lovely strain of ham in both of us. As soon as he'd accomplished his conference goal, I'd alert Pauline it was time to serve a buffet dinner.

Pauline is the understanding woman who keeps this house, and what a job she does! There was a time, when I was first alone, when she did not take a day off for six months. Some people are overwhelmed by strong personalities, Pauline is stimulated. Our three-ring international circus has interested her, she enjoys the flow of visitors from everywhere. She has great devotion, she's as much a perfectionist as I am, and she puts up with me, the first "madame" she's ever known who cooks in her own kitchen.

When Alfred and I were home for an evening alone, I'd listen to him discuss business. It was wonderful to know he trusted me, and I was his sounding board for sales problems, personnel, the techniques of advertising in widely varied situations, and the scale of Pepsi-Cola operations not only in this country but as far as the African jungles. It *is* women who buy a majority of the products sold in this world, so a marketing man welcomes a woman's point of view, and Alfred invited mine. He had instinct for spotting a good marketing man. He welded together a team of executives and gave them his enthusiasm like a transfusion. Company progress depended on this team, so did Alfred's well-being.

His world and mine was opening wider every moment. He had his heart set on an expanding international organization, and there was no question about my traveling with him. I'd waited a long time to be a wife. He'd waited a long time for a wife who would want to travel with him and who had some knowledge of the incredible working hours that go into a dedicated job. I who had dreaded flying, flew with my husband more than two hundred thousand miles, so we could officiate at plant openings in the States and abroad.

Hard to do? Not a bit. I'd always said that if I ever found a perfect love, I'd give up everything for it. Alfred loved my strength, he didn't resent it. He always said I looked, acted and behaved like a lady, but, thank God, I could think like a man. And he felt reinforced by that thinking, he had someone to talk *with*.

Two hundred thousand miles—Africa or Mexico, Beirut or Joplin, Missouri, Switzerland, the Belgian Congo, people were waiting to say hello. You should have seen the look on my husband's face when we arrived at Lourenco Marques in Mozambique, East Africa! It was seven in the morning, hot, humid and sticky, purple thunderclouds presaged a downpour, but there were thousands at the airport, screaming their welcome. It took an hour to extricate us and get us to our press conference. This was part of our schedule wherever we went—press conferences the first thing in the morning. Alfred would speak to the financial editors and news reporters, I would speak to women editors and movie critics. Early in our marriage I heard Alfred at a conference in the den saying definitely, "No, I won't ask my wife to do this."

"Do what?" I said, beckoning him into the other room.

"I won't use your talent and name to sell our product."

"And why not?" I said.

"That's not why I married you!"

"Of course it isn't. But *if* this is something I have, *if* it's useable, *if* it's saleable, use it."

It was a pleasure to work with him, to help him handle the multiple facets of a business situation. "My bride!" he told an associate when we came back from Africa. "She wrapped 'em up in little spitballs, pally." He hadn't expected to share his business, he'd had no idea I'd care. Now he shared with me as if the company were our child. At conventions, when the other Pepsi wives discovered that I went to business meetings, they began attending too.

In our organization there are seventy-five district managers, ten regional managers, twenty plant managers, and five hundred ten independent owner-managers. Everywhere we went he carried a team of experts and presided at meetings dedicated to marketing and advertising. By the time of our last tour we found 33⅓ percent of the wives were attending these sessions right with me and enjoying them. Some confided that they'd been afraid they weren't business-minded. Attending sessions, they found that any woman who loves a man can be business-minded. With a little concentration, a wife can equip herself to understand a man's business problems and many Pepsi wives have found as I have, the stimulation and excitement of big business.

In Denmark we had a press conference, and one of the reporters, enjoying an ice-cold drink, asked why our product wasn't sold in Denmark? Alfred was busy with another group, so I answered simply that we were taxed out of the market, which seemed hardly fair considering that America imports so much Danish beer, silver, laces and other products. The next day my comments were streaming in bold black headlines across the front pages of Danish newspapers. Alfred told a press conference that "I don't like to think of my wife in terms of a business asset, but she is definitely a tremendous part of our goodwill."

For the first time in my life a man was giving me emotional security. A woman has to be loved. *If* she's told so and believes it, she's happy. He was loving me for what I am, and he was the first thing in my life.

Gunnar Ohberg says:

"Alfred was the catalyst. He brought Joan's personality to maturity. He made her all woman. They worked strictly *mano a mano.*"

Dr. Henry Nachtigall says:

"Joan was the catalyst. She brought out in Alfred something that was never there before, a humility, a sensitivity, the ability to feel and understand. She brought his personality to maturity."

They're both right. Love was the catalyst and brought both of us up to the best we could be. Ours was a romance that accelerated constantly within marriage, rather than, as in so many cases, dwindling down within marriage. We attained a precious height—the ability to love each other beyond the love of self.

TWELVE

You can't do a line drawing of Alfred. A full painting is called for. Few men in life touch and affect so many. He listened, grasped concepts quickly, cracked through all negative thought and apprehension. He said he bought only champions, I felt he made them. He created an atmosphere in which a man could grow. And a woman too.

His talent was people, his religion was people. He was never confused between the relative value of a dollar and the value of a man. "Historically," he told me, "two people standing together have always been able to lick the world. The important thing isn't money, not plants, product, trucks or glass. It's men. When you can't get a knife between two guys, and when they *know* it, they're invincible."

"Like us," I said, and he bought that.

His philosophy rubbed off on everyone. And it was a philosophy based on his own zest and naturalness—he never violated nature.

In Mexico, three years ago, I was so avid for a picnic in the wilderness that Alfred gave in, somewhat reluctantly, I thought. I found a lush, beautiful spot, reminiscent of *Green Mansions* and, Romantic

Annie, sat there with my feet in the cool water of a little brook, eating fried chicken. Alfred kept glancing about, appraising the undergrowth. The twins were with us, and the minute we'd finished our lunch he sent them plodding up the incline to our car. When I loitered, he gave me a quick hurrying pat on the rear.

"Honey, it's hot, don't make me hurry," I moaned.

At which, he picked me up and literally threw me four feet. He quickly followed, pushed me into the car and slammed the door. This wasn't *like* Alfred. I sat in the car silent, I don't like being shoved. He appraised my petulance and corrected it in nothing flat.

"Honey," he said, *"tarantulas* are deadly poison."

Medicine and medical science engrossed Alfred, and one of his closest friends was Henry Nachtigall, M.D., FACP (Fellow of The American College of Physicians), medical director of Pepsi-Cola. With the doctor he'd make the rounds at the hospital, not morbidly, but with mature insight. He was devoted to Henry, he wanted to know *his* world. Also he was interested in medicine in terms of a health program for the company. People in business wear a heavy suit of tension, and that tension affects disastrously glands and muscles. To have a great organization and not safeguard it, he said, is like having expensive machinery and no expert to protect it. The only one Alfred short-changed was himself. He was constantly drawing on extra reserves of energy and traveling too fast to catch up.

Herbert Barnet was aware of this. Herbert had become president of the company in 1955 when Alfred became Chairman of the Board and they worked together in close and perfect harmony. Herbert, the doctor and I all tried to help my husband avoid fatigue, but Alfred was always fighting beyond his weight and he stimulated others to do the same.

In his organization he wanted only the best. His phrasemaking was classic. "You can't start with a punk, you can never teach a punk to be a good guy," he'd say. "A guy who'll steal with you will steal from you." "As a company expands, the guys who haven't got it to start with, crumble. You can hear them splatter. They march bravely to the front and cave in."

Like most unusual people I don't think he knew exactly the source of his inspiration. It was born at the instant and stemmed from an acute sensitivity. To one man who was very dear to him and who had just recovered from a serious operation he said, "Don't you ever be sick like that again, remember, you are immortal."

He could be ruthless with the opposition: "You don't stab the king, you kill him," but he could turn around and show a delicate consideration for someone, the matron of the building perhaps, who used to serve his lunch in the days when he'd first joined the company. I was with him once when he caught sight of her at work with her dust mop as we came off the elevator. He strode across the hall and kissed her. "Him, the Chairman," as she said.

You never knew where he might go, to California or Istanbul on a moment's notice. He mislaid tickets, arrived without them and was admitted just the same. He was a man with no ceiling, as Luke, our pilot says, coming out of the weather shack smiling, "V.A.C.U." (visibility and ceiling unlimited).

In the fall of 1956 we went abroad. I had signed, before we were married, to make a film in England. *The Story of Esther Costello.* Alfred had much work to do on the Continent and we could make the trip together. The press met us at Southampton and accompanied us back to London on the boat train. Waiting at the Dorchester were hundreds of fans who cheered when a Pepsi truck came down the street carrying our luggage. I kept the clipping from the London *Daily Mail.*

Durable and amazing, [went the story]. She arrived in the almost forgotten manner of the great stars. She brought 28 suitcases, 48 film costumes, one trunk of furs and a millionaire husband.

How Alfred laughed at that description of us! We had been worried, frankly, because I'd never made a picture in Britain. We had more than an inkling of an idea what their attitude might be. American actresses had been getting a very rough press. Our apprehension was short-lived. I was given a luncheon at once by the London Critics Circle—a rare honor, as our British friends explained to us. These critics are usually the honored guests rather than the gracious hosts. Top critics turned out en masse for this luncheon at the Café Royal, and Rossiter Shepherd, chairman of the Circle's film section, presented me with a beautiful citation. Alfred kept holding my hand under the table, he knew how I felt in prospect of my twelve-minute speech to be televised over BBC. The following night, producers Jimmy and John Woolf threw a welcoming party at Les Ambassadeurs, there was open-air dancing and champagne, friends from everywhere.

Then on October 29 I was to be presented to Queen Elizabeth. I was thrilled, but anxious. That half-way curtsy was rehearsed more than any scene for any picture I ever made. My worry was needless. I found the Queen so warm and gracious, also Princess Margaret, and both far more beautiful than they photograph. We were presented in the foyer of the Empire Theater, then were again presented on the stage, to the audience, including the Royal Family. Stages have always appalled me, but somehow I managed, first to bow to the audience, then to the Queen's box, then to back offstage—something that only occurred to me as I found myself doing it, but a lucky gesture, for it brought down the house.

Our picture was to take three months and I had a work permit for that period, but because of constant strikes and labor unrest, my permit had to be renewed and we actually finished shooting two days before that second permit expired.

What made *The Story of Esther Costello* a delight, in spite of all outside annoyances, was working with Heather Sears. This twenty-one-year-old girl gave a memorable performance with her "mute," wistful smile, her shining "sightless" eyes. It was a reward to work with one so young who knew so much about character and acting. But while in the film I was breaking successfully through the wall of silence to this child, I was having trouble in reality with a child of my own. Christopher ran away from school.

Alfred had been taxiing into London every weekend from Canada, Madrid, Rome, Egypt or New York—where he went to attend board meetings—now he had joined me for a brief respite while I finished the picture. When we heard about Christopher, Alfred left at once for America. He talked with the boy, trying to establish a rapport, and found a school for him in Arizona with emphasis on horses, sports and outdoor activities. Alfred felt, as I did, that Christopher's run-aways had something to do with a lack of physical activity, that he needed a more rugged outdoor life. With Chris in this new school, Alfred returned to New York to Pepsi business, then he checked once more on Christopher before leaving the country.

He'd been gone three weeks—the only time we were ever separated like that—and made it back to London just in time for Thanksgiving. He brought me a home-cooked turkey, mince pie, pumpkin pie and the news that all was well with Christopher. "We can have a happy Thanksgiving, darling." Well now, we'd just started that Thanksgiving feast when the telephone rang. It was Arizona calling. Christopher had done it again!

My son was one of the few problems in this world that I couldn't solve. Alfred started out thinking I had been too strict a disciplinarian, he ended up thinking I hadn't been half strict enough.

Christopher just plainly didn't like school, and his pattern was to run. Each school told me the same thing: "This boy doesn't *want* to attend classes, he *won't* attend classes and we can't *carry* him to classes." At nineteen, he has found for the first time that school has a purpose—he can't get a job without a high school diploma and he's admitted it. I've just received a letter that says, "Mother, you said it all enough times so that I should have remembered . . . that education was important, that life wasn't just one long game. Now that I need a good job, I find you were right, I cannot get one without that little piece of paper called a diploma."

After Alfred's and my arduous schedules in Europe, we went to Jamaica for a week's rest. Here, our glass-louvered doors stood open to the magic of Half Moon Bay, the limestone walks bordered with lace-leaf plants, the magenta spikes of cocoa plants, bougainvillea and hibiscus. We loved our cottage, and beyond, the turquoise water of the offing, then the white ring of surf breaking endlessly on the coral barrier reef, and beyond that, Caribbean indigo.

We'd swim four or five times a day, walk along the beach, sunbathe, read to each other. But there were days when we did nothing. . . . Just watched the sea, hand in hand, watched the tropical rain clouds, an occasional passerby, a graceful woman with a bundle on her head, a white-coated waiter carrying a huge breakfast tray on his head, a native fisherman selling deep-sea conches from his dug-out canoe. We played gin rummy for hours. A woman can do a great deal for a man if he understands how to help her help him. And at night we'd breathe the lovely air and listen to the Calypso singers, the hoarse melodic voices, the careless perfection of their timing. . . .

It's sheer heaven to find love and be loved in return. We were totally content with each other, with the beauty of the bay, the rhythm of the restless trade winds, the soft murmur of the water.

Alfred was capable of love because he honored himself. Does that sound selfish? It isn't. We all want to give, but we give out of spiritual riches—not out of spiritual poverty. There are many things you learn in a good marriage. I learned that you don't use sex, you give it. When you finally find someone you love and give enough of yourself, you can eventually have the most beautiful marriage in the world.

From the peace and calm of Jamaica we were to plunge into eight weeks of Alfred's ADorama tour, the climax of all he'd done for Pepsi-Cola. I knew how strenuous this would be, how strenuous our life *was*—we worked right through weekends always—and I made my husband promise me that once this tour was concluded, we'd try a new schedule, work four weeks, rest a week, straight through the year. Dr. Nachtigall was so pleased with this plan.

And the ADorama tour *was* the ultimate in pressure, travel-ing from city to city, as tough as a political campaign. In each city Alfred conducted his brilliant discussions on advertising for the bottlers. His last speech was in Washington and he was terribly tired, I could sense this without his saying, as I could sense his every thought and gesture.

He knew I knew. He looked at me that night in Washington and said, "I don't know what to say tomorrow, darling. I'm so tired."

So I urged him to go to bed; and when he had, I wrote him some notes to glance at later. "I know you'll be up about four as you always are, dearest. Your fruit and cheese and milk are in the cooler. And for your speech, darling, I'm jotting down a few suggestions. You'd think of these things anyhow, but there may be constant interruptions in the morning and these notes may serve as reminders." I also attached lists of names so he'd have them at his fingertips.

At breakfast he seemed refreshed, but later I saw he was fighting for energy after a long morning of discussions, and I whispered, "Alfred, I've had you alone so little, let's have a quiet lunch, just the two of us in our suite." I knew he'd say yes—I'd already ordered lunch at breakfast time. That afternoon he presented the Multiple Sclerosis Society citation to Senator John F. Kennedy and then he made his last ADorama speech—not only a brilliant speech but one that came right from his heart. I sat there proudly, as always at the very back of the hall, with an empty seat beside me for Alfred when he was finished. That day he gave each of his key men credit for his specific brand of talent, thanked all of them who'd traveled with him so hard and fast on these one-night stands. And then he said, looking straight down the hall:

"And I want to thank you, my darling wife, for your untiring dedication to me as a man and to Pepsi. You've helped me so. Everyone who's ever met you knows how much."

I sat there weeping. Here was the recognition, the love and gentleness I'd longed for. A minute later Alfred was seated beside me, holding my hand, and I suddenly realized the whole room was standing, applauding his warm speech.

We concluded in Washington that night, a Friday, and returned to New York the following day. Monday we were to leave for Jamaica and rest. Alfred had had ten years of uncompromising activity. He'd built Pepsi-Cola from a company trailing its nearest competitor one to six, to a first-rate company now edging up on its competition one to two, and in some areas outselling it. Sales were increased three-fold, profits tenfold; he changed the company's approach from quantity to quality, lowered the sweetness of the product, standardized that product, put it in vending machines, changed advertising policies and opened a vast world market, whose plants were put into the ownership, into the hands of local people.

But there was still so much more he wanted to accomplish. He and Herbert were working on a ten-year plan. Alfred asked Dr. Nachtigall to come to the house that first afternoon of our return to discuss a ten-year plan for the conservation of energy for all Pepsi executives. Alfred was so weary, he was subdued as I had never seen him, but he still made his points, what he wanted for that company.

I'll always remember them saying good-bye. Alfred was halfway up the steps when I reminded him he hadn't taken leave of Henry. He turned, came down a step or two, and Henry ran up.

"I never say good-bye to you, my friend!" Alfred said, and for a moment, they grasped each other's arms.

Alfred had an appointment with an advertising man from five to eight. Then I cooked dinner and Pauline tiptoed around, serving us at the card table in the living room while we watched Perry Como on TV. The room was dark, except for points of light on the paintings, and the television screen. Our great windows quivered with the myriad lights that salt a New York sky.

After dinner we went upstairs. I wasn't sleepy, I was so excited about Jamaica. Alfred's birthday was the following Friday. I'd already packed the presents. Now he suggested we play a hand of gin rummy.

He fell asleep playing. As I took the cards from that strong hand of his, he woke, took my hand and said:

"Darling, there has never been a man as happy as I. Thank you for making me so happy." Then he gave me a very special look. "I want you to know this, Joan—no man has ever loved a woman as I love you. I never knew what marriage was."

"Neither did I," I said. Tears of happiness ran down both our faces.

I kissed my love and turned out the light. Twelve thirty. I never saw him alive again. At nine fifteen next morning when I wakened, he wasn't beside me. I tiptoed into his room. He was lying on the floor, a strange, gray mottled color. I ran for Pauline, called the doctor, ran back upstairs, covered him with blankets—he was so cold.

"Get warm, darling, get warm," I pleaded, patting him.

I got more blankets, sat on the floor, patting and patting my husband and reassuring him, "It's all right, darling. Please God, it's going to be all right."

But it was not all right.

The thought haunting me was that he might have called out and I had not heard. Impossible, Dr. Nachtigall said, death was instant.

After a while I was guided downstairs into some strange vacuum. Herbert Barnet had come, and Vice-President Emmett O'Connell and his wife, Toni, our lawyer, Bud Morris, and his wife, Florence. They were trying to reach me, trying to help, but I kept seeing Alfred. He was on the floor upstairs, that great warm vital human being.

Suddenly I came out of the fog. The children! I must phone the twins, not let them hear this on radio or TV. I dialed our home in California. Poor little girls. I remembered their loving to skate with us in Switzerland . . . fishing with us in Acapulco . . . leaning over the rail watching the flying fish when we passed the Azores . . . sailing down the Rhine as in a fairy tale.

Cindy answered the phone.

"Cindy, I have some bad news, dear."

"You're crying, Mummie, what is it?"

"Cindy, your daddy died this morning."

Silence.

"Are you there, darling? Do you understand?"

"Yes, Mummie." A strange voice, strangled with grief.

"Now, Cindy, darling, get your sister and let me tell her. . . . Cathy? Cathy, dear, your daddy died this morning."

Cathy sobbed as though she'd been kicked in the stomach.

"It's all right, darling, scream, let it go." I wanted to scream right with her.

"Mummie, are you all right?"

"Daddy is still upstairs, I don't know."

I could never go up those stairs again, I could never live in this house, I'd take the children and run somewhere, I could never go up those stairs.

Cathy said, "Mummie, we want to be with you."

They came on the first plane and they never let go of me. They've seen me cry so little—I was the one, when they cried, who always said, "Happy face, happy face, no tears!"

Had he called my name? Had he possibly called and I not heard? Dr. Nachtigall explained again. Impossible.

"I'm glad you phoned the children," Herbert said, and then suddenly the same idea struck us both. *Our Pepsi family!* They mustn't hear it on radio or TV. Herbert grabbed a phone, Emmett another.

People came streaming in. . . . I never knew the extent and meaning of friendship until that day.

Men from the mortuary had now come and gone. I turned to the doctor who had never left the room, never been more than a few feet away from me.

"Henry?"

He caught my glance, met me at the foot of the stairs and put out his hand. I took it for an instant and then let it go. If I was to do this, I must do it *alone* and I must do it *now*. I turned and started up those stairs. I walked into the room where I had found Alfred on the floor. I turned around and there was Henry.

"I didn't think I'd make it," I said.

"I didn't think so either, bless you, and where did you get the courage?"

"This is the home Alfred and I built together with happiness and joy," I told him, "and I said to myself, 'I'm going up those stairs, what's more, we're going up together.' And you know what? We did."

Exactly two days after Alfred's death, at the recommendation of Herbert Barnet, I was elected by stockholders of the corporation to the Board of Pepsi-Cola. If anyone thought this a sentimental gesture to Alfred's widow, President Herbert Barnet set them straight. It was strictly, as he puts it, "a calculated business deal."

Herbert was perfectly aware that Pepsi had never had a woman on the Board before. "But you're part of the Pepsi organization, Joan," he said. "You've brought bottlers and executives closer than they've ever been. You've done a great job and we want you to continue doing it. As a matter of fact, we want you to expand." That's what he said in the beginning, and I said:

"But how about those big businessmen with an aversion to women in business, men with a definite dubiety regarding a woman?"

"You'll give them more than they've bargained for," he said. "We all know you have heart. What they don't know is—you have a little IBM machine ticking away in that head of yours too, a zest for business and the mind of a cash register."

From the first Board meeting until today, Herbert has given me the sense of security and achievement so terribly necessary. "We're a family, Joan," he has told me many times. "We understand each other, we have a wonderful rapport."

We do indeed. Herbert had lost his adored wife, Annette, the year before I lost Alfred. He'd been a tortured soul, knowing for her last two years that she had leukemia and keeping that knowledge from her and from their two young sons. This is a gallant and courageous man, and better than anyone he understands what I have lived through—understands doubly because Alfred and he were like brothers.

I think one of the memorable nights of my life was at our convention this year in San Francisco when we stood together, Herbert and I, welcoming two thousand people to our convention, greeting them all by name. (I don't know how Herbert has trained his amazing memory. I've tried to train mine by identifying each name with some object which suggests that name. In a pinch I run rapidly through the letters of the alphabet until I find the letter that suggests the object.)

Working with Herbert is a rare privilege. I treasure his constant thoughtfulness for my well-being, my welfare and my happiness, I treasure his confidence and faith. I treasure the card that came this year with his flowers on the anniversary of Alfred's death: "The future, Joan, lies before you."

As Official Hostess for the company, my job includes *bottler* relations . . . *marketing* relations . . . *public* relations . . . a constant contact with the movie and theatrical world and the press. We open twenty to thirty bottling plants a year . . . we host ten or twelve parties a year, often in connection with the opening of an art exhibit in the lobby of our beautiful building at 500 Park Avenue. I go to a Variety Club anniversary dinner in Philadelphia where I'm one dame with a thousand men, white chiffon and sable, entirely surrounded by black dinner jackets and white shirt fronts . . . a Heart Ball in Charlotte, North Carolina . . . a cancer benefit in Palm Beach, Florida . . . the United Jewish Appeal, Las Vegas . . . the Theater Owners of America convention in Los Angeles . . . the Cherry Blossom Festival, Washington . . . the Shakespeare Festival, Central Park . . . the Women's Auxiliary of Variety banquet, Philadelphia, to be named Woman of the Year . . . Strategic Air Command, Omaha . . . to New Orleans to be named an Honorary Citizen . . . the Israel Bond Rally, Miami Beach . . . a food convention, Chicago . . . the Cerebral Palsy Clinic . . . the Kaiser Cookout, Honolulu . . . Women's Auxiliary Variety Charity Show, Las Vegas . . . the Apres Ball for the Postgraduate Center for Psychotherapy . . . the annual Christmas Cotillion in Philadelphia at which I lit the famous Christmas tree and received the Star of Malta for "achieving a personal goal in spite of obstacles which might have proved insurmountable" . . . to Atlantic City as grand marshal and a judge of the Miss America Contest . . .

As I was leaving for this one, the phone rang and a friend said, "Do I hear that you're packing again?" I assured him he was correct, that I was off to Atlantic City. "What for?" he asked. "Miss America," I said. There was only a slight pause, then my friend, fervently, "Oh, honey, I *hope* you win!"

I take planes like taxis . . . to Buenos Aires to open a new bottling plant . . . to Caracas, Venezuela, to open the ABC TV channel there . . . to Lausanne, Switzerland, or Milan, Italy. Wherever I go, the routine Alfred and I followed on our tours continues: the first morning, a press conference, then radio interviews and TV interviews about anything and everything.

Flashbulbs pop, TV cameras turn, I receive plaques and pose with a dozen dignitaries before breakfast . . . change clothes and face enormous groups of people crowded into convention halls . . . sit with the civic figures of the city at lunch . . . change clothes and face dignitaries from all over the world at cocktail time . . . bathe, redress and don a ball gown in the evening. I'm pulled, pushed and hugged, and it's all stimulating and rewarding because it's people.

That's why it's good to travel, why it was such a thrill this year to help open the new bottling plants in Lausanne—our first in Switzerland—and in Milan and Busto Arsizio—our first in Italy. I was traveling with a distinguished group of company executives and their wives. Everywhere we were met with smiles, with children and flowers and recognition. When we threw open our doors at the Hotel Principe de Savoia for the press conference in Milan, two hundred and fifty members of the press came in. I've participated in many press conferences, but never one as warm as this.

"What does it mean?" I whispered to Mitchell Cox, our vice-president in charge of public relations.

He laughed. "Well, they certainly haven't come here to meet *me*." And they did give us generous space: *L'Ore, Epoca, Oggi, Il Giorno, Settimana Incom, Lo Sport Illustrato*.They all recounted the career of what they call "La celebre Stella cinematografica americana," but they also spoke of my other career as a "donna d'affari" which brought me as an "ambassador" to Italy and of course mentioned "Nuova beveta gassea Pepsi-Cola."

Normally I wouldn't have expected much attention from a sports periodical, but we became involved in that great sporting event, the Tour of Italy race, which represents to Italy what the Kentucky Derby, the Indianapolis Memorial Day Race and the Rose Bowl Game all rolled into one, represent to us. A group of us were seated in the stadium, awaiting the finish. So was everyone else in Milan, I'm sure. And the rest of Europe was glued to TV, for the event was being covered by Eurovision, which combines TV coverage for England, Ireland, Scotland and the continent. While we waited, there was a series of preliminary races and the winner of all the preliminaries, awarded a handsome bouquet, began cycling slowly around the arena. He had very bright eyes, and suddenly they spied me. Leaping from his bike he presented me with *his* flowers! That whole sea of humanity burst into wild applause.

And again when Arnaldo Pambianco pedaled into the stadium at the finish of the great race, the ovation was thunderous. Fans went wild. They hugged and kissed Arnaldo, and presented him to me for the victory bouquet, which mine was the privilege of bestowing, and for the victory kiss—I bestowed that, too. It just so happened that Eurovision picked up that kiss and then panned to the Pepsi-Cola sign.

Oh, I love Italy, the warmth and naturalness of the people. One day, I was having lunch with a correspondent from *Time* and Mitchell Cox. We ate at a charming garden restaurant, Savini's, and I was fascinated by the man at a nearby table whose head was so magnificent you could only dream of how a sculptor might capture it.

"Who is he?" I asked the *Time* man.

He was Giovanni Martinelli, the great tenor of the Met, lunching quietly with one of his students. He was so beautiful with his great shoulders and chest, his shock of hair like Einstein's. The *Time* man went over and told Mr. Martinelli that I was there and would like to meet him. It was very exciting, we greeted each other and chatted like old friends.

That's how the world is for me. It's filled with old friends and new friends, more family with every trip I take. The mail grows more and more interesting, and the visitors. People from all over the world come to visit me in New York.

For of course I continue living in New York, in the apartment that was Alfred's and mine, the apartment that reflects him and our life together—seven minutes from the Pepsi building. I'd never have an excuse for being late to a Board meeting, would I?

Last year I sold my home in California. A great deal of my life was reflected in that house and I never thought I could part with it. I went through years of treasures and for a moment, held memories in my hands. But I have changed. The wonderful years with Alfred taught me that you don't need *things,* you carry all you have with you in your heart and spirit.

Janie says I've come a long way from Kansas City. It doesn't seem like such a long road, actually, though there have been moments when I thought it would never end. But those were good moments, too, in retrospect. Essentially I'm interested in the present, in the future, in my wonderfully rewarding life as mother, actress and businesswoman. Alfred left me a legacy of all his dreams for this company. And I have a few dreams of my own.

Tomorrow is my destination. I'll wake to it as I wake to each new day of my life, with this prayer, "Thank you, God, for this lovely day. What can I contribute to it?"

FILMOGRAPHY

1. July 1925 **PRETTY LADIES** Metro-Goldwyn
From the story by Adela Rogers St. Johns. Adapted by Alice D. G.
Miller. Director, Monta Bell. Cameraman, Ira H. Morgan.

Maggie Keenan . . . . ZaSu Pitts
Al Cassidy . . . . Tom Moore
Ann Pennington . . . . Ann Pennington
Selma Larson . . . . Lilyan Tashman
Aaron Savage . . . . Bernard Randall
Adrienne . . . . Helen D'Algy
Maggie's Dream Lover . . . . Conrad Nagel
Frances White . . . . Norma Shearer
Roger Van Horn . . . . George K. Arthur
Bobby . . . . Lucille LeSueur
Warren Hadley . . . . Paul Ellis
Paul Thompson . . . . Roy D'Arcy
Fay . . . . Gwendolyn Lee
Diamond Tights Girl . . . . Dorothy Seastrom
Will Rogers . . . . Lew Harvey
Frisco . . . . Chad Huber
Mr. Gallagher . . . . Walter Shumway
Mr. Shean . . . . Dan Crimmins
Eddie Cantor . . . . Jimmy Quinn

2. November 1925 **OLD CLOTHES** Metro-Goldwyn
From the story by Willard Mack. Producer, Jack Coogan, Sr.
Director, Eddie Cline. Cameraman, Frank B. Good.

Max Ginsberg	Max Davidson
Mrs. Burke	Lillian Elliott
Mary Riley	Joan Crawford
Nathan Burke.	Alan Forrest
Dapper Dan	James Mason
The Adjuster.	Stanton Heck
"Dynamite"	A Horse
Timothy Kelly.	Jackie Coogan

3. November 1925 **THE ONLY THING** Metro-Goldwyn
From the novel by Elinor Glyn. Story by Elinor Glyn and picture
made under her personal supervision. Director, Jack Conway.
Cameraman, Chester Lyons.

Princess Thyra	Eleanor Boardman
Duke of Chevenix	Conrad Nagel
The King	Edward Connelly
Sir Charles Vane	Louis Payne
Gigberto	Arthur Edmond Carew
Princess Erek	Vera Lewis
Princess Anne.	Carrie Clarke Ward
Countess Arline	Constance Wylie
Governess	Dale Fuller
Gibson.	Ned Sparks
Prime Minister.	Mario Carillo
Kalkur.	David Mir
Captain of the Guards.	Michael Pleschkoff
Young Arnold.	Buddy Smith
Young Lady Catherine	Joan Crawford
Young Porteous	Frank Braidwood
Young Cheney	Derke Glynne
Thyra's Maid	Mary Hawes

4. December 1925 **SALLY, IRENE AND MARY** Metro-Goldwyn
*From the musical play by Eddie Dowling and Cyrus Woods. Adapted
by Edmund Goulding. Director, Edmund Goulding. Cameraman,
John Arnold.*

Sally	Constance Bennett
Irene	Joan Crawford
Mary	Sally O'Neil
Jimmy Dugan	William Haines
Glen Nester	Douglas Gilmore
Charles Greenwood	Ray Howard
Mrs. O'Brien	Aggie Herrin
Mrs. Dugan	Kate Price
Mrs. O'Dare	Lillian Elliott
Marcus Morton	Henry Kolker
Tom O'Dare	Sam DeGrasse
Maggie Edna	Mae Cooper

5. June 1926 **THE BOOB** Metro-Goldwyn-Mayer
*Adapted by Kenneth Clarke from the story by George Scarborough
and Annette Westbay. Director, William A. Wellman. Cameraman,
William Daniels. Titled by Katherine Hiliker and H. H. Caldwell.*

Amy	Gertrude Olmstead
Peter Good	George K. Arthur
Jane	Joan Crawford
Cactus Jim	Charles Murray
Harry Benson	Antonio D'Algy
Village Soda Clerk	Hank Mann
Fat Girl	Babe London

6. June 1926 **TRAMP, TRAMP, TRAMP** First National
*Story by Frank Capra, Tim Whelan, Hal Conklin, J. Frank Holliday,
Gerald Duffy and Murray Roth. Produced by Harry Langdon Corp.
Director, Harry Edwards. Cameramen, Elgin Lessley and George
Spear.*

Harry	Harry Langdon
Betty Burton.	Joan Crawford
John Burton	Edwards Davis
Roger Caldwell	Carlton Griffith
Harry's Father, Amos Logan.	Alec B. Francis
Taxi Driver	Brooks Benedict
Nick Kargas	Tom Murray

7. June 1926 **PARIS** (MGM)

Story by Edmund Goulding. Director, Edmund Goulding. Cameraman, John Arnold.

Jerry	Charles Ray
The Girl.	Joan Crawford
The Cat	Douglas Gilmore
Rocco	Michael Visaroff
Marcelle	Rose Dione
Pianist.	Jean Galeron

8. March 1927 **THE TAXI DRIVER** (MGM)

Sory by Robert Terry Shannon. Adapted by A. P. Younger. Director, Harry Millarde. Cameraman, Ira H. Morgan.

Joan Crawford, Owen Moore, Douglas Gilmore, Marc MacDermott, William Orlamond, Gertrude Astor, Rockliffe Fellowes, Claire McDowell, Bert Roach

9. April 1927 **WINNERS OF THE WILDERNESS** (MGM)

Story by John Thomas Neville. Director, W. S. Van Dyke. Cameraman, Clyde De Vinna.

Colonel O'Hara	Tim McCoy
Renee Contrecoeur.	Joan Crawford
General Contrecoeur	Edward Connelly
Governor de Vaudreuil	Frank Currier
Captain Dumas	Roy D'Arcy
Mimi.	Louise Lorraine
George Washington	Edward Hearn
General Braddock	Will R. Walling

Timothy . . . . Tom O'Brien
Pontiac . . . . Chief Big Tree
Governor Dinwiddie . . . . Lionel Belmore

10. May 1927 **THE UNDERSTANDING HEART** MGM
From the story by Peter B. Kyne. Adapted by Edward T. Lowe, Jr.
Director, Jack Conway. Cameraman, John Arnold.

Monica Dale . . . . Joan Crawford
Bob Mason . . . . Rockcliffe Fellows
Tony Garland . . . . Francis X. Bushman, Jr.
Kelcey Dale. . . . . Carmel Myers
Sheriff Bentley . . . . Richard Carle
Uncle Charley . . . . Harvey Clark

11. June 1927 **THE UNKNOWN** MGM
Story by Tod Browning. Scenario by Waldemar Young. Director,
Tod Browning. Cameraman, Merritt Gerstad.

Alonzo . . . . Lon Chaney
Malabar . . . . Norman Kerry
Estrellita . . . . Joan Crawford
Zanzi . . . . Nick de Ruiz
Cojo. . . . . John George
Gypsy . . . . Frank Lanning

12. July 1927 **TWELVE MILES OUT** MGM
From the play by William Anthony McGuire. Adapted by Sada
Cowan. Director, Jack Conway. Cameraman, Ira H. Morgan.

Jerry Fay . . . . John Gilbert
Red McCue . . . . Ernest Torrence
Jane . . . . Joan Crawford
Mayme . . . . Betty Compson
Luke . . . . Bert Roach
Daisy . . . . Eileen Percy
John Burton . . . . Edward Earle
Irish. . . . . Tom O'Brien
French. . . . . Harvey Clark

13. October 1927 **SPRING FEVER** MGM

From the play by Vincent Lawrence. Scenario by Albert Lewin and Frank Davies. Director, Edward Sedgwick. Titles by Ralph Spence. Cameraman, Ira H. Morgan.

Jack Kelly	William Haines
Allie Monte	Joan Crawford
Eustace Tewksbury	George K. Arthur
Mr. Waters	George Fawcett
Martha Lomsdon	Eileen Percy
Johnson	Edward Earle
Pop Kelly	Bert Woodruff
Oscar	Lee Moran

14. January 1928 **WEST POINT** MGM

From the story by Raymond L. Schrock. Director, Edward Sedgwick. Cameraman, Ira H. Morgan. Titles by Joe Farnham. Editor, Frank Sullivan.

Bill Wheeler	William Haines
Betty Channing	Joan Crawford
Perry	Neil Neely
Tex McNeil	William Bakewell
Bob Chase	Ralph Emerson
Hugh Anderson	Edward Richardson
Dana Stephens	Baury Bradford Richardson
Captain Munson	Leon Kellar
Coach Towers	Major Raymond G. Moses, Corps of Engineers, USA
Major Mullens	Major Philip B. Fleming, Corps of Engineers, USA

15. February 1928 **ROSE MARIE** MGM

From the operetta by Otto Harbach and Oscar Hammerstein II. Scenario by Lucien Hubbard. Director, Lucien Hubbard. Cameraman, John Arnold. Editor, Carl F. Pierson.

Rose Marie	Joan Crawford

Jim Kenyon . . . . James Murray
Sergeant Malone . . . . House Peters
Etienne Doray . . . . Creighton Hale
Black Bastien . . . . Gibson Gowland
Lady Jane . . . . Polly Moran
Henri . . . . Lionel Belmore
Emile . . . . William Orlamond
Wanda . . . . Gertrude Astor
Jean . . . . Ralph Yearsley
Hudson . . . . Sven Hugo Borg
Gray . . . . Harry Gribbon

16. May 1928 **ACROSS TO SINGAPORE** MGM

From the story by Ben Ames Williams. Continuity by E. Richard Schayer.
Director, William Nigh. Cameraman, John Seitz. Editor, Ben Lewis.

Joel Shore . . . . Ramon Novarro
Priscilla Crowninshield . . . . Joan Crawford
Capt. Mark Shore . . . . Ernest Torrence
Jeremiah Shore . . . . Frank Currier
Noah Shore . . . . Dan Wolheim
Mathew Shore . . . . Duke Martin
Joshua Crowninshield . . . . Edward Connelly
Finch . . . . James Mason

17. June 1928 **THE LAW OF THE RANGE** MGM

From the story by Norman Houston. Scenario by E. Richard
Schayer. Director, William Nigh. Cameraman, Clyde DeVinna.
Titles, Robert Hopkins. Editor, Dan Sharits.

Jim Lockhart . . . . Tim McCoy
Betty Dallas . . . . Joan Crawford
Solitaire Kid . . . . Rex Lease
Mother Lockhart . . . . Bodil Rosing
Cohen . . . . Tenen Holtz

18. August 1928 **FOUR WALLS** MGM
From the story by Dana Burnet and George Abbott. Continuity
by Alice D. G. Miller. Director, William Nigh. Cameraman, James
Howe. Titles, Joe Farnham. Editor, Harry Reynolds.

Benny .... John Gilbert
Frieda .... Joan Crawford
Mrs. Horowitz .... Vera Gordon
Bertha .... Carmel Myers
Sullivan .... Robert Emmet O'Connor
Monk .... Louis Natheaux
Roma .... Jack Byron

19. October 1928 **OUR DANCING DAUGHTERS**
Cosmopolitan Production MGM
Story and scenario by Josephine Lovett. Director, Harry Beaumont.
Cameraman, George Barnes. Titles, Marion Ainslee and Ruth
Cummings. Editor, William Hamilton.

Diana .... Joan Crawford
Ben Black .... Johnny Mack Brown
Beatrice .... Dorothy Sebastian
Anne .... Anita Page
Norman .... Nils Asther
Anne's Mother .... Dorothy Cummings
Diana's Father .... Huntley Gordon
Freddie's Mother .... Evelyn Hall
Freddie's Father .... Sam De Grasse
Freddie .... Edward Nugent

20. December 1928 **DREAM OF LOVE** MGM
From the play Adrienne Lecouvreur *by Eugène Scribe and Ernest*
Legouvé. Continuity by Dorothy Farnum. Director, Fred Niblo.
Cameramen, Oliver Marsh and William Daniels. Titles, Marion
Ainslee, Ruth Cummings. Editor, James MacKay.

Adrienne .... Joan Crawford
Mauritz .... Nils Asther

Duchess .... Aileen Pringle
Duke .... Warner Oland
Countess .... Carmel Myers
Count .... Harry Reinhardt
Baron .... Harry Myers
Michonet .... Alphonse Martell
Ivan .... Fletcher Norton

21. March 1929 **THE DUKE STEPS OUT** MGM

From the story by Lucian Cary. Adapted by Raymond Schrock and Dale Van Every. Director, James Cruze. Cameraman, Ira H. Morgan. Titles, Joe Farnmham. Editor, George Hively.

Duke .... William Haines
Susie .... Joan Crawford
Barney .... Karl Dane
Jake .... Tenen Holtz
Tommy Wells .... Eddie Nugent
Poison Kerrigan .... Jack Roper
Bossy Edwards .... Delmer Daves
Professor Widdicomb .... Luke Cosgrave
Mr. Corbin .... Herbert Prior

22. August 1929 **OUR MODERN MAIDENS** MGM

Story and screenplay by Josephine Lovett. Producer, Hunt Stromberg. Director, Jack Conway. Cameraman, Oliver Marsh. Titles, Ruth Cummings, Marion Ainslee. Editor, Sam S. Zimbalist.

Billie .... Joan Crawford
Abbott .... Rod LaRocque
Gil .... Douglas Fairbanks, Jr.
Kentucky .... Anita Page
Reg. .... Edward Nugent
Blondie .... Josephine Dunn
B. Bickering Brown .... Albert Gran

23. November 1929 **HOLLYWOOD REVUE OF 1929** MGM
(June 1929 premiere and road show before general release date)
Dialogue by A1 Boasberg and Robert Hopkins. Producer, Harry Rapf.
Director, Charles F. Reisner. Cameramen, John Arnold, Irving G. Reis
and Maximilian Fabian. Art directors, Cedric Gibbons and Richard
Day. Music and lyrics by Gus Edwards, Joe Goodwin, Nacio Herb
Brown, Arthur Freed, Dave Snell, Louis Alter, Jessie Greer, Ray Klages,
Martin Broones, Fred Fisher, Jo Trent, Avy Rice, Ballard MacDonald.
Orchestra and musical score by Arthur Lange. Costumes, David Cox.
Dances and ensembles by Sammy Lee. Editor, William Gray.

Conrad Nagel, Cliff Edwards, Bessie Love, Charles
King, Joan Crawford, Polly Moran, William Haines,
Gus Edwards, Buster Keaton, Lionel Barrymore, Anita
Page, Jack Benny, Karl Dane, Brox Sisters, George K.
Arthur, Albertina Rasch Ballet, Gwen Lee, Natacha
Natova and Company, Ernest Belcher's Dancing The
Rounders Tots, Norma Shearer, Marie Dressier, John
Gilbert, Marion Davies, Laurel and Hardy

24. November 1929 **UNTAMED** MGM
From the story by Charles E. Scoggins. Adapted by Sylvia Thalberg
and Frank Butler. Dialogue by Willard Mack. Director, Jack
Conway. Cameraman, Oliver Marsh. Titles, Lucile New-mark.
Editors, William Gray, Charles Hockberg.

Bingo	Joan Crawford
Andy	Robert Montgomery
Ben Murchison.	Ernest Torrence
Howard Presley	Holmes Herbert
Bennock	John Miljan
Marjory	Gwen Lee
Paul	Edward Nugent
Gregg	Don Terry
Mrs. Mason	Gertrude Astor
Jollop	Milton Farney
Dowling	Lloyd Ingram

Milly .... Grace Cunard
Moran .... Tom O'Brien
Billcombe .... Wilson Benge

25. March 1930 **MONTANA MOON** MGM
Story and screenplay by Sylvia Thalberg and Frank Butler. Dialogue,
Joe Farnham. Director, Malcolm St. Clair. Cameraman, William
Daniels. Music and lyrics by Nacio Herb Brown and Arthur Freed.
Editors, Carl L. Pierson and Leslie F. Wildier.
Joan........................... Joan Crawford
Larry..................... Johnny Mack Brown
Elizabeth .... Dorothy Sebastian
Jeff .... Ricardo Cortez
"The Doctor".................... Benny Rubin
Froggy Cliff Edwards *Hank* .... Karl Dane
Mr. Prescott .... Lloyd Ingraham

26. July 1930 **OUR BLUSHING BRIDES** MGM
Story by Bess Meredyth. Screenplay, Bess Meredyth and John
Howard Lawson. Additional dialogue by Edwin Justus Mayer.
Director, Harry Beaumont. Cameraman, Merritt B. Gerstad.
Editors, George Hively, Harold Palmer.
Jerry .... Joan Crawford
Connie .... Anita Page
Franky .... Dorothy Sebastian
Tony .... Robert Montgomery
David .... Raymond Hackett
Marty........................... John Miljan
Mrs. Weaver .... Hedda Hopper
Monsieur Pantoise .... Albert Conti
Joe Munsey .... Edward Brophy
The Detective........ Robert Emmett O'Connor
Evelyn Woodforth .... Martha Sleeper
Mannequins Gwen Lee, Mary Doran, Catherine
Moylan, Norma Drew, Claire Dodd, Wilda Mansfield

27. December 1930 **PAID** MGM

From the play Within the Law *by Bayard Veiller. Adapted by Lucien Hubbard and Charles MacArthur. Dialogue, Charles MacArthur. Director, Sam Wood. Cameraman, Charles Rosher. Editor, Hugh Wynn.*

Mary Turner	Joan Crawford
Joe Garson	Robert Armstrong
Agnes Lynch	Marie Prevost
Bob Gilder	Kent Douglass
Inspector Burke	John Miljan
District Attorney Demarest	Hale Hamilton
Edward Gilder	Purnell B. Pratt
Polly	Polly Moran
Cassidy	Robert Emmett O'Connor
Eddie Griggs.	Tyrell Davis
Carney	William Bakewell
Red	George Cooper
Bertha.	Gwen Lee
Helen Morris	Isabel Withers

28. February 1931 **DANCE, FOOLS, DANCE** MGM

From the story by Aurania Rouverol. Continuity, Richard Schayer. Dialogue, Aurania Rouverol. Director, Harry Beaumont. Cameraman, Charles Rosher. Editor, George Hively.

Bonnie	Joan Crawford
Bob	Lester Vail
Bert Scranton	Cliff Edwards
Rodney	William Bakewell
Stanley Jordan	William Holden
Jake Luva	Clark Gable
Wally.	Earle Foxe
Parker	Purnell B. Pratt
Selby	Hale Hamilton
Della	Natalie Moorhead
Sylvia	Joan Marsh
Whitey	Russell Hopton

29. July 1931 **LAUGHING SINNERS** MGM
From the play Torch Song *by Kenyon Nicholson. Continuity, Bess
Meredyth. Dialogue, Martin Flavin. Director, Harry Beaumont.
Cameraman, Charles Rosher. Editor, George Hively.*

Ivy	Joan Crawford
Howard	Neil Hamilton
Carl	Clark Gable
Ruby	Marjorie Rambeau
Cass Wheeler	Guy Kibbee
Mike	Cliff Edwards
Fred Greer	Roscoe Karns
Edna	Gertrude Short
Joe	George Cooper
Humpty	George F. Marion
Tink	Bert Woodruff

30. August 1931 **THIS MODERN AGE** MGM
*From the story "Girls Together" by Mildred Cram. Continuity and
dialogue, Sylvia Thalberg and Frank Butler. Director, Nicholas
Grinde. Cameraman, Charles Rosher. Editor, William LeVanway.*

Valentine	Joan Crawford
Diane	Pauline Frederick
Bob	Neil Hamilton
Tony	Monroe Owsley
Mr. Blake	Hobart Bosworth
Mrs. Blake	Emma Dunn
Andre De Graignon	Albert Conti
Marie	Adrienne D'Ambricourt
Alyce	Marcelle Corday

31. November 1931 **POSSESSED** MGM
From the play The Mirage *by Edgar Selwyn. Adapted by Lenore
Coffee. Director, Clarence Brown. Cameraman, Oliver T. Marsh.*

Marian	Joan Crawford
Mark Whitney	Clark Gable

Al Manning .... Wallace Ford
Wally .... Skeets Gallagher
Travers .... Frank Conroy
Vernice .... Marjorie White
John Driscoll .... John Miljan
Mother .... Clara Blandick

32. May 1932 **LETTY LYNTON** MGM

*From the novel by Marie Belloc Lowndes. Adapted by John Meehan
and Wanda Tuchock. Director, Clarence Brown. Cameraman, Oliver
T. Marsh. Costumes, Adrian. Editor, Conrad A. Nervig.*

Letty Lynton................... Joan Crawford
Jerry Darrow .... Robert Montgomery
Emile Renaul .... Nils Asther
Mr. Haney .... Lewis Stone
Mrs. Lynton .... May Robson
Miranda .... Louise Closser Hale
Mrs. Darrow.................... Emma Dunn
Mr. Darrow .... Walter Walker
Hennessey .... William Pawley

33. September 1932 **GRAND HOTEL** MGM

*From the novel and play by Vicki Baum. Continuity, William A.
Drake. Director, Edmund Goulding. Cameraman, William Daniels.
Costumes, Adrian. Editor, Blanche Sewell.*

Grusinskaya .... Greta Garbo
Flaemmchen .... Joan Crawford
Preysing .... Wallace Beery
Baron .... John Barrymore
Kringelein .... Lionel Barrymore
Doctor.......................... Lewis Stone
Senf .... Jean Hersholt
Meirheim .... Robert McWade
Zinnowitz .... Purnell Pratt
Pimenov .... Ferdinand Gottschalk

Suzette .... Rafaela Ottiano
Chauffeur.................... Morgan Wallace
Gerstenkorn .... Tully Marshall
Rohna .... Frank Conroy
Schweiman................... Murray Kinnell
Dr. Waltz.................... Edwin Maxwell

34. October 1932 **RAIN** United Artists
From the play Rain *adapted by John Colton and Clemence Randolph*
from the story "Miss Thompson" by W. Somerset Maugham.
Screenplay, Maxwell Anderson. Director, Lewis Milestone.
Cameraman, Oliver T. Marsh. Editor, W. Duncan Mansfield.

Sadie Thompson .... Joan Crawford
Reverend Davidson .... Walter Huston
Sergeant O'Hara .... William Gargan
Mrs. Davidson .... Beulah Bondi
Dr. McPhail .... Matt Moore
Mrs. McPhail................... Kendall Lee
Joe Horn....................... Guy Kibbee
Quartermaster Bates............ Walter Catlett
Griggs .... Ben Hendricks, Jr.
Hodgson .... Fred Howard

35. April 1933 **TODAY WE LIVE** MGM
From the story by William Faulkner. Screenplay, Edith Fitzgerald
and Dwight Taylor. Director, Howard Hawks. Cameraman, Oliver T.
Marsh. Editor, Edward Curtiss.

Diana .... Joan Crawford
Bogard........................ Gary Cooper
Claude .... Robert Young
Ronnie........................ Franchot Tone
McGinnis .... Roscoe Karns
Applegate .... Louise Closser Hale
Major .... Rollo Lloyd
Eleanor .... Hilda Vaughn

36. November 1933 **DANCING LADY** MGM

From the novel by James Warner Bellah. Screenplay, Allen Rivkin and P. J. Wolfson. Producer, David O. Selznick. Director, Robert Z. Leonard. Cameraman, Oliver T. Marsh. Music by Burton Lane, Harold Adamson, Richard Rodgers, Lorenz Hart, Jimmy McHugh, Dorothy Fields. Conducted by Lou Silvers. Costumes, Adrian. Editor, Margaret Booth.

Janie	Joan Crawford
Patch Gallegher	Clark Gable
Tod Newton	Franchot Tone
Mrs. Newton	May Robson
Rosette	Winnie Lightner
Fred Astaire	Fred Astaire
Ward King	Robert Benchley
Steve	Ted Healy
Vivian Warner	Gloria Foy
Art	Art Jarrett
Bradley, Sr.	Grant Mitchell
Bradley, Jr.	Maynard Holmes
Nelson Eddy	Nelson Eddy
Stooges	Moe Howard, Jerry Howard, Larry Fine
Arthur	Sterling Holloway

37. May 1934 **SADIE MCKEE** MGM

Based on the story "Pretty Sadie McKee" by Viña Delmar. Screenplay by John Meehan. Producer, Lawrence Weingarten. Director, Clarence Brown. Cameraman, Oliver T. Marsh. Costumes, Adrian. Editor, Hugh Wynn.

Sadie	Joan Crawford
Tommy	Gene Raymond
Michael	Franchot Tone
Brennan	Edward Arnold
Dolly	Esther Ralston
Stooge	Earl Oxford
Opal	Jean Dixon

Phelps . . . . Leo Carrillo
Ricorri. . . . . Akim Tamiroff
Mrs. Craney . . . . Zelda Sears
Mrs. McKee . . . . Helen Ware
Maid . . . . Helen Freeman
Café Entertainers Gene Austin, Candy and Coco

38. August 1934 **CHAINED** MGM

From the story by Edgar Selwyn. Screenplay, John Lee Mahin.
Producer, Hunt Stromberg. Director, Clarence Brown. Cameraman,
George Folsey. Costumes, Adrian. Editor, Robert J. Kern.

Diane Lovering . . . . Joan Crawford
Mike Bradley . . . . Clark Gable
Richard Field . . . . Otto Kruger
Johnnie Smith. . . . . Stuart Erwin
Amy. . . . . Una O'Connor
Mrs. Field . . . . Marjorie Gateson
Pablo. . . . . Akim Tamiroff

39. December 1934 **FORSAKING ALL OTHERS** MGM

From the story by Edward Barry Roberts and Frank Morgan Cavett.
Screenplay, Joseph L. Mankiewicz. Producer, Bernard H. Hyman.
Director, W. S. Van Dyke. Cameramen, Gregg Toland and George
Folsey. Costumes, Adrian. Editor, Tom Held.

Mary. . . . . Joan Crawford
Jeff. . . . . Clark Gable
Dill . . . . Robert Montgomery
Shep. . . . . Charles Butterworth
Paula. . . . . Billie Burke
Connie . . . . Frances Drake
Eleanor . . . . Rosalind Russell
Wiffens . . . . Tom Rickets
Johnson. Arthur Treacher
Bella . . . . Greta Moyer

40. June 1935 **NO MORE LADIES** MGM

From the play by A. E. Thomas. Screenplay, Donald Ogden Stewart and Horace Jackson. Producer, Irving Thalberg. Directors: Edward H. Griffith and George Cukor. Cameraman, Oliver T. Marsh. Costumes, Adrian. Editor, Frank E. Hull.

Marcia	Joan Crawford
Sherry	Robert Montgomery
Edgar	Charlie Ruggles
Jim	Franchot Tone
Fanny	Edna May Oliver
Theresa	Gail Patrick
Oliver	Reginald Denny
Lady Diana Moulton	Vivienne Osborne
Caroline	Joan Burfield
Lord Moulton	Arthur Treacher
Duffy	David Horsley
Sally	Jean Chatburn

41. October 1935 **I LIVE MY LIFE** MGM

Based on the short story Claustrophobia *by A. Carter Goodloe. Developed by Gottfried Reinhardt and Ethel Borden. Screenplay, Joseph L. Mankiewicz. Producer, Bernard H. Hyman. Director, W. S. Van Dyke. Cameraman, George Folsey. Costumes, Adrian. Editor, Tom Held.*

Kay	Joan Crawford
Terry	Brian Aherne
Bentley	Frank Morgan
Betty	Aline MacMahon
Grove	Eric Blore
Gene	Fred Keating
Mrs. Gage	Jessie Ralph
Gallup	Arthur Treacher
Alvin's Mother	Hedda Hopper
Doctor	Frank Conroy

Professor .... Etienne Girardot
Pete .... Edward Brophy
Max........................ Sterling Holloway
Miss Morrison .... Hilda Vaughn
Clerk .... Vince Barnett
Yaffitz .... Lionel Stander
Uncle Carl .... Hale Hamilton.

42. August 1936 **THE GORGEOUS HUSSY** MGM
Based on the novel by Samuel Hopkins Adams. Screenplay,
Ainsworth Morgan and Stephen Morehouse Avery. Producer,
Joseph L. Mankiewicz. Director, Clarence Brown. Cameraman,
George Folsey. Art director, Cedric Gibbons. Musical score, Herbert
Stothart. Costumes, Adrian. Editor, Blanche Sewell.

Peggy O'Neal .... Joan Crawford
Timberlake..................... Robert Taylor
Jackson .... Lionel Barrymore
John Eaton .... Franchot Tone
John Randolph .... Melvyn Douglas
"Rowdy" Dow................... James Stewart
Mrs. Beall .... Alison Skipworth
Sunderland.................... Louis Calhern
Rachel Jackson .... Beulah Bondi
Cuthbert .... Melville Cooper
Daniel Webster .... Sidney Toler
Major O'Neal.................. Gene Lockhart
Louisa Abbot .... Clara Blandick
John C. Calhoun .... Frank Conroy
Maybelle..................... Nydia Westman
Martin Van Buren........... Charles Trowbridge
Secretary Ingham............ Willard Robertson
Mrs. Bellamy .... Ruby DeRemer
Mrs. Wainwright .... Betty Blythe
Mrs. Daniel Beall................ Zeffie Tilbury

43. November 1936 **LOVE ON THE RUN** MGM

From the story by Alan Green and Julian Brodie. Screenplay, John Lee Mahin, Manuel Seff and Gladys Hurlbut. Producer, Joseph L. Mankiewicz. Director, W. S. Van Dyke. Cameraman, Oliver T. Marsh. Costumes, Adrian. Editor, Frank Sullivan.

Sally Parker	Joan Crawford
Michael Anthony	Clark Gable
Barnabus Pells	Franchot Tone
Baron	Reginald Owen
Baroness	Mona Barrie
Igor	Ivan Lebedeff
Lieutenant of Police	Charles Judels
Editor	William Demarest

44. February 1937 **THE LAST OF MRS. CHEYNEY** MGM

Adapted from the play The Last of Mrs. Cheyney *by Frederick Lonsdale. Screenplay by Leon Gordon, Samson Raphaelson and Monckton Hoffe. Producer, Lawrence Weingarten. Director, Richard Boleslawski. Cameraman, George Folsey. Art director, Cedric Gibbons. Music, Dr. William Axt. Editor, Frank Sullivan.*

Fay Cheyney	Joan Crawford
Charles	William Powell
Arthur	Robert Montgomery
Lord Kelton	Frank Morgan
Duchess	Jessie Ralph
Willie	Nigel Bruce
Joan	Colleen Clare
Kitty	Benita Hume
Cousin John	Ralph Forbes
Maria	Aileen Pringle
William	Melville Cooper
Ames	Leonard Carey
Anna	Sara Haden
Inspector Witherspoon	Lemsden Hare

George. . . . . Wallis Clark
Clerk . . . . Barnett Parker

45. October 1937 **THE BRIDE WORE RED** MGM
Based on the unpublished play The Girl from Trieste *by Ferenc Molnar. Screenplay, Tess Slesinger and Bradbury Foote. Producer, Joseph L. Mankiewicz. Director, Dorothy Arzner. Cameraman, George Folsey. Art Director, Cedric Gibbons. Music, Franz Waxman. Costumes, Adrian. Editor, Adrienne Fazan.*

Anni . . . . Joan Crawford
Guilio . . . . Franchot Tone
Rudi Pal . . . . Robert Young
Contessa Di Meina . . . . Billie Burke
Admiral Monti. . . . . Reginald Owen
Maddelena Monti . . . . Lynne Carver
Count Armalia. . . . . George Zucco
Maria . . . . Mary Phillips
Nobili . . . . Paul Porcasi
Pietro . . . . Dickie Moore
Alberto . . . . Frank Puglia

46. January 1938 **MANNEQUIN** MGM
Developed from an unpublished story by Katharine Brush. Screenplay by Lawrence Hazard. Producer, Joseph L. Mankiewicz. Director, Frank Borzage. Cameraman, George Folsey. Costumes, Adrian. Editor, Frederic Y. Smith.

Jessie Cassidy . . . . Joan Crawford
John L. Hennessey . . . . Spencer Tracy
Eddie Miller . . . . Alan Curtis
Briggs . . . . Ralph Morgan
Beryl . . . . Mary Phillips
"Pa" Cassidy. Oscar O'Shea
Mrs. Cassidy. . . . . Elizabeth Risdon
Clifford . . . . Leo Gorcey

47. November 1938 **THE SHINING HOUR** MGM
Based on the play by Keith Winter. Screenplay by Jane Murfin and Ogden Nash. Producer, Joseph L. Mankiewicz. Director, Frank Borzage. Cameraman, George Folsey. Music, Franz Waxman. Dance arranged by De Marco. Costumes, Adrian. Editor, Frank E. Hull.

Olivia Riley.................... Joan Crawford
Judy Linden .... Margaret Sullavan
David Linden................... Robert Young
Henry Linden................. Melvyn Douglas
Hanna Linden .... Fay Bainter
Roger Q. Franklin .... Allyn Joslyn
Belvedere.................... Hattie McDaniel
Charlie Collins.................. Oscar O'Shea
Benny Collins................ Frank Albertson
Bertie........................... Harry Barris

48. March 1939 **THE ICE FOLLIES OF 1939** MGM
From the story by Leonard Praskins. Screenplay by Leonard Praskins, Florence Ryerson and Edgar Allan Woolf. Producer, Harry Rapf. Director, Reinhold Schunzel. Cameramen, Joseph Ruttenberg, Oliver T. Marsh. Music, Roger Edens. Costumes, Adrian. Editor, W. Donn Hayes.

Mary McKay .... Joan Crawford
Larry Hall...................... James Stewart
Eddie Burgess..................... Lew Ayres
Douglas Tolliver, Jr................ Lewis Stone
Kitty Sherman .... Bess Ehrhardt
Mort Hodges................... Lionel Stander
Barney .... Charles D. Brown
"The International Ice Follies" with Bess Ehrhardt,
Roy Shipstad, Eddie Shipstad and Oscar Johnson

49. September 1939 **THE WOMEN** MGM
Based on the play by Clare Boothe. Screenplay by Anita Loos and Jane Murfin. Producer, Hunt Stromberg. Director, George Cukor.

Cameramen, Oliver T. Marsh, Joseph Ruttenberg. Art director, Cedric Gibbons. Music, Edward Ward, David Snell. Costumes, Adrian. Editor, Robert J. Kerns.

Mary (Mrs. Stephen Haines)	Norma Shearer
Crystal Allen	Joan Crawford
Sylvia (Mrs. Howard Fowler)	Rosalind Russell
The Countess De Lave	Mary Boland
Miriam Aarons	Paulette Goddard
Edith (Mrs. Phelps Potter).	Phyllis Povah
Peggy (Mrs. John Day)	Joan Fontaine
Little Mary	Virginia Weidler
Mrs. Morehead.	Lucile Watson
Nancy Blake	Florence Nash
Jane	Muriel Hutchinson
Ingrid	Esther Dale
Exercise Instructress	Ann Moriss
Miss Watts	Ruth Hussey
Olga.	Dennie Moore
Maggie	Mary Cecil
Miss Trimmerback.	Mary Beth Hughes
Pat.	Virginia Grey
Lucy.	Marjorie Main
Mrs. Van Adams	Cora Witherspoon
Dolly De Peyster.	Hedda Hopper

50. March 1940 **STRANGE CARGO** MGM

Based on the book Not Too Narrow, Not Too Deep *by Richard Sale. Screenplay, Lawrence Hazard. Producer, Joseph L. Mankiewicz. Director, Frank Borzage. Cameraman, Robert Planck. Art, Cedric Gibbons. Music, Franz Waxman. Editor, Robert J. Kern.*

Julie.	Joan Crawford
Verne	Clark Gable
Cambreau.	Ian Hunter
M'sieu Pig.	Peter Lorre

Hessler	Paul Lukas
Moll.	Albert Dekker
Flaubert	J. Edward Bromberg
Telez	Eduardo Ciannelli
Ufond	John Arledge
Grideau.	Frederic Worlock
Marfeu	Bernard Nedell
Fisherman	Victor Varconi

51. May 1940 **SUSAN AND GOD** MGM

Based on the play by Rachel Crothers. Screenplay by Anita Loos. Producer, Hunt Stromberg. Director, George Cukor. Cameraman, Robert Planck. Art, Cedric Gibbons. Music, Herbert Stothart. Costumes, Adrian. Editor, William H. Terhune.

Susan	Joan Crawford
Barrie	Fredric March
Charlotte	Ruth Hussey

53. August 1941 **WHEN LADIES MEET** MGM

Based on the play by Rachel Crothers. Screenplay by S. K. Lauren and Anita Loos. Producers, Robert Z. Leonard, Orville O. Dull. Director, Robert Z. Leonard. Cameraman, Robert Planck. Art, Cedric Gibbons. Music, Bronislau Kaper. Costumes, Adrian. Editor, Robert Kern.

Mary Howard	Joan Crawford
Jimmy Lee.	Robert Taylor
Clare Woodruff	Greer Garson
Rogers Woodruff	Herbert Marshall
Bridget Drake.	Spring Byington
Walter Del Canto.	Rafael Storm
Janet Hopper	Florence Shirley
Homer Hopper.	Leslie Francis
Mathews	Olaf Hytten
Mabel Guiness	Mona Barrie

54. June 1942 **THEY ALL KISSED THE BRIDE** Columbia
From the story by Gina Kaus and Andrew P. Solt. Screenplay, P. J.
Wolfson. Producer, Edward Kaufman. Director, Alexander Hall.
Cameraman, Joseph Walker. Art directors, Lionel Banks and Cary
Odell. Music, M. Stoloff. Costumes, Irene. Editor, Viola Lawrence.

Margaret J. Drew	Joan Crawford
Michael Holmes	Melvyn Douglas
Marsh	Roland Young
Mrs. Drew	Billie Burke
Johnny Johnson	Allen Jenkins
Crane	Andrew Tombes
Vivian Drew	Helen Parrish
Mahoney	Emory Parnell
Susie Johnson	Mary Treen
Secretary	Nydia Westman
Dr. Cassell	Ivan Simpson
Stephen Pettingill	Roger Clark
Taxi Driver	Gordon Jones
Private Policeman	Edward Gargan

55. December 1942 **REUNION IN FRANCE** MGM
Based on original screen-story by Ladislas Bus-Fekete. Screenplay,
Jan Lustig, Marvin Borowsky and Marc Connelly. Producer, Joseph
L. Mankiewicz. Director, Jules Dassin. Cameraman, Robert Planck.
Art Director, Cedric Gibbons. Music, Franz Waxman. Costumes,
Irene. Editor, Elmo Veron.

Michele de la Becque	Joan Crawford
Pat Talbot	John Wayne
Robert Cortot	Philip Dorn
Schultz	Reginald Owen
General Schroeder	Albert Basserman
Windier	John Carradine
Juliette	Ann Ayars
Durand	J. Edward Bromberg
Grebeau	Moroni Olsen

Stegel...................... Howard Da Silva
Fleuron...................... Henry Daniell

56. May 1943 **ABOVE SUSPICION** MGM

Based on the novel by Helen MacInnes. Screenplay, Keith Winter, Melville Baker, Patricia Coleman. Producer, Victor Saville. Director, Richard Thorpe. Cameraman, Robert Planck. Art, Randall Duell. Music, Bronislau Kaper. Costumes, Irene, Gile Steele. Editor, George Hively.

Frances Myles.................. Joan Crawford
Richard Myles .... Fred MacMurray
Hassert Seidel.................. Conrad Veidt
Sig Von Aschenhausen .... Basil Rathbone
Dr. Mespelbrunn .... Reginald Owen
Countess.................. Cecil Cunningham
Peter Galt.................... Richard Ainley
Aunt Ellen .... Ann Shoemaker
Aunt Hattie .... Sara Haden
A. Werner..................... Felix Bressart
Thornley .... Bruce Lestor
Frau Kleist .... Johanna Hoper
Ottillie........................... Lotta Palfi
Man in Paris .... Alex Papana

57. December 1944 **HOLLYWOOD CANTEEN** Warner Bros.

Original screenplay by Delmer Daves. Producer, Alex Gottlieb. Director, Delmer Daves. Cameraman, Bert Glennon. Art director, Leo Kuter. Musical director, Leo F. Forbstein. Musical numbers created by LeRoy Prinz. Music adapted by Ray Heindorf. Editor, Christian Nyby.

Joan Leslie .... Joan Leslie
"Slim" .... Robert Hutton
Sergeant .... Dane Clark
Angela.......................... Janis Paige
GUEST STARS Andrews Sisters, Paul Henreid, Jack

Benny, Peter Lorre, Joe E. Brown, Ida Lupino, Eddie
Cantor, Irene Manning, Kitty Carlisle, Joan McCracken,
Jack Carson, Dennis Morgan, Joan Crawford, Eleanor
Parker, Bette Davis, Roy Rogers and Trigger, John
Garfield, Barbara Stanwyck, Sydney Greenstreet,
Jane Wyman

58. October 1945 **MILDRED PIERCE** Warner Bros.
*From the novel by James M. Cain. Screenplay by Ranald
MacDougall. Producer, Jerry Wald. Director, Michael Curtiz.
Cameraman, Ernest Haller. Art Director, Anton Grot. Music,
Max Steiner. Costumes, Milo Anderson. Editor, David Weisbart.*

Mildred Pierce	Joan Crawford
Wally Fay	Jack Carson
Monte Beragon	Zachary Scott
Ida	Eve Arden
Veda Pierce	Ann Blythe
Bert Pierce	Bruce Bennett
Mr. Chris	George Tobias
Maggie Binderhof	Lee Patrick
Inspector Peterson	Moroni Olsen
Kay Pierce	Jo Ann Marlow
Mrs. Forrester	Barbara Brown

59. December 1946 **HUMORESQUE** Warner Bros.
*Based on story by Fanny Hurst. Screenplay, Clifford Odets, Zachary
Gold. Producer, Jerry Wald. Director, Jean Negulesco. Cameraman,
Ernest Haller. Art director, Hugh Reticker. Music conducted by
Franz Waxman. Musical director, Leo F. Forbstein. Music advisor,
Isaac Stern. Miss Crawford's costumes, Adrian. Editor, Rudi Fehr.*

Helen Wright	Joan Crawford
Paul Boray	John Garfield
Sid Jeffers	Oscar Levant
Rudy Boray	J. Carroll Naish
Gina	Joan Chandler

Phil Boray . . . . Tom D'Andrea
Florence . . . . Peggy Knudsen
Esther Boray . . . . Ruth Nelson
Monte Loeffler . . . . Craig Stevens
Victor Wright . . . . Paul Cavanagh
Bauer . . . . Richard Gaines
Rozner . . . . John Abbott
Paul Boray (as a child) . . . . Bobby Blake
Phil Boray (as a child) . . . . Tommy Cook
Eddie . . . . Don McGuire
Hagerstrom . . . . Fritz Leiber
Night Club Singer . . . . Peg La Centra
Orchestra Leader . . . . Nestor Paiva
Teddy . . . . Richard Walsh

60. July 1947 **POSSESSED** Warner Bros.

Based on a story "One Man's Secret!" by Rita Weiman. Screenplay by Silvia Richards and Ranald MacDougall. Producer, Jerry Wald. Director, Curtis Bernhardt. Cameraman, Joseph Valentine. Art director, Anton Grot. Music, Franz Waxman. Miss Crawford's costumes, Adrian. Editor, Rudi Fehr.

Louise Howell . . . . Joan Crawford
David Sutton . . . . Van Heflin
Dean Graham . . . . Raymond Massey
Carol Graham . . . . Geraldine Brooks
Dr. Harvey Williard . . . . Stanley Ridges
Harker . . . . John Ridgely
Dr. Ames . . . . Moroni Olsen
Dr. Max Sherman . . . . Erskine Sanford
Wynn Graham . . . . Gerald Perreau
Nurse Rosen . . . . Isabel Withers
Elsie . . . . Lisa Golm
Asst. D.A. Douglas Kennedy
Norris . . . . Monte Blue
Dr. Craig . . . . Don McGuire

```
Coroner's Asst. . . . . . . . . . . . . . . . . Rory Mallinson
Interne . . . . . . . . . . . . . . . . . . . . . . Clifton Young
Coroner. . . . . . . . . . . . . . . . . . . . . . Griff Barnett
```

61. December 1947 **DAISY KENYON** 20th Century-Fox
From the novel by Elizabeth Janeway. Screenplay by David Hertz.
Producer-director, Otto Preminger. Cameraman, Leon Shamroy.
Art directors, Lyle Wheeler and George Davis. Musical score, David
Raskin. Musical director, Alfred Newman. Costumes, Charles
LeMaire. Editor, Louis Loeffler.

```
Daisy Kenyon. . . . . . . . . . . . . . . . . Joan Crawford
Dan O'Mara. . . . . . . . . . . . . . . . . . Dana Andrews
Peter . . . . . . . . . . . . . . . . . . . . . . . . Henry Fonda
Lucile O'Mara . . . . . . . . . . . . . . . . . Ruth Warrick
Mary Angelus. . . . . . . . . . . . . . . . . Martha Stewart
Rosamund . . . . . . . . . . . . . . . . Peggy Aim Garner
Marie . . . . . . . . . . . . . . . . . . . . . . Connie Marshall
Coverly . . . . . . . . . . . . . . . . . . . . . . . . . Nicholas Joy
Lucile's attorney. . . . . . . . . . . . . . . . . . Art Baker
Attorney . . . . . . . . . . . . . . . . . . . . . Robert Karnes
Mervyn. . . . . . . . . . . . . . . . . . . . . . John Davidson
Marsha . . . . . . . . . . . . . . . . . . . . . . Victoria Horne
Judge . . . . . . . . . . . . . . . . . . . . . . Charles Meredith
Dan's attorney . . . . . . . . . . . . . . . . . . Roy Roberts
Thompson. . . . . . . . . . . . . . . . . . . . . Griff Barnett
```

62. April 1949 **FLAMINGO ROAD** Warner Bros.
From the play by Robert and Sally Wilder. Screenplay by
Robert Wilder. Producer, Jerry Wald. Director, Michael Curtiz.
Cameraman, Ted McCord. Art director, Leo K. Kuter. Musical
score, Max Steiner. Musical director, Ray Heindorf. Miss Crawford's
costumes designed by Travilla, executed by Sheila O'Brien. Editor,
Folmar Blangsted.

```
Lane Bellamy . . . . . . . . . . . . . . . . . Joan Crawford
Fielding Carlisle. . . . . . . . . . . . . . . . . Zachary Scott
```

Titus Semple............... Sydney Greenstreet
Lute Mae Sanders............... Gladys George
Annabelle Weldon............ Virginia Huston
Doc Waterson..................... Fred Clark
Millie...................... Gertrude Michael
Gracie.......................... Alice White
Boatright...................... Sam McDaniel
Pete Ladas .... Tito Vuolo
and introducing David Brian as *Dan Reynolds*

63. August 1949 **IT'S A GREAT FEELING** Warner Bros.
*From a story by I. A. L. Diamond. Screenplay, Jack Rose and
Mel Shavelson. Producer, Alex Gottlieb. Director, David Butler.
Cameraman, Wilfrid M. Cline. Art director, Stanley Fleischer.
Music, Ray Heindorf. Editor, Irene Morra.*

CAST:
Dennis Morgan
Doris Day
Jack Carson,
Bill Goodwin
Irving Bacon
Claire Carleton
Harlan Warde
Jacqueline deWit

GUEST APPEARANCES BY:
Gary Cooper
Edward G. Robinson
Joan Crawford
Danny Kaye
Errol Flynn
Ronald Reagan
Jane Wyman
Eleanor Parker
Patricia Neal

64. May 1950 **THE DAMNED DON'T CRY** Warner Bros.
Story, Gertrude Walker. Screenplay, Harold Medford, Jerome Weidman. Producer, Jerry Wald. Director, Vincent Sherman. Cameraman, Ted McCord. Art director, Robert Haas. Music, Daniele Amfitheatrof. Wardrobe, Sheila O'Brien. Editor, Rudi Fehr.

Ethel Whitehead	Joan Crawford
Lorna Hansen Forbes	Joan Crawford
George Castleman	David Brian
Nick Prenta	Steve Cochran
Martin Blackford	Kent Smith
Grady	Hugh Sanders
Patricia Longworth	Selena Royle
Sandra	Jacqueline deWit
Mr. Whitehead	Morris Ankrum
Mrs. Castleman	Edith Evanson
Roy	Richard Egan
Tommy	Jimmy Moss
Mrs. Whitehead	Sara Perry
Walter Talbot	Eddie Marr

65. November 1950 **HARRIET CRAIG** Columbia)
Based on the play Craig's Wife *by George Kelly. Screenplay, Anne Froelick, James Gunn. Producer, William Dozier. Director, Vincent Sherman. Cameraman, Joseph Walker. Art director, Walter Holscher. Music, Morris T. Stoloff. Wardrobe, Sheila O'Brien. Editor, Viola Lawrence.*

Harriet Craig	Joan Crawford
Walter Craig	Wendell Corey
Celia Fenwick	Lucile Watson
Billy Birkmire	Allyn Joslyn
Wes Miller	William Bishop
Clare Raymond	K. T. Stevens
Mrs. Harold	Viola Roache
Henry Fenwick	Raymond Greenleaf
Lottie	Ellen Corby
Mrs. Frazier	Fiona O'Shiel

Danny Frazier	Patric Mitchell
Harriet's Mother	Virginia Brissac
Dr. Lambert	Katharine Warren
Mr. Norwood	Douglas Wood
Mrs. Norwood	Kathryn Card
Mr. Winston	Charles Evans
Mrs. Winston	Mira McKinney

66. May 1951 **GOODBYE MY FANCY** Warner Bros.
Based on the play by Fay Kanin. Screenplay, Ivan Goff, Ben Roberts. Producer, Henry Blanke. Director, Vincent Sherman. Cameraman, Ted McCord. Art Director, Stanley Fleischer. Music, Ray Heindorf. Wardrobe, Sheila O'Brien. Editor, Rudi Fehr.

Agatha Reed	Joan Crawford
Dr. James Merrill	Robert Young
Matt Cole	Frank Lovejoy
Woody	Eve Arden
Virginia Merrill	Janice Rule
Ellen Griswold	Lurene Tuttle
Claude Griswold	Howard St. John
Miss Shackleford	Viola Roache
Miss Birdeshaw	Ellen Corby
Dr. Pitt	Morgan Farley
Mary Nell Dodge	Virginia Gibson
Prof. Dingley	John Qualen
Clarisse Carter	Ann Robin
Jon Wintner	Mary Carver

67. February 1952 **THIS WOMAN IS DANGEROUS** Warner Bros.
Original story, Bernard Firard. Screenplay, Geoffrey Homes, George Worthing Yates. Producer, Robert Sisk. Director, Felix Feist. Cameraman, Ted McCord. Art director, Leo K. Kuter. Music, David Buttolph. Wardrobe, Sheila O'Brien. Editor, James C. Moore.

Beth Austin	Joan Crawford
Dr. Ben Halleck	Dennis Morgan

Matt Jackson .... David Brian
Franklin .... Richard Webb
Ann Jackson..................... Mari Aldon
Will Jackson.................... Philip Carey
Joe Crossland .... Ian MacDonald
Admitting Nurse .... Katherine Warren
Dr. Ryan .... George Chandler
Ned Shaw .... William Challee
Susan Halleck.................. Sherry Jackson
McGill....................... Stuart Randall
Club Manager .... Douglas Fowley

68. August 1952 **SUDDEN FEAR** RKO

Based on the novel by Edna Sherry. Screenplay, Lenore Coffee, Robert Smith. Producer, Joseph Kaufman. Director, David Miller. Cameraman, Charles Lang, Jr. Art Director, Boris Leven. Music composed and directed by Elmer Bernstein. Wardrobe, Sheila O'Brien. Editor, Leon Barsha.

Myra Hudson.................. Joan Crawford
Lester Blaine..................... Jack Palance
Irene Neves................... Gloria Grahame
Steve Kearney.................. Bruce Bennett
Ann........................ Virginia Huston
Junior Kearney................ Touch Connors

69. October 1953 **TORCH SONG** MGM

From the story "Why Should I Cry?" by I. A. R. Wylie. Screenplay, John Michael Hayes, Jan Lustig. Producers, Henry Berman, Sidney Franklin, Jr. Director, Charles Walters. Cameraman, Robert Planck. Art director, Cedric Gibbons. Music, Adolph Deutsch. Costumes, Helen Rose. Editor, Albert Akst.

Jenny Stewart .... Joan Crawford
Tye Graham .... Michael Wilding
Cliff Willard..................... Gig Young
Mrs. Stewart............... Marjorie Rambeau

Joe Denner . . . . Henry Morgan
Martha . . . . Dorothy Patrick
Philip Norton . . . . James Todd
Gene, Dance Director . . . . Eugene Loring
Monty Rolfe . . . . Paul Guilfoyle
Charlie Maylor . . . . Benny Rubin
Peter . . . . Peter Chong
Anne . . . . Maidie Norman
Celia Stewart . . . . Nancy Gates
Chuck Peters . . . . Chris Warfield
Singer at Party . . . . Rudy Render

70. May 1954 **JOHNNY GUITAR** Republic
Based on the novel by Roy Chanslor. Screenplay, Philip Yordan.
Producer, Herbert J. Yates. Director, Nicholas Ray. Cameraman,
Harry Stradling. Art director, James Sullivan. Music, Victor Young.
Song, Peggy Lee and Young. Wardrobe, Sheila O'Brien. Editor,
Richard L. Van Enger.

Vienna . . . . Joan Crawford
Johnny Guitar . . . . Sterling Hayden
Emma Small . . . . Mercedes McCambridge
Dancin' Kid . . . . Scott Brady
John McIvers . . . . Ward Bond
Turkey Ralston . . . . Ben Cooper
Bart Lonergan . . . . Ernest Borgnine
Old Tom . . . . John Carradine
Corey . . . . Royal Dano
Marshall Williams . . . . Frank Ferguson
Eddie . . . . Paul Fix
Mr. Andrews . . . . Rhys Williams
Pete . . . . Ian MacDonald

71. September 1955 **FEMALE ON THE BEACH**
Universal-International
Based on the play The Besieged Heart *by Robert Hill. Screenplay, Robert Hill and Richard Alan Simmons. Producer, Albert Zugsmith. Director, Joseph Pevney. Cameraman, Charles Lang. Art director, Alexander Golitzen. Music, Joseph Gershenson. Wardrobe, Sheila O'Brien. Editor, Russell Schoengarth.*

Lynn Markham	Joan Crawford
Drummond Hall	Jeff Chandler
Amy Rawlinson	Jan Sterling
Osbert Sorenson	Cecil Kellaway
Queenie Sorenson	Natalie Schafer
Lieutenant Galley	Charles Drake
Eloise Crandall	Judith Evelyn
Frankovitch	Stuart Randall
Mrs. Murchison	Marjorie Bennett
Pete Gomez	Romo Vincent

72. November 1955 **QUEEN BEE** Columbia
Based on the novel by Edna Lee. Screenplay and director, Ranald MacDougall. Producer, Jerry Wald. Cameraman, Charles Lang. Art director, Ross Bellah. Music, Morris Stoloff. Gowns, Jean Louis. Editor, Viola Lawrence.

Eva Phillips	Joan Crawford
Avery Phillips	Barry Sullivan
Carol Lee Phillips	Betsy Palmer
Judson Prentiss	John Ireland
Jennifer Stewart	Lucy Marlow
Ty McKinnon	William Leslie
Sue McKinnon	Fay Wray
Miss Breen	Katherine Anderson
Ted	Tim Hovey
Trissa	Linda Bennett

Miss George . . . . Willa Pearl Curtis
Sam . . . . Bill Walker
Dr. Pearson. . . . . Olan Soule

73. July 1956 **AUTUMN LEAVES**
(William Goetz Productions, Columbia)
*Story and screenplay, Jack Jevne, Lewis Meltzer, Robert Blees.
Producer, William Goetz. Director, Robert Aldrich. Camerman,
Charles Lang. Art director, Bill Glasgow. Music composed by Hans
Salter. Conductor, Morris Stoloff. Gowns, Jean Louis. Editor, Michael
Luciano.*

Milly . . . . Joan Crawford
Burt Hanson. . . . . Cliff Robertson
Virginia . . . . Vera Miles
Mr. Hanson . . . . Lorne Greene
Liz . . . . Ruth Donnelly
Dr. Couzzens . . . . Sheppard Strudwick
Mr. Wetherby . . . . Selmer Jackson
Nurse Evans . . . . Maxine Cooper
Waitress . . . . Marjorie Bennett
Mr. Ramsey . . . . Frank Gerstle
Colonel Hillyer. . . . . Leonard Mudie
Dr. Masterson . . . . Maurice Manson
Desk Clerk . . . . Bob Hopkins

74. October 1957 **THE STORY OF ESTHER COSTELLO**
Valiant Films, Columbia
*Romulus Production. From the novel by Nicholas Monsarrat.
Screenplay, Charles Kaufman. Producer-director, David Miller.
Cameraman, Robert Krasker. Art directors, George Provis, Tony
Masters. Music, Lambert Williamson. Gowns, Jean Louis. Editor,
Ralph Kemplen.*

Margaret Landi. . . . . Joan Crawford
Carlo Landi . . . . Rossano Brazzi

Esther Costello . . . . Heather Sears
Harry Grant. Lee Patterson
Wenzel . . . . Ron Randell
Mother Superior . . . . Fay Compton
Paul Marchant. . . . . John Loder
Father Devlin . . . . Denis O'Dea
Ryan . . . . Sidney James
Matron in Art Gallery. . . . . Bessie Love
Mr. Wilson . . . . Robert Ayres
Jennie Costello . . . . Maureen Delaney
Irish Publican. . . . . Harry Hutchinson
Irish Pub Customer . . . . Tony Quinn
Esther Costello (as a child) . . . . Janina Faye
Tammy . . . . Estelle Brody
Mrs. Forbes. . . . . June Clyde
Susan North . . . . Sally Smith
Christine Brown. . . . . Diana Day
Nurse Evans . . . . Megs Jenkins
Dr. Stein . . . . Andrew Cruikshank
Signor Gatti . . . . Victor Rietti
Mary Costello. . . . . Sheila Manahan

75. October 1959 **THE BEST OF EVERYTHING** 20th Century-Fox
*From the novel by Rona Jaffe. Screenplay, Edith Sommer and Mann
Rubin. Producer, Jerry Wald. Director, Jean Negulesco. Cameraman,
William C. Mellor. Art directors, Lyle R. Wheeler, Jack Martin
Smith, Mark-Lee Kirk. Music, Alfred Newman. Costumes, Adele
Palmer. Editor, Robert Simpson.*

Caroline Bender. . . . . Hope Lange
Mike . . . . Stephen Boyd
Gregg. . . . . Suzy Parker
Barbara. . . . . Martha Hyer
April . . . . Diane Baker
Mr. Shalimar . . . . Brian Aherne

Dexter Key .... Robert Evans
Eddie .... Brett Halsey
Sidney Carter .... Donald Harron
Mary Agnes .... Sue Carson
Jane .... Linda Hutchings
Paul .... Lionel Kane
Ronnie Wood .... Ted Otis
Brenda .... June Blair
Judy Masson .... Myrna Hansen
Girls in Typing Pool .... Alena Murray,
                    Rachel Stephens, Julie Payne
Scrubwoman .... Nora O'Mahoney
Louis Jordan as *David Savage*
Joan Crawford as *Amanda Farrow*